Gendered Policies in Europe

Reconciling Employment and Family Life

Edited by

Linda Hantrais
Director, European Research Centre
Department of European Studies
Loughborough University

Consultant Editor: Jo Campling

First published in Great Britain 2000 by
MACMILLAN PRESS LTD
Houndmills, Basingstoke, Hampshire RG21 6XS and London
Companies and representatives throughout the world

A catalogue record for this book is available from the British Library.

ISBN 0–333–73982–5

First published in the United States of America 2000 by
ST. MARTIN'S PRESS, INC.,
Scholarly and Reference Division,
175 Fifth Avenue, New York, N.Y. 10010

ISBN 0–312–22923–2

Library of Congress Cataloging-in-Publication Data
Gendered policies in Europe : reconciling employment and family life /
edited by Linda Hantrais.
        p.   cm.
Includes bibliographical references and index.
ISBN 0–312–22923–2 (cloth)
1. Work and family—Government policy—European Union countries.
2. Family policy—European Union countries.   3. Sex role in the work
environment—European Union countries.   I. Hantrais, Linda.
HD4904.25.G46   1999
331.25—dc21   99–43351
                                                                  CIP

Selection, editorial matter, Preface and Chapter 1 © Linda Hantrais 2000
Chapters 2–10 © Macmillan Press Ltd 2000

This book is printed on paper suitable for recycling and made from fully managed and sustained
forest sources.

10   9   8   7   6   5   4   3   2   1
09   08   07   06   05   04   03   02   01   00

Printed and bound in Great Britain by
Antony Rowe Ltd, Chippenham, Wiltshire

90 0404715 7

This book is to be returned on
or before the date stamped below

UNIVERSITY OF PLYMOUTH

PLYMOUTH LIBRARY

Tel: (01752) 232323
This book is subject to recall if required by another reader
Books may be renewed by phone
CHARGES WILL BE MADE FOR OVERDUE BOOKS

Gendered Policies in Europe

Also by Linda Hantrais

* CONTEMPORARY FRENCH SOCIETY

CROSS-NATIONAL RESEARCH METHODS IN THE SOCIAL SCIENCES (*co-editor with Steen Mangen*)

FAMILIES AND FAMILY POLICIES IN EUROPE (*with Marie-Thérèse Letablier*)

MANAGING PROFESSIONAL AND FAMILY LIFE: A Comparative Study of British and French Women

* SOCIAL POLICY IN THE EUROPEAN UNION

THE UNDERGRADUATE'S GUIDE TO STUDYING LANGUAGES

LE VOCABULAIRE DE GEORGES BRASSENS
Vol 1: Une étude statistique et stylistique
Vol 2: Concordance et index des rimes

* *From the same publishers*

Contents

List of Figures   vi

Notes on Contributors   vii

Preface   x

1 **From equal pay to reconciliation of employment and family life**   1
   Linda Hantrais

2 **The European Union and the equal opportunities process**   27
   Maria Stratigaki

3 **Reconciliation policies from a comparative perspective**   49
   Marlene Lohkamp-Himmighofen and Christiane Dienel

4 **From equality to reconciliation in France?**   68
   Marie-Thérèse Lanquetin, Jacqueline Laufer and Marie-Thérèse Letablier

5 **Equal opportunities policies and the management of care in Germany**   89
   Kirsten Scheiwe

6 **The paradoxes of Italian law and practice**   108
   Alisa Del Re

7 **From hard to soft law and from equality to reconciliation in the United Kingdom**   124
   Barbara Bagilhole and Paul Byrne

8 **Reconciliation policies in Spain**   143
   Celia Valiente

9 **Adaptation or diffusion of the Swedish gender model?**   160
   Christina Bergqvist and Ann-Cathrine Jungar

10 **Taking stock and looking ahead**   180
   Monica Threlfall

Bibliography   201

Index   221

v

List of Figures

1.1 Trends in economic activity rates by age groups, for women in 1985–1995 and for men in 1995, in EU member states 6

1.2 Changing EU legislation on gender 11

3.1 Maternity leave, paternity leave and parental leave and allowances in EU member states, 1997 52

10.1 Models of full or partial reconciliation between paid work and family life for both sexes 191

vi

Notes on Contributors

Barbara Bagilhole is Senior Lecturer in Social Policy and Equal Opportunities in the Department of Social Sciences at Loughborough University. Her research focuses on equal opportunities in the areas of gender, race and disability, with particular reference to equal opportunities policies and practices in employment. She is the author of *Equal Opportunities and Social Policy: issues of gender, 'race' and disability* (Addison Wesley Longman, 1997).

Christina Bergqvist is Lecturer in Politics at Uppsala University and the National Institute for Working Life in Stockholm. Her research activities cover gender, interest formulation and policy-making in Nordic welfare states. She is editor of *Equal Democracies? Gender and Politics in the Nordic Countries* (Norwegian University Press, 1999).

Paul Byrne is Senior Lecturer in Politics in the Department of European Studies at Loughborough University. His research includes public policy, political institutions and structures, and social movements, with particular reference to the analysis of policy environments and policy formulation. He is the author of *Social Movements* (Routledge, 1997).

Alisa Del Re is a researcher and lecturer in Political Science at the University of Padoua. She is the convenor and co-director of the international research group 'État et rapports sociaux de sexe', which has carried out a number of projects on social policies in Europe. Her publications include *Les femmes et l'état-providence: les politiques sociales en France dans les années trente* (L'Harmattan, 1994); *Quelle citoyenneté pour les femmes? La crise des États-providence et de la représentation politique en Europe* (with J. Heinen, eds, Harmattan, 1996); *Genere e democrazia* (with F. Bimbi, eds, Rosemberg and Sellier, 1997).

Christiane Dienel is a demographer and researcher in the European Community Unit of the Landesregierung Brandenburg, and president of the Gesellschaft für Familienforschung. Her publications include an analysis of family policy in EC member states, *Zwölf Wege der Familienpolitik in Europa* (vols 1 and 2, Kohlhammer, 1993) and a comparative study of the family–employment relationship among career women in France, Germany, Great Britain and Czechoslovakia, *Frauen in Führungspositionen in Europa* (Juventa, 1996).

Linda Hantrais holds a chair in the Department of European Studies at Loughborough University. She is Director of its European Research Centre and convenor of the Cross-National Research Group. Her research interests are in comparative, cross-national research, particularly with reference to social policy in the European Union. Her publications include *Social Policy in the European Union* (Macmillan, 1995) and *Families and Family Policies in Europe* (with M-T. Letablier, Longman, 1996).

Ann-Cathrine Jungar is a researcher in the Department of Government at Uppsala University. Her research interests include the study of governmental coalitions, and she has worked on a project analyzing the repercussions of European Union membership on the Nordic form of democratic government.

Marie-Thérèse Lanquetin is a lawyer by training and a researcher at the Institut de Recherche sur l'Entreprise et les Relations Professionnelles (IREP) at the Université de Paris X Nanterre. She has been a member of the network of legal experts with the Commission's Equal Opportunities Unit since 1986. Her publications include numerous articles on equal opportunities legislation in *Droit social*.

Jacqueline Laufer is a professor with the Groupe HEC (Paris) in the School of Management. Her main research interests are women in management and equal opportunities strategies at European and national level. Her publications include *L'entreprise et l'égalité des chances: enjeux et démarches* (La Documentation Française, 1992).

Marie-Thérèse Letablier is a researcher at the Centre d'Études de l'Emploi, Paris, where she is conducting comparative studies of working time, particularly with reference to the impact of flexibility on working practices. Her publications include *Families and Family Policies in Europe* (with L. Hantrais, Longman, 1996).

Marlene Lohkamp-Himmighofen is a Referentin with the Federal Ministry of Education and Research in Bonn, and she is a core team member of the Gesellschaft für Familienforschung (GEFAM). Her research has focused primarily on women's labour market activity and the family–employment relationship. Her publications include contributions on these topics and on family policy, law and practice in *Zwölf Wege der Familienpolitik in Europa* (vols 1 and 2, Kohlhammer, 1993) and in *Cross-National Research Papers* (vol. 5 nos 3, 4, 1999).

Kirsten Scheiwe is a researcher in legal studies at the Mannheim Centre for European Social Research (MZES). Her interests embrace the interdisciplinary and comparative analysis of legal institutions and their gender dimension in the field of family law, labour law and social security, legal strategies for regulating the family–employment relationship and their gender implications. Her publications include a chapter in D. Sainsbury (ed.), *Gender and Welfare States* (Sage, 1994).

Maria Stratigaki worked for the European Commission between 1991 and 1999, and she is affiliated with the Department of Social Policy and Social Anthropology at Panteion University, Athens. Her research interests include computerization, work organization and the gender division of labour, European equality policy and gender aspects of social policy. She has published articles on women's work and technology.

Monica Threlfall is Senior Lecturer in Politics in the Department of European Studies, Loughborough University. Her research interests include Spanish politics and gender issues, particularly with reference to the PSOE, and European social policy and employment patterns. She is editor of *Mapping the Women's Movement: feminist politics and social transformation in the North* (Verso, 1996).

Celia Valiente is a lecturer and researcher in sociology in the Faculdad de Ciencias Sociales y Jurídicas, Universidad Carlos III de Madrid. Her main research interests are in women and public policies in Spain, with a particular focus on Spanish public policy formulation and implementation at national level. Her publications include *Políticas Públicas de Género en Perspectiva Comparada* (Universidad Autónoma de Madrid, 1997).

Preface

As recognition grows of the impact that European legislation can have on the everyday lives of men and women in the member states of the European Union (EU), the body of interdisciplinary literature on European integration has been expanding rapidly. The European legislative framework has been closely scrutinized, as have national policy environments. Theoretical insights have been extensively documented, and have often been elucidated by empirical examples. In the area of gender studies, scholarly interest has focused on women, law and politics in the EU, on women and welfare/social policies, and on women and citizenship. Less attention has been paid to policies designed to promote the reconciliation of employment with family life.

Through its funding of transnational projects, the European Commission's Equal Opportunities Unit, in Directorate General V (Employment, Industrial Relations and Social Affairs), has provided a major impetus for the collection of information and monitoring of changing gender relations. Under the European Community Fourth action Programme on Equal Opportunities between Women and Men, interest shifted from equal opportunities to mainstreaming, defined as the promotion and development of methods and strategies aimed at integrating a gender dimension in all policies and activities. A danger of the mainstreaming approach is that equality policy may become more difficult to identify and track. The present book, therefore, seeks to capture and take stock of the development of gendered policies at EU and national level over the second half of the twentieth century, before mainstreaming supplants equal opportunities and reconciliation of employment and family life on the policy agenda.

The emphasis throughout the book is on the policy process, with the aim of providing a tightly focused, informative and critical account of the ways in which policy is formulated, enacted and implemented from an international and interdisciplinary perspective. The authors track the inputs of national and EU policy actors, including the social partners and pressure groups, to gender policy formation. The chapters also analyse outputs and outcomes of EU policy at national level as they impact on gender issues in law and practice. The chapters follow the progression from the formulation of policy on equal pay at EU level in the late 1950s to the implementation of reconciliation measures in the 1990s. The contributors show how the policy process operates, and elucidate the interactive relationship between EU and national institutions and their policy actors.

The first three chapters in the book present the European framework for policy formation and implementation in the area of equal opportunities, and more especially the reconciliation of employment and family life. Chapter 1 provides an overview of the institutional settings and economic context in which gender issues have moved onto the political agenda at European and national level. Chapter 2 analyses the role played by national governments and, more especially, European institutions in the development of European policy on equality, and raises the question of whether mainstreaming should replace or complement positive action. Chapter 3 focuses on existing measures for maternity and parental leave and benefits in the 15 EU member states, and also in Poland and the Czech Republic, and defines six different concepts of reconciliation policy.

Chapters 4 to 9 provide national case studies, representing different geographical areas in the European Union, a variety of welfare regimes and disparate stages in the development of equality policy. The contributors assess critically the roles played by the many policy actors in promoting or resisting change. They examine the impact of differing policy styles, and of the institutions and methods adopted for policy implementation. In the first of the national case studies, Chapter 4 examines how equality has been conceptualized in France. The authors analyse the development of gender equality policy in employment and assess the effectiveness of measures to reconcile paid work and family life. Chapter 5 concentrates on the management of policy on caring in Germany to illustrate changing approaches in gender relations and equal opportunities policies, with particular reference to childcare and long-term care insurance. Chapter 6 reviews the shifting interest in Italy between the concepts of equality of opportunity and positive action, and the utopian ideal of combining equality and difference. Chapter 7 investigates the development in the United Kingdom from the hard law associated with equal opportunities policies, to soft law, as reconciliation policies moved onto the agenda. Chapter 8 analyses the policy context and the ways in which policy actors in Spain have promoted and resisted reconciliation policies. In the last of the country case studies, Chapter 9 focuses on the vision of equal parenthood in Sweden, and shows how Swedish membership has had both an impact on EU policy and been influenced by it. The final chapter appraises the EU's equality work. It analyses reconciliation as a policy instrument, and proposes a set of models for reconciling paid work and family life by both sexes. In conclusion, the author assesses the outlook for equality politics at national and European level.

The contributors are all internationally recognized experts in the field of policy analysis and equal opportunities. They bring to the book a wealth of knowledge and understanding of the ways in which the gender policy process operates in disparate policy environments, located in different socio-cultural and economic contexts. They provide not only national insights but also a mix of disciplinary expertise such that no single author could muster. They are to be thanked for the care and attention they have devoted to researching and drafting their contributions, for their patience and forbearance in answering the editor's queries, and for reflecting on the niceties of the interactive policy process.

Many other people have helped to bring this book to fruition. Our thanks are due to Jo Campling for her valuable support as consultant editor, and to Catherine Hoskyns for her expert advice on the European chapters. Karel Thomas took responsibility for producing the graphs in Chapter 1, and Liz Such provided research assistance. Laurie McGarry responded unstintingly to requests for information on European source materials, and staff at Eurostat ensured that our datasets were as complete as possible.

LINDA HANTRAIS

1 From Equal Pay to Reconciliation of Employment and Family Life

Linda Hantrais

The 'herstory' of gendered policies in the member states of the European Union (EU) cannot be dissociated from the process of European enlargement and integration. Nor can it be fully understood without reference to the changing balance of power between and within European institutions, and the multiple pressures exerted by the many social, economic and political actors involved in the policy process at European and national level.

Equal pay and equal treatment for men and women have long been on the European agenda. Since the 1970s, the EU has built up a strong body of equality legislation, thereby establishing the rights of women as paid workers. With the extension of membership to countries that have developed different legal and social security institutions, consensus over the acceptability of binding EU-level legislation on equal opportunities issues has been more difficult to achieve. In addition, welfare retrenchment, prolonged economic recession, deregulation and Economic and Monetary Union (EMU) have called equality policies into question and raised doubts about their effectiveness. At the same time, the focus has shifted from equal pay and equal treatment to more equal sharing of paid and unpaid work. The agreement reached in the 1990s over the need to integrate the gender perspective into all aspects of EU policy (mainstreaming) could be interpreted as a sign that governments have acknowledged the wisdom of recognizing the contribution made by women to economic and social life, under the influence of leaders in the world equality rankings, such as Finland and Sweden (United Nations Development Programme, 1995). Alternatively, it could be seen as a means of pacifying women's lobbies by giving the impression that gender issues are being taken into account, but without necessarily formulating and implementing binding legislation.

1

Close scrutiny of European legislation confirms the conceptual shift from what could broadly be termed women's policy, in the sense of measures designed to bring women into line with men as workers, to gender policy aimed at tackling socially constructed inequalities at work and in the home. Over the years, attention has moved on from the principle of equal pay, enshrined in the 1957 Treaty of Rome, through positive action and positive discrimination intended to help women achieve greater equality of opportunity and redress inequality of outcomes, to the mainstreaming approach incorporated in the 1997 Treaty of Amsterdam. In the context of education and training, Teresa Rees (1998) has graphically described the equal treatment approach of the early years of the EEC as 'tinkering', the attempt to integrate women into male-dominated organizations and cultures through positive action as 'tailoring', and the recasting of mainstream provision as 'transforming' difference. She warns, though, that mainstreaming could be used to dismantle many of the 'hard-won mechanisms' supporting equal opportunities.

The central aim of this book is to contribute to the understanding of the way in which the policy process has changed and developed, by tracking the inputs of member states and pressure groups to policy formation at European level over time, and by analysing outputs at national level as they impact on gender issues in law and practice. Particular attention is paid to measures for reconciling employment and family life at the intersection between national and European-level policy processes.

The body of literature on equal opportunities in the European context expanded rapidly during the 1990s as realization grew of the impact that European law can have on the everyday lives of men and women in EU member states. While adding to the general literature on the subject, the present volume complements and extends work on the integration of gender in the EU (for example Hoskyns, 1996) and on sex equality policy in Western Europe (for example García-Ramon and Monk, 1996; Gardiner, 1997). It traces the development of EU policy on women's rights over the second half of the twentieth century, analysing the relationship between national and European-level policy formulation, the role of different policy actors and the outcomes of equality and reconciliation measures.

This introductory chapter is one of three contributions providing an overview of the European context for equality policy formulation and implementation. It sets the scene by presenting the evolving institutional framework and economic context in which gender issues have moved onto the political agenda at European and national level. It then tracks the shift in European legislation from equal rights to reconciliation measures, and examines the impact of the different waves of membership on gender policy. The chapter raises a number of questions that are developed throughout the book. What have been the forces for and against change in EU equality policy? Who are the policy actors at national and transnational level? How have EU institutions responded to the pressures for and against change? To what extent has EU legislation on gender issues resulted in a stronger body of legislation at national level? Has the need for consensus at European level led to a levelling down of measures to match the resources of the least advanced countries? To what extent have gender policies produced unwanted outcomes and perverse effects for women in EU member states? What has been the impact of reconciliation policies? These questions are returned to in the concluding chapter by Monica Threlfall, who draws on the evidence adduced in the country chapters to exemplify different national responses.

THE CHANGING INSTITUTIONAL FRAMEWORK FOR GENDER POLICY

The EU has aptly been described by Paul Pierson and Stephan Leibfried (1995) as a multitiered system of governance rather than as an international organization. These two authors debate the widely held view that national sovereignty has progressively been eroded as the institutions of the EU have extended their competence, leaving few areas of public policy outside its reach. They show how individual member states have been able to influence both the European agenda and the passage of legislation. Insistence on the subsidiarity principle has, for example, enabled member states to oppose contentious legislation and water down its prescriptions. In a study that analyses the impact of European policy-making and the influence of EU institutions on the wider process of European integration, Laura Cram (1997) also selects social policy as an area where national governments strongly opposed the extension of EU competence. She concludes that the EU has, paradoxically, extended the scope of its actions, despite the absence of explicit treaty obligations, largely through reliance on soft law rather than binding legislation.

Another metaphor frequently applied to EU policy development is that of a multilevel game, in which national governments are both gatekeepers for their own country's interests and key actors in the international arena (Putnam, 1988). On the basis of a comparison of state-centric and multilevel governance, Gary Marks *et al.* (1996) also argue that the sovereignty of individual member states has been diluted, as supranational institutions increase their powers, and more policy decisions are taken collectively. State-centrists (for example Moravcsik, 1993; Caporaso, 1996) would maintain that intergovernmental negotiation and co-ordination have produced gains that might not otherwise have arisen. Proponents of multilevel governance respond that 'national governments are constrained in their ability to control supranational institutions they have created at the European level', and that the decision-making process involves 'multiple intermeshing competencies, complementary policy functions, and variable lines of authority' (Marks *et al.*, 1996, pp. 352, 366).

Extending the analysis to equality policy, Bob Reinalda (1997) has analysed how co-operation and policy co-ordination have been applied in the equal opportunities area. He argues that international organizations are actors capable of exercising an autonomous influence over national states and their policies, at times setting standards that may be bolder than national ones, as exemplified by the decisions of the European Court of Justice (ECJ). It can be argued that agreement over international standards is, however, dependent on negotiated compromise between member states, and that such standards can only be effective if international and domestic enforcement mechanisms and penalties for non-compliance are applied, particularly in the case of women's policy. As many commentators have noted, the role played by non-governmental pressure groups as policy actors is not to be underestimated. It may be decisive not only at national level, for example by bringing cases before the ECJ, but also at transnational level when national groups join forces to lobby intergovernmental institutions, as illustrated by the interstate feminism of the 1970s (Hoskyns, 1996).

While being contained by the subsidiarity principle, the powers of EU institutions in the social policy field were significantly extended by the Single European Act (SEA) and the Treaty on European Union, which introduced majority voting in areas where, previously, unanimity was required, notably for social provisions. The role accorded to the European Parliament has also been enhanced as a result of changes in procedures under the SEA. Agenda setting has developed into a shared and contested competence among European institutions (European Council, Council of Ministers, European Commission and European Parliament), and interest group representation has proliferated. Arguably, the European Commission has come to play the key role in setting the agenda and in moving forward legislation in the social area. At the same time, the ECJ has used its powers of judicial review to interpret and refine European directives and clarify the legitimacy of national law and practice, thereby further expanding European authority. In Chapter 2, Maria Stratigaki examines how the institutions created by the EEC have developed their respective competencies as policy actors in the gender equality area, and how the cumulative effect of their actions has been to achieve mainstreaming of gender policy.

THE CHANGING SOCIO-ECONOMIC CONTEXT
FOR GENDER POLICY

Since the 1970s and 1980s, the institutional framework for gender policy-making has developed against a background of increasing deregulation and globalization of markets. Over the period, economic growth slowed down, and unemployment became a major priority for most governments, as confirmed at the Essen Summit in 1994 (European Council, 1994). National social protection systems came increasingly under scrutiny, as EU member states entered a period of welfare retrenchment, while at the same time striving to meet the criteria laid down for EMU.

The period from the late 1970s also brought far-reaching changes to the place of women in society: more women were entering the labour force and developing more continuous working patterns. In the 1970s, when labour markets were still expanding, governments had been prepared to consider ways of supporting women as workers to satisfy the demand for labour. During the economic recession of the 1980s, in many countries, female employment was again of interest to policymakers, because women afforded a more flexible and less costly supply of labour.

The decade from the mid-1980s to mid-1990s saw marked change in women's patterns of education and training, employment and unemployment, as recorded by Eurostat (1997c) using data drawn from the Community labour force surveys. Between 1985 and 1995, more women were acquiring higher levels of educational qualifications. However, in 1995, women with an equivalent level of educational achievement to men were still displaying consistently lower economic activity rates than their male counterparts, even for the younger age groups, particularly in Greece, as shown in Figure 1.1. While female

Figure 1.1 Trends in economic activity rates by age group, for women in 1985–1995 and for men in 1995, in EU member states

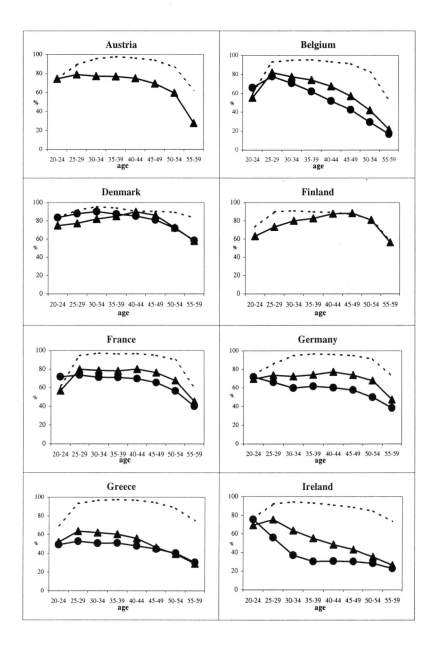

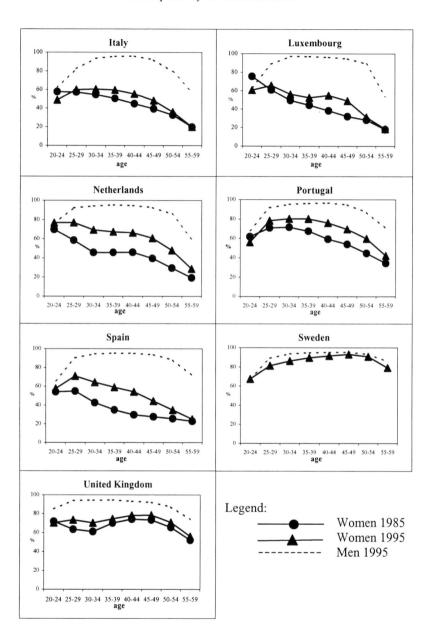

Sources: Eurostat, *Labour Force Survey 1995*, 1997c, table 003;
1985 data, Eurostat personal communication.

economic activity rates were increasing, those for men were falling, bringing overall rates for men and women closer together, especially in Finland (4.6 points difference), Sweden (5.2 points) and East Germany (6.3 points) in the mid-1990s. Disparities remained much more marked in Greece, Ireland, Italy, Luxembourg and Spain (over 30 points). The increase in women's economic activity rates was accompanied in most EU member states (except Finland and the United Kingdom) in the mid-1990s by higher unemployment rates than for men. Women in Spain were particularly prone to suffer from long-term unemployment: by 1995, 30.5 per cent of Spanish women of working age were unemployed, of whom 60.0 per cent for 12 months or more.

In the mid-1990s, women's working patterns varied from one member state to another and according to age. As illustrated by Figure 1.1, in many countries, female economic activity rates peaked for women in their mid-twenties and then fell as women left the labour force to begin raising a family; in Denmark, Finland, France, Germany, Portugal, Sweden and the United Kingdom, rates increased for women in their thirties and forties. Women were also much more likely than men to adjust their work-time patterns to fit their family commitments, by working shorter hours and part-time. Again rates for part-time varied markedly between member states: from 67.2 per cent in the Netherlands, 44.3 per cent in the United Kingdom and 43.0 per cent in Sweden, to 8.4 per cent in Greece, in 1995. Labour markets continued to be segregated both horizontally and vertically, with women concentrated in less secure, low-paid jobs, essentially in the service sector, which accounted for over 80 per cent of female employment across the EU. Nor was the greater commitment of women to paid work accompanied by a marked redistribution of household labour. According to data from European Community Household Panel (Eurostat, 1997b) and Eurobarometer (1996) surveys, everywhere women still performed the vast majority of domestic tasks and were the primary homemakers. Overall, Sweden, Denmark, Finland and Portugal were the member states where women's working patterns appeared to have moved closest to those of men. Disparities in terms of gender equality and sharing of tasks between men and women had remained most marked in Greece, Italy, Spain, Luxembourg and Ireland.

The greater economic independence associated with women's labour market activity was reflected in changing family-building patterns. Alternative, non-institutionalized family forms were becoming more widespread, though with important regional differences. According to Eurostat (1997a) demographic statistics, marriage rates had fallen to 5.1 per 1000 population in 1995, compared to 7.9 in 1960. Age at marriage was being postponed, and mean age at first marriage had risen to 28.7 years for men and 26.3 for women by the mid-1990s, an increase of 2 years in each case since 1960. Mean age of women at childbearing had also risen, reaching 28.9 years by 1995, the age at which women's economic activity rates were peaking. Completed fertility rates had fallen to the lowest levels ever recorded (1.63 in Germany and Italy in 1995), and the proportion of third and higher order births had declined rapidly, particularly since 1985 in the countries (Ireland, Portugal and Spain), where family size was largest. Many women appeared to be opting not to have children and to be refusing to confine themselves to a homemaker role. Divorce rates had risen to relatively high levels in the Nordic states and the United Kingdom (more than 4 in 10 marriages contracted in 1980 were expected to end in divorce, compared to 2 in 10 for the 1960 cohorts). Unmarried cohabitation had become a widespread living arrangement in the Nordic states, affecting about 1 in 4 of all couples, and was particularly prevalent among the younger age groups.

The proportion of extramarital births had risen to over 50 per cent of all live births in Sweden by the mid-1990s, and to more than a third of births in Denmark, Finland, East Germany and the United Kingdom, but only to 3 per cent in Greece. Lone parenthood, most often as a result of divorce or separation, became a widespread phenomenon in the 1990s, affecting more than 10 per cent of families in all except the Mediterranean states. Overall, postponement of family formation and the development of non-institutionalized family forms had been taken furthest in Sweden, Denmark and France, while patterns of family-building remained much more conventional in Southern Europe, particularly in Portugal and Greece.

These changes in economic activity and family-building patterns were posing important challenges for public policy in the mid-1990s. Policy-makers were seeking to ensure the efficacy of gender policies in a situation where high (male) unemployment continued to be a major concern, and where women constituted a more flexible labour supply for employers interested in recruiting part-time and temporary workers to keep down costs. Governments had to decide whether to target support on women as working mothers, by pursuing policies designed to maintain full-time, continuous female economic activity, involving minimal leave, public childcare and eldercare on demand, or whether to encourage women to leave the labour force to raise their own children, through paid parental leave and part-time work. Another possibility was to promote policies intended to maximize individual choice between different options by offering arrangements for parental leave and reducing economic activity during the childrearing phase for both men and women who temporarily leave the labour force when their children are young, but with a guarantee of reinstatement, and generous provision of childcare and household services to support parents who remain in the labour market. In Chapter 3, Marlene Lohkamp-Himmighofen and Christiane Dienel examine how different countries have chosen between these policy options and comment of the outcomes for women as workers and as mothers. In Chapter 10, Monica Threlfall analyses different models of reconciliation adopted by both men and women on an individual basis.

CHANGING EU POLICY ON GENDER

Many writers in the 1990s were critical of comparative analysis of state welfare regime typologies, such as that constructed by Gøsta Esping-Andersen (1990), on the grounds that these classification systems, like the welfare states they describe, are gender blind (for example Lewis, 1992; the contributions to Sainsbury, 1994; or the overview by Duncan, 1995). The same criticism could be made of the EEC in its early years. During the construction of European institutions, social provisions and equal pay were incorporated into the Treaty of Rome primarily for economic reasons and not to help parents find solutions to the problems of reconciling paid work with family life.

The ground had already been prepared in international debates for policies to establish equal rights between women and men. Convention 100 of the General Conference of the International Labour Organization (ILO), adopted in 1951, concerned 'equal remuneration for men and women workers for work of equal value'. ILO conventions represent standards which signatory states agree they will aspire to achieve. Failure to do so may incur international opprobrium but not financial penalties. The EEC Treaty Article 119, which referred only to 'equal pay for equal work' and not for 'equal value', did not have an immediate effect either. It represented a concession and a means of conciliating the French government. At no point in the discussions was reference made to the interests of women or to social justice (Hoskyns, 1996, p. 57). Equality issues did not become a topic of serious concern for member states until the 1970s, when the main output was in the form of Council directives, as summarized in Figure 1.2. By the 1990s, directives were being supplemented and developed through soft law and case law, as illustrated by the cases brought before the ECJ which are discussed in this volume and also listed in the figure. Mainstreaming was being written into treaty commitments and was being expressed in the equality rhetoric of resolutions and decisions. The development and expansion of the EU broadened interest out from the equal pay/treatment theme and equality at work to reconciliation between family life and employment and greater sharing in the home.

Figure 1.2 Changing EU legislation on gender

PRIMARY LEGISLATION

Treaty establishing the European Economic Community, signed in Rome on 25 March 1957: Article 119 on the application of the principle that men and women should receive equal pay for equal work.

Treaty on European Union, signed in Maastricht on 7 February 1992, Protocol and Agreement on Social Policy, concluded by the member states, with the exception of the United Kingdom: Article 2 on equality between men and women with regard to labour market opportunities and treatment at work; Article 6 on equal pay for equal work.

Treaty of Amsterdam amending the Treaty on the European Union, the Treaties establishing the European Communities and certain related acts, signed in Amsterdam on 2 October 1997: Articles 2, 3, 13, 137, 141 (*Official Journal of the European Communities* C 340, 10.11.97).

SECONDARY LEGISLATION AND POLICY DOCUMENTS

Council Resolution of 21 January 1974 concerning a social action programme (*OJEC* C 13/1 12.2.74).

Council Directive 75/117/EEC of 10 February 1975 on the approximation of the laws of the Member States relating to the application of the principle of equal pay for men and women (*OJEC* L 45/19 19.2.75).

Council Directive 76/207/EEC of 9 February 1976 on the implementation of the principle of equal treatment for men and women as regards access to employment, vocational training and promotion and working conditions (*OJEC* L 39/40 14.2.76).

Council Directive 79/7/EEC of 19 December 1978 on the progressive implementation of the principle of equal treatment for men and women in matters of social security (*OJEC* L 6/24 10.1.79).

Council Recommendation 84/635/EEC of 13 December 1984 on the promotion of positive action for women (*OJEC* L 331/34, 19.12.84).

Council Directive 86/378/EEC of 24 July 1986 on the implementation of the principle of equal treatment for men and women in occupational social security schemes (*OJEC* L 225/40 12.8.86).

Council Directive 86/613/EEC of 11 December 1986 on the application of the principle of equal treatment between men and women engaged in an activity, including agriculture, in a self-employed capacity, and on the protection of self-employed women during pregnancy and motherhood (*OJEC* L 359/56, 19.12.86).

Communication from the Commission of 8 August 1989 on family policies, COM(89) 363 final.

Community Charter of the Fundamental Social Rights of Workers, adopted in Strasbourg on 9 December 1989 by the member states, with the exception of the United Kingdom; Title I §16 on equal treatment for men and women.

Council Resolution of 21 May 1991 on the third medium-term Community action programme on equal opportunities for women and men (1991–1995) (*OJEC* C 142/1 31.5.91).

Council Recommendation 92/241/EEC of 31 March 1992 on child care (*OJEC* L 123/16 8.5.92).

Council Recommendation 92/442/EEC of 27 July 1992 on the convergence of social protection objectives and policies (*OJEC* L 245/49 26.8.92).

Council Directive 92/85/EEC of 19 October 1992 on the introduction of measures to encourage improvements in the safety and health at work of pregnant workers and workers who have recently given birth or are breastfeeding (*OJEC* L 348/1 28.11.92).

Council Recommendation 92/131/EEC of 27 November 1991 on the protection of the dignity of women and men at work (*OJEC* L 49/1 24.2.92).

Council Directive 93/104/EC of 23 November 1993 concerning certain aspects of the organization of working time (*OJEC* L 307/18 13.12.93).

Council Decision 95/593/EC of 22 December 1995 on a medium-term Community action programme on equal opportunities for men and women (1996 to 2000) (*OJEC* L 335/37 30.12.95).

Council Directive 96/34/EC of 3 June 1996 on the Framework Agreement on parental leave concluded by UNICE, CEEP and the ETUC (*OJEC* L 145/4 19.6.96).

Council Directive 97/80/EC of 15 December 1997 on the burden of proof in cases of discrimination based on sex (*OJEC* L 14/6 20.1.98)

Council Directive 97/81/EC of 15 December 1997 concerning the Framework Agreement on part-time work concluded by UNICE, CEEP and the ETUC (*OJEC* L 14/9 20.1.98)

SELECTED CASES BROUGHT BEFORE THE EUROPEAN COURT OF JUSTICE

Case 80/70 Gabrielle Defrenne v Belgian State [1971] ECR I–445, on the status of social security retirement pensions in relation to equal pay.

Case 43/75 Gabrielle Defrenne v Société Anonyme Belge de Navigation Aérienne Sabena [1976] ECR I–455, on the application of the equal pay principle in the case of termination of contracts.

Case 96/80 Mrs J.P. Jenkins v Kingsgate (Clothing Productions) Ltd. [1981] ECR I–911, on the difference in pay between full-time and part-time workers.

Cases C–312/86 and C–318/86 Commission of the European Communities v French Republic [1988] ECR I–3359 and ECR I–6315, on Directive 76/207 concerning equal treatment of men and women.

Case C–262/88 Douglas Harvey Barber v Guardian Royal Exchange Assurance Group [1990] ECR I–1889, on discrimination over pensionable age for workers made redundant.

Case C–177/88 E.J.P. Dekker v Stichting Vormingscentrum voor Jong Volwassenen (VJV-Centrum) Plus [1990] ECR I–3941, on the refusal to employ a pregnant woman.

Case C–188/89 A. Foster and Others v British Gas plc. [1990] ECR I–3313, on the right to continue work after the age of retirement.

Case C–345/89 Criminal proceedings against Alfred Stoeckel, Tribunal de police d'Illkirch, Preliminary ruling [1991] ECR I–4047, on legislation prohibiting night work for women.

Case C–271/91 M.H. Marshall v Southampton and South West Hampshire Area Health Authority [1993] ECR I–4367, on the upper limit of compensation in cases of discrimination.

Case C–408/92 Constance Christina Ellen Smith and Others v Avdel Systems Ltd [1994] ECR I–4435, on retrospective action with regard to discrimination in relation to benefits under occupational pensions.

Case C–450/93 Eckhard Kalanke v Freie Hansestadt Bremen [1995] ECR I–3051, on positive discrimination in the appointment and promotion of men and women.

Case C–180/95 Nils Draehmpaehl v Urania Immobilienservice OHG [1997] ECR I–2195, on the burden of proof and compensation.

Case C–409/95 Hellmut Marschall v Land Nordrhein-Westfalen [1997] ECR I–6363, on priority for women in promotion.

Case C–197/96 Commission of the European Communities v French Republic [1997] ECR I–1489, on the failure of a member state to fulfil its obligations with regard to the prohibition on night work.

Case C–136/95 Caisse nationale d'assurance vieillesse des travailleurs salariés (CNAVTS) v Evelyne Thibault [1998] ECR I–2011, on the right and assessment of performance during maternity leave.

Linda Hantrais

From equal opportunities measures...

The intention behind the equal pay principle contained in Article 119 under the social policy section of the 1957 EEC Treaty was to create fair and equal competition between member states by preventing any one country from gaining a competitive edge by paying women at lower rates than men. It provided a foundation and reference point for subsequent equality legislation. No important measures were, however, developed in the equal opportunities area until the mid-1970s, when the growing debate on the subject coincided with increasing interest in social affairs, the early signs of economic recession and the rapid expansion of women's labour market participation. The postwar baby boom had, by then, come to an end and the full effects of the oil crises were not yet being felt. The Community's social action programme of 1974 recognized that economic growth was not benefiting all sectors of the European population, not least women. The focus of attention was, therefore, broadened to cover access to employment and vocational training and advancement, as well as working conditions, in a series of equal opportunities action programmes and legislation.

Equality between the sexes, as embodied in Council Directive 75/117/EEC on equal pay and Council Directive 76/207/EEC on equal treatment for men and women in access to employment, vocational training and promotion, took some account of the special needs of women who were seeking to combine motherhood with paid work. Equal treatment under the terms of the directives meant that discrimination was prohibited on the grounds of sex by reference, in particular, to marital or family status.

Council Directive 79/7/EEC, which finally came into force in 1984, addressed the principle of equal treatment for men and women in matters of social security. It was supplemented in 1986 by two further directives, 86/378/EEC and 86/613/EEC, which extended the principle of equal treatment to occupational schemes and self-employed men and women. Although all three directives undoubtedly made an important contribution to equality legislation by giving women access to individualized rights, they were not concerned to help parents combine paid work with family life.

Under Article 118a of the SEA, signed in Luxembourg and the Hague in 1986, qualified majority voting was introduced for areas of legislation concerned with the working environment and health and safety at work. It was a procedure that could be used when it might otherwise be difficult to obtain unanimous agreement in the Council of

Ministers, as was the case with Council Directive 92/85/EEC, which was designed to protect women as working mothers by guaranteeing they were not exposed to health risks, including night work. The way in which this directive has been implemented at national level is examined with regard to maternity leave in Chapter 3.

Legislation on equal treatment in matters of social security did not directly address the issue of part-time working conditions, another important area of concern for women seeking to combine family responsibilities and employment. From the early 1970s, several unsuccessful attempts had been made to bring forward legislation on working time. The provisions of the SEA were again used to enable progress to be made with contentious legislation in this area, by treating it as a health and safety measure. Council Directive 93/104/EC, concerning certain aspects of the organization of working time, laid down minimum daily, weekly and yearly rest periods and regulations for night and shift work. While no explicit link was made between work-time arrangements and family life, some progress was achieved towards greater recognition of working hours as an important component in the family–employment relationship.

The equal treatment directives were founded on the premise that action was needed to ensure women had access to the same employment rights as men. The restrictions built into EU law and the apparent reluctance of national governments to make more generous provision indicated that the unpaid domestic work performed by women had still not been fully recognized as a basis for entitlements in their own right.

... to reconciliation of employment with family life

Reference was made to the need for measures to enable family responsibilities to be reconciled with job aspirations in the 1974 Council Resolution establishing a social action programme (*OJEC* C 13, 12.02.74, p. 2), but it did not produce any concrete results at the time. As social affairs secured a stronger position on the European agenda, particularly in the late 1980s, attention began to shift towards unpaid work, an area previously outside the remit of the Community's institutions. The European Commission had drafted a Communication on family policies in 1989 (COM(89) 363 final), in which explicit reference was made to the need for measures to help parents reconcile paid work and family life and to encourage greater sharing of family responsibilities. The communication recognized the importance of the contribution women made to the economy, while also being a necessity at household level. Under the heading 'equal treatment' (§16), the 1989

Community Charter of the Fundamental Social Rights of Workers also referred explicitly to the need for measures to enable 'men and women to reconcile their occupational and family obligations'.

A number of other documents drafted during the early 1990s kept reconciliation measures on the policy agenda at European level, particularly in the context of equal opportunities. A Council Resolution of 21 May 1991 on the third medium-term Community action programme on equal opportunities for women and men, covering the period 1991–95, enjoined member states to implement policies to reduce barriers to women's employment, 'through measures designed to reconcile family and occupational responsibilities of both women and men' (*OJEC* C 142, 31.5.91, p. 2). It called upon both sides of industry to 'pursue and intensify the social dialogue on the issues of reconciling occupational and family responsibilities and protecting the dignity of women and men at work' (*OJEC* C 142, 31.5.91, p. 3).

The Agreement on Social Policy annexed to the Treaty on European Union, and signed in Maastricht on 7 February 1992 by 11 of the 12 member states, made no reference to women as mothers. However, the Council's concern that differences in social security cover from one member state to another might prevent mobility of labour did prompt it to publish a recommendation in the same year on the convergence of social protection objectives and policies (*OJEC* L 245/49, 26.8.92). In a short section on the family, one of the two aims set out was to remove obstacles to occupational activity by providing measures to help parents reconcile their family and professional responsibilities.

When the Maastricht Treaty came into force, childcare was the only family–employment area where the Council had adopted proposals for action brought forward by the Commission. The childcare recommendation was an equal opportunities measure designed to help parents reconcile employment, education and training with family obligations arising from caring for children. The recommendation covered not only the provision of public and private childcare facilities but also special leave, the environment, the structure and organization of the workplace and the sharing of family, professional and educational responsibilities. Levels of childcare provision were not specified, but the Commission was assigned the task of monitoring and reporting on national measures. The task undertaken since 1986 by the European Childcare Network was upgraded to become part of the Commission's brief, and the network was renamed in 1991 to indicate its broader remit as the European Commission Network on Childcare and Other Measures to Reconcile Employment and Family Responsibilities.

The 1994 White Paper on European Social Policy indicated that the Commission was prepared to go further in ensuring implementation of childcare. It was planning to undertake 'an economic assessment both of the job-creation and reflationary potential of child and dependent-care infrastructures and services', as well as looking into target levels of provision and the possible use of fiscal and financial instruments to improve infrastructures and services before making further proposals (European Commission, 1994a, p. 43). The White Paper confirmed that the Commission intended to pursue its activities in this area, again within the context of equality of opportunity between women and men. A subsection in the document was devoted to 'Reconciling employment and household/family life', on the grounds that it was in the interests of society as a whole that working life and family life should be 'more mutually reinforcing' (European Commission, 1994a, pp. 42–3). Two key issues were explicitly addressed: how to manage and support the relationship between working time and time spent caring for children and older people; how to encourage more effective sharing of responsibilities for care between men and women. These aims were reiterated in the Council Decision 95/593/EC of 22 December 1995 on a medium-term Community action programme on equal opportunities for men and women (1996 to 2000) and became an integral part of the programme (see Chapter 2).

Although the childcare recommendation contained references to special leave from work, for more than a decade a proposal from the Commission for a Council directive concerning parental leave and leave for family reasons had remained on the table (*OJEC* C 333/6, 9.12.83). The version before the Council in 1994 provided for an entitlement to a minimum of three months' leave up to the child's second birthday, either full- or part-time, with a guarantee of reinstatement and insurance cover for sickness, unemployment, invalidity and old age benefits. Parental leave was presented as an entitlement and not an obligation, and payment of an allowance was a possibility rather than a mandatory requirement. Provision of leave for other family reasons, contained in the same draft directive, covered cases such as the illness of a spouse, death of a close relative, marriage or illness of a child. Such leave was to be counted as paid leave for the purposes of wages, social security contributions and benefits, and pension rights. When Council Directive 96/34/EC was eventually agreed in 1996, the period over which the leave could be taken was extended up to the time when the child reached the age of eight (see Chapter 2). An important stipulation was that the right should be granted to each parent on a non-transferable basis. No reference was made to any payment during the leave period, but member states were given discretion to decide under what conditions leave should be granted, enabling them to retain the individual arrangements already in operation (see Chapter 3).

The Treaty of Amsterdam, adopted in 1997, confirmed the commitment to promote equality between men and women in the labour market and at work, to eliminate inequalities and avoid discrimination (Articles 2, 3, 13, 137). Article 141, which replaced Article 119 in the Treaty of Rome, included a paragraph on the right of member states to take measures to assist the 'underrepresented sex' in pursuing an occupational activity. It did not, however, identify reconciliation measures as an equality provision. The employment strategy agreed at the Extraordinary European Council Meeting on Employment held in Luxembourg, also in 1997, recognized the contribution of women to employment growth, and the need to ensure their 'employability' (European Council, 1997, Part II). In this case, a paragraph was included on the reconciliation of work and family life, recommending that the implementation of directives and agreements between social partners should be 'accelerated and monitored regularly' (§76). The provision of care services and of measures to facilitate the return to work was identified as a key area for attention.

The incorporation of gender issues into the 1998 Employment Guidelines, adopted by a Council Resolution on 15 December 1997, signalled an important development for gender policy, giving legitimacy to reconciliation measures in the general discussion about job creation. The new commitment to the concept of 'mainstreaming' required 'the systematic consideration of the differences between the condition, situation and needs of women and men in all Community policies, at the point of planning, implementing and evaluation' (European Commission, 1997a, p. 8). Further aims underpinning the mainstreaming approach were to avoid the possible negative consequences of policy and to monitor the actual gender impact of policies that are often considered to be gender neutral.

Council Directive 97/81/EC, implementing the framework agreement on part-time work concluded between the social partners in December 1997, provides an appropriate illustration of the progress made in linking flexibility in work organization with family responsibilities. However, it demonstrates the importance of arguing the case in terms of the interests of employers. In the agreement, explicit reference was made to the need to protect part-time workers not only on the grounds of equal treatment and equal opportunities for men and women, but also because of the benefits to be gained by enterprises from measures facilitating the reconciliation of paid and unpaid work.

In sum, even though the subject has not been explicitly broached in primary legislation in EEC and EU treaties, over the years European institutions have shown a growing interest in the family–employment relationship. The rhetoric in official documents has evolved from global and rather anodyne statements about the need for measures to ensure that the family responsibilities 'of all concerned' could be reconciled with job aspirations, as in the 1974 social action programme, through more forceful policy statements in the White Paper on European Social Policy, encouraging national governments to take positive action to ensure a more equal sharing of parental responsibilities, to a blanket acceptance in the late 1990s in various policy documents of the need to integrate the gender dimension in all EU policies.

THE IMPACT OF MEMBER STATES ON GENDER POLICY FORMATION

If EU governance is essentially a multilevel game and a process involving negotiation and the multiple intermeshing of competencies and interests between member states, the composition, or country mix, of its membership is an important factor in determining the nature of the compromises reached. In the 40 years since it was founded in the late 1950s, the EEC has undergone four waves of enlargement. Each new group of countries brought with it a differentiated set of interests and expectations, in terms of its political culture and policy environment, which have influenced the approach to gender issues at supranational level and, in turn, determined how European legislation has been implemented at national level. While some countries have been movers and shakers, pressing for policy innovation at EU level, others have opposed and resisted European authority, and a third group have been obliged to adapt and develop their national policy frameworks to accommodate gender issues. The changing country mix has contributed not only to institutional change at European level but also to the development of domestic policy innovation.

First-wave EEC membership and the development of women rights

The six founder members of the EEC – Belgium, France, Germany, Italy, Luxembourg and the Netherlands – and also Austria, which did not join until the 1990s, shared a certain similarity of approach to the organization of welfare. Their social protection systems were mainly derived from the Bismarckian, statist, corporatist model, in accordance with the principle that workers are guaranteed benefits and a substitute income related to their previous earnings through a contractual insurance scheme (Clasen and Freeman, 1994). This 'continental' insurance model was founded on the assumption that employment qualified workers for welfare benefits as well as wages, and that benefits were funded primarily, if not exclusively, by employer and employee contributions as part of labour costs. Within such systems, married women's rights to protection were derived essentially from the labour force activity of their spouse, the male breadwinner. Women who engaged in economic activity could gain rights in their own name but, because they were generally employed in lower paid, often part-time jobs, and tended to leave employment when they married and had children, their individual earned rights were as a rule inferior to those of their spouses. In addition, the advantages accorded to sole-earner couples (Germany, Netherlands) or the allowances paid to women who stayed at home to raise children (France in the 1950s) served as a work disincentive for women, dissuading them from earning their own rights. Since the distribution of social security resources is determined essentially by labour market participation and employment-related rights, and since women's contribution to household (re)production is not attributed a monetary value, they are, per capita, likely to be receiving a relatively small proportion of the social spending budget.

Although this group of member states share several of the broad characteristics of the continental welfare model, their social protection systems are far from being uniform. They differ both structurally and in terms of their funding arrangements: the social costs of labour are, for example, likely to be much higher in France and Italy where contributions fall heavily on employers (Eurostat, 1998b). Despite systemic similarity, they have developed different approaches to gender issues, which are reflected in their input to policy at European level and the extent to which they have adapted their own legal frameworks to comply with European legislation.

France and Germany have been prime movers in European policy development, with France exercising strong pressure for member states to take account of the social dimension. The inclusion of the equal pay clause (Article 119) in the original Treaty of Rome was due, in no small part, to the insistence of the French, who had adopted provisions on equal pay at a much earlier date and feared unfair competition from their partners. It was perhaps no coincidence that two high profile French women, Evelyne Sullerot and Jacqueline Nonon, were responsible, in the early 1970s, for successfully pushing forward measures at European level for women in employment that took account of women's caring responsibilities (Hoskyns, 1996, p. 100). The French interest in demographic issues has also been in evidence in moves to extend EU competence to family policy. French equality legislation has closely mirrored developments at EU level, particularly with regard to reconciliation policies. By the late 1990s, the French could be described as having confirmed their position as an exemplar of the 'modified' breadwinner model (Lewis, 1992), due to well-established policies recognizing the rights of women as mothers and as workers. However, equal sharing of leave and of tasks in the home, the representation of women in decision-making positions and the desegregation of labour markets have continued to be distant goals for proponents of equal opportunities, as demonstrated by Marie-Thérèse Lanquetin, Jacqueline Laufer and Marie-Thérèse Letablier in this volume. Chapter 4 illustrates how different concepts of equality have been brought into conflict in France. The authors argue that, if sex equality employment law has not been effectively used to implement rights, the failure is due in no small part to a lack of political will.

The gender policies pursued by Germany have been described as promoting 'equality of difference', and as counteracting 'both national and EU equal-employment rules and measures' (Ostner and Lewis, 1995, p. 186). When the equal pay and equal treatment directives were being negotiated in the 1970s, German representatives insisted that the legal provisions in the German constitution were adequate, even though they discriminated against women by protecting the male breadwinner and by reinforcing the role of women as homemakers. Germany has effectively circumvented EU directives and used national legislation to safeguard the breadwinner principle, a point demonstrated by Kirsten Scheiwe in Chapter 5.

Italy, the third of the case study countries in the book, examined in Chapter 6 by Alisa Del Re, represents another form of adaptation to European integration and to gender issues. The Italian Constitution of 1947 also contained an equal pay clause, but the Italian government was more concerned in the 1950s with freedom of movement than with women's rights. Public opinion has been largely favourable towards the Community; European political and economic integration has provided incentives for social and economic policy, but women are far from being major beneficiaries from membership. Italy is among the member states with the worst records for transposing directives in the employment and social policy fields (European Commission, 1994a, p. 64). As in France, one of the paradoxes of its equality record is that innovative and generous policy measures do not appear to have resulted in any marked improvement of opportunities for women. On the contrary, they may have contributed to the exclusion of women from the labour market, as well as adversely affecting family building.

Second-wave EC membership and the development of equality policy

The second wave of membership of the European Community (EC) in the 1970s coincided with a fresh impetus in the social area and the first equal pay and equal treatment directives. The states that became members of the Community in 1973 – Denmark, Ireland and the United Kingdom – and also the two other Nordic states that joined in the 1990s, shared a general conception of social protection closer to what can be described as the citizenship or universal welfare model. According to the Beveridge scheme for social welfare in Britain (and also in Ireland) and to the Scandinavian model as practised in Denmark, the right to a pension, health care and family allowances was granted on the basis of social citizenship, independently from income earned by labour market activity. The implication was that employment provided a living wage, while welfare benefits were distributed through taxation to all citizens on equal terms whatever their employment status.

The social security systems in these three countries were also distinguished from the 'continental' model by their preference for fiscal resources and the universal provision of health care rather than insurance contributions and income-related benefits. The three member states had in common their voluntarist tradition in labour market regulation, based on negotiated contractual arrangements between employers and workers rather than legal statutes (Rhodes, 1995, p. 98). The Danish system, however, placed emphasis on income maintenance, whereas, in Ireland and the United Kingdom, the aim was to ensure subsistence by providing low flat-rate payments or means-tested social assistance. Despite the similarity in the underlying principle, according to Esping-Andersen's (1990) classification, the British welfare regime could be described as 'liberal' on the grounds that welfare has mainly operated as a residual safety net for the poor. The assumption in the British and Irish systems, as in the continental male-breadwinner model countries, was that women would be homemakers and, at most, secondary earners. In Denmark, the universalist, citizenship approach was taken much further and worked to the advantage of women, justifying its place among the countries with a 'weak' breadwinner model (exemplified by Sweden in Lewis, 1992).

In the United Kingdom, as illustrated by Barbara Bagilhole and Paul Byrne in Chapter 7, 'Europe' has been a source of dissension within and between the main political parties. Britain vehemently opposed proposals for social policy measures under the Thatcher government, and systematically blocked legislation in areas of equality policy, where it felt that national interests would not be served. In the late 1990s, the United Kingdom was still characterized by the strong male-breadwinner model, with relatively little state support to help mothers combine employment with family life. An unexpected, though not illogical outcome, was that British men seemed to be contributing to a greater extent to household tasks than, for example, some of their counterparts in countries where the male-breadwinner model was weaker (Eurobarometer, 1996; Eurostat, 1997b).

Despite the opposition of British governments to the growing competence of European institutions as social policy actors, the blocking tactics practised by the United Kingdom appear to have delayed rather than prevented some of the equality directives from being taken forward. It has been suggested that British representatives may have been expressing misgivings shared by other member states. Martin Rhodes (1995, p. 116) has speculated that, with the introduction of the procedures allowed for in the SEA and the Treaty on European Union, the 11 other member states would no longer be able to 'rely on the British veto to prevent their high-minded espousal of principles from coming to expensive fruition'. The impact of EC social legislation has, nonetheless, been felt strongly by the United Kingdom in the area of equal opportunities through the enforcement of legal rights following cases brought before the ECJ (Meehan and Collins, 1996). The United Kingdom was the EC member state (excluding Portugal and Spain) which held the record in 1997 for the number of judgements rendered by the ECJ for legal cases concerned with equal opportunities. The United Kingdom had received 31 rulings, compared to 30 for Germany, 2 for Ireland and 1 each for France, Luxembourg and Greece (European Commission, 1998a, p. 122).

For Ireland, by contrast, European membership served as an impetus for policy innovation in areas where change might not otherwise have been realized. Ireland is widely quoted as one of the countries where fundamental changes have been forced on policy-makers, and where, as a consequence, women have benefited greatly from being in the EC (Hoskyns, 1988; Gardiner, 1997, p. 11). In Denmark, as in the other Nordic states (see Bergqvist and Jungar in this volume), women have been the strongest opponents to European integration, fearing a levelling down of their rights.

Third-wave EC membership and the alignment of equality policy

Greece, Portugal and Spain, which joined the EC in the 1980s in the third wave of membership, were characterized by less advanced and less coherent social security systems, compared to most of the earlier members, and by underdeveloped gender policies. They continued to rely heavily on traditional forms of support through family and kinship networks, the Church and discretionary provision at local level. Social protection was broadly based on corporatism, as in the continental model, with employers carrying the major burden of the cost of providing benefits, but in Spain and Portugal, as in Italy and the second-wave member states, health care was largely provided by the state and funded from taxation. In the early 1990s, a relatively large proportion of the population was still not covered by social insurance, and neither Greece nor Portugal had a general social assistance scheme.

In all three countries, accession to the EC coincided with the development of new democracies. Integration has been strongly supported by the European Structural Funds and was dependent on the conditionality they imposed. Welfare spending has been heavily influenced by the need to meet the Maastricht criteria, which Greece failed to do. As in Ireland, but to a lesser extent, EC membership has helped to shape equality policy. In Chapter 8, Celia Valiente shows how governments in Spain have responded, and have sent the right signals, by setting up the Instituto de la Mujer and transposing EC directives into national law. Equality has not, however, been a government priority, and even less so the reconciliation of paid and unpaid work.

Fourth-wave EU membership and the advancement of equality policy

While Austria's social protection system was close to that of the continental member states, the other two countries that joined the EU in the 1990s – Finland and Sweden – belonged to the Nordic welfare state model, based on the universalist, citizenship principle, with relatively generous levels of benefit, funded mainly from taxation. Equality of rights, obligations and opportunities in all fields of life is seen as an essential component of the Nordic model and of its conception of democracy, exemplified in this book by the Swedish case. Equality means that differences between women and men should not lead to inequality in status or treatment in society. Economic independence is the basis on which equality is founded, implying not only that women should be able to enjoy the same status in the labour force as men, but also that the distribution of unpaid work between women and men should be changed to ensure more equal sharing (Vibe Lande, 1995).

The development of equality policy in these three countries has taken place mainly outside the EC, as illustrated by Christina Bergqvist and Ann-Cathrine Jungar in Chapter 9 with reference to Sweden. Since the early 1990s, Swedish governments have been trying to roll back the state. They have been following economic policies which have enabled the country to meet the Maastricht criteria, but which may have placed the 'Swedish model' under threat. Swedish membership of the EU may have been decisive for gender policy in Europe: the acceptance of the mainstreaming approach, and the emphasis on more equal sharing between women and men at the workplace and in the home can be largely attributed to the pressure exerted by the Nordic states. This proof that they can influence EU policy has gone some way towards allaying fears in Sweden that the advances made in gender equality outside the EU would be placed in jeopardy if they had to be defended in the European arena. As the Swedish contributors suggest, EU membership may also have influenced the national policy process by forcing legislative change.

GENDER POLICY OUTCOMES

The chapters in this volume illustrate how national policy priorities have differed from one member state to another. One of the reasons why reconciliation measures were such latecomers to the policy agenda may be that member states were unable to reach agreement over the legitimacy of intervention at European level in areas where national governments differed markedly in their approach (Hantrais and Letablier, 1996). Another possible explanation for the considerable variation from one country to another in the outcomes of EU reconciliation policies may be that policies decided at European level have been watered down to match the means of the slowest, or least willing, partners. They also reflect the contentiousness of the issues under debate at national level. The shift towards soft law has given member states greater leeway in implementation. The net result is, however, that the compromise solutions reached at EU level are generally considered as having moved forward the gender equality cause, though not necessarily to the extent and at the speed that most women would have liked.

Governments are not simply reacting to pressures from women's lobbies (social justice arguments), but are also influenced by human resource arguments in a situation where women are increasingly breadwinners (and sometimes the sole earner in a family), while still being expected to perform the role of unpaid carers. In a climate of tighter monetary control over public spending and high levels of unemployment, equal opportunities, sharing and reconciliation measures are being implemented by governments concerned to find solutions to labour market problems. They may also be trying to find ways of reducing dependency on welfare and tackling the social problems associated with family breakdown by developing a stronger sense of individual and family responsibility. In some cases, the outcome of positive action or positive discrimination measures may have been to confirm women's difference and 'justify' their concentration in lower status, casual jobs. Another perverse effect of equality policies may have been the polarization of the female labour force (full-time, well-qualified, well-paid versus part-time, casualized, flexible workers), or the polarization of families between dual-earner, single-earner and no-earner households. The chapters in this book suggest that none of the gender policy mixes attempted so far has produced outcomes that satisfy all parties. The challenge, therefore, remains posed for policy-makers in the twenty-first century.

2 The European Union and the Equal Opportunities Process

Maria Stratigaki

In the 1970s, as the women's movement gained momentum, the European Community (EC) began to include equality between women and men among its social policy concerns. Since the 1970s, equality policy has shifted from the focus on equal pay and equal treatment in the labour market to the reconciliation of paid work and family life. This chapter examines the role played by European institutions in the policy process and negotiation procedures that brought about this shift. It shows how the institutions of the European Union (EU) have both promoted and resisted change, and how the interaction between the intentions of the initiators of policy, interpretations of policy-makers and lobbying of women's organizations provides the framework for policy formation.

The first part of the chapter describes the role of national governments, the European Commission, the European Parliament, the social partners and women's organizations in the development of European policy on equality. Specific reference is made to their role in promoting either equal treatment or reconciliation. It is argued that a clear shift from the equal treatment objective in the 1970s and 1980s to the reconciliation objective in the 1990s can be identified in the policies dealing with women and paid work. This shift is linked to the progression in the equality instruments used from positive action to gender mainstreaming. Equal treatment presupposed the desegregation of the labour market, with positive action as the policy instrument for implementing it. Reconciliation of paid work and family life required the coordination of all policies relating to employment and work organization, an aim that could be achieved through gender mainstreaming.

The second part of the chapter illustrates the roles played by different social actors and their interaction at critical points in equal opportunities policy development. The cases chosen are particularly relevant to policy shifts in the 1990s. Firstly, the strong alliance between policy-makers in supporting the Third Action Programme marked a substantial development for policy on reconciliation. Secondly, with the Kalanke ruling (Case C–450/93 Eckhard Kalanke v Freie Hansestadt Bremen [1995]), the European Court of Justice (ECJ) attacked positive action, which had been a major policy instrument for equal treatment. Thirdly, the implementation of the Agreement on Social Policy made it possible to adopt two directives on parental leave and part-time work attributing a new role to the social partners in law-making at European level. Finally, the development of gender mainstreaming marked the beginning of broader policy concerns for achieving equality; it also raised the question of whether mainstreaming should replace or complement positive action.

FROM EQUAL TREATMENT TO RECONCILIATION OF FAMILY AND EMPLOYMENT: THE POLICY ACTORS

In 1957, the founding members of the European Economic Community (EEC) introduced equal pay for women and men in the Treaty of Rome. Forty years later, in November 1997, the heads of state at their Extraordinary European Council Meeting on Employment, accepted equality between women and men, including reconciling paid work and family life, as one of the four pillars of the employment guidelines (European Council, 1997, p. 13). Over this period, the number of policy actors involved in gender issues at European level has been significantly extended. Their role has also changed as power has shifted from one institution to another.

National governments and the Council of Ministers

The role of national governments is exercised primarily in the drafting of treaties, in intergovernmental conferences and through the formal work of the Council of Ministers, particularly in adopting EU wide directives, and at the European Council's biannual regular meetings of heads of state. Article 119 on equal pay was introduced in the Treaty of Rome at the initiative of the French government. The underlying aim was to reduce competition between industries in member states, since the French had already implemented equal pay legislation. Other member states could then compete on more equal terms, with regard to labour costs in the emerging common market. The equal pay article was, however, moved from the section in the Treaty of Rome dealing with distortion of competition to that on social policy, with the aim of strengthening the social dimension of the treaty (Hoskyns, 1996, p. 57).

The first enlargement of the Community in 1973, when Denmark, Ireland and the United Kingdom became members, coincided with the initiation of EC social policy through the adoption in 1974 of a Council Resolution concerning a social action programme, which included equality between women and men. Social movements in Europe in the aftermath of 1968 played an important part in bringing social policy onto the European agenda. The first United Nations' World Conference on Women, in Mexico in 1975, provided an international impetus for the promotion of equality policy. However, member states, unlike the Commission, were becoming more reluctant to engage with equality issues. Exercising their influence primarily through the Council of Ministers, national governments effectively reduced the scope and content of Commission proposals for legislation.

The three directives on equality adopted by the Council in the 1970s (75/117/EEC, 76/207/EEC, 79/7/EEC) were pushed through by external forces. Women's organizations entered the European arena and pressed for legislation, and women officials in the Commission initiated and brought forward Commission proposals based on favourable rulings by the ECJ: for example Case 80/70 Gabrielle Defrenne v Belgian State [1971] and Case 43/75 Gabrielle Defrenne v Société Anonyme Belge de Navigation Aérienne Sabena [1976]. In the recitals of the first two directives, the objective of harmonizing living and working conditions was clearly stated as a background to the directives.

In 1984, the Council adopted Recommendation 84/635/EEC on positive action for women as a tool for equal treatment and desegregation of the labour market in European equality policy. In its proposals for the recommendation, the Commission had tried to fill the gap in the equal treatment directive with regard to positive action, thus preparing the ground for the subsequent Kalanke ruling (Hoskyns, 1996, pp. 103–7). The Commission decided to propose a non-binding instrument. Economic pressures to increase the number of women in the labour market in response to growth in the service sector, together with the demands of the women's movement on the eve of the United Nations' World Conference on Women, in Nairobi in 1985, should, however, have been sufficient reasons to persuade the Council of Ministers of the need to produce a directive aimed at promoting positive action.

This role played by the Council of Ministers with regard to equality policy during this period changed only when women began exercising political pressure. In 1994, during the German presidency, and on the eve of another United Nations' international conference, this time in Beijing, women ministers in charge of equality (including representatives from Scandinavian countries) met informally in Berlin to discuss equality issues. Shortly afterwards, the heads of state at their meeting in Essen recognized that equality between women and men and the fight against unemployment were 'the paramount tasks of the European Union and its Member States' (European Council, 1994, p. 4). These political declarations were made in response to warnings issued by Jacques Delors on the future of the EU in the White Paper on Growth, Competitiveness and Employment (European Commission, 1994b). They succeeded in mobilizing the relevant Commission services to try and integrate gender equality into employment policy (European Commission, 1995).

The role of national governments in taking forward equality again became crucial in the drafting of the Treaty of Amsterdam. Belgium, Finland and Sweden displayed the most progressive positions in terms of equality provisions (European Women's Lobby, 1997). In line with their proposals, positive action and mainstreaming were finally incorporated into the Treaty (Vogel-Polsky, 1997, pp. 3–4). The simultaneous reinforcement of employment policy in the Treaty helped to ensure a constructive framework, allowing the Council to accept the Commission's proposal in the 1998 employment guidelines, which included equality and reconciling paid work and family life as one of four pillars (European Commission, 1998c, p. 12).

The European Court of Justice

The ECJ played a positive role in promoting equality in the 1970s. It underpinned the adoption of the equal pay and equal treatment directives, and also contributed to their implementation by its judgements throughout the 1980s (Hoskyns, 1996, pp. 68, 90, 132–5). When the Treaty of Rome was drafted in 1957, member states were unable to predict that the transfer of power to the ECJ, a new and ambitious European institution, would cause them so many problems with its rulings. One of the most important of these was the second Defrenne judgement (Case 43/75), where the ECJ identified a violation of the Treaty in complicity with the European institutions (Vogel-Polsky and Vogel, 1991, p. 106; Hubert, 1998, p. 60).

The ECJ's interpretation of the equality directives continued to provoke problems for member states until the early 1990s. One of the most serious was the Barber ruling (Case C–262/88 Douglas Harvey Barber v Guardian Royal Exchange Assurance Group [1990]), which considered private occupational pensions as 'pay' entailing additional financial costs in what was a strong economic sector. The ECJ limited the retrospective effect of the judgement to cases that had already been commenced by 17 May 1990, the date of the judgement. This retrospective restriction was confirmed by member states in protocol no. 2 concerning Article 119, which they inserted into the Maastricht Treaty (Commission of the European Communities, 1995, p. 520). The use of the treaty amendment to limit, irreversibly, the effect of a directive was unprecedented and could be considered as an extreme reaction to the judgement.

The European Commission

With its exclusive right of initiative, the European Commission has been a major player in European women's policy. Gender equality has become an area of social policy which, together with health and safety, has one of the strongest legal bases. From the time of the 1974 social action programme through to the 1998 employment guidelines, the Commission proposed a series of directives, recommendations and action programmes in the field of equality. In most cases, the initial drafts were prepared by women officials committed to action on equality issues. They mobilized every possible source of support, from representatives of national governments and national experts to professionals and academics, in an attempt to ensure a broad political consensus. They had to overcome resistance from their hierarchical superiors and the reluctance of national politicians (Hoskyns, 1996, chapters 3–6).

In the 1980s, the role of the Commission was expanded to new areas and policy instruments by the adoption of two action programmes for equal opportunities in 1982 and 1986 (Commission of the European Communities, 1982, 1986). The programmes were drafted under pressure from women's movements, and were driven by United Nations' deliberations claiming that equality between women and men in the labour market would be possible only if, and when, the gender division of labour within the family was also challenged. Sharing of family responsibilities between women and men was included in both programmes. Equal treatment for women and men was one of the 12 rights in the 1989 Community Charter of the Fundamental Social Rights of Workers (§16), drafted by Directorate General V, in line with Delors' social priorities during his second term of office. In the charter, 'reconciliation' measures were proposed as an important means of promoting the right to equal treatment. Both the programmes and the charter enjoyed greater political visibility in Europe than their weak legal status and restricted funding might suggest. For example, member states were required to report annually to the Commission on the actions taken with regard to each of the workers' rights included in the charter.

The introduction of new issues in EC equality policy and the implementation of the action programmes were facilitated by the work of the administrative unit (Women's Bureau) set up within Directorate General V in 1976 (Hoskyns, 1996, p. 108). The unit was given the task of establishing and developing contacts with the outside world. The personality and commitment of its successive heads have proved to be of crucial importance in taking forward policies. One or two national civil servants have usually been invited to spend up to three years on secondment in the unit. These officials bring with them their own national traditions concerning equality issues, and may work on topics that are of interest to their governments.

Actions on childcare and reconciliation of paid work and family life have been systematically pursued within the unit by national experts from the United Kingdom. The co-ordinator of the expert network in this field was also British. The United Kingdom was the only member state sufficiently interested in equality to allow the secondment of a national expert on a regular basis, either from the Equal Opportunities Commission in Great Britain or Northern Ireland, or the Department of Employment. In addition, economic restructuring during the Thatcher era made reconciliation and its implications for flexibility a popular theme in equality policy-making in the United Kingdom.

The Commission has had to try and find a balance between the contradictory demands of the European Parliament and the Council of Ministers, and its margins for manœuvre have, therefore, frequently been constrained. Unanimous voting in the Council has meant that the Commission has been forced to propose solutions that would be acceptable to all member states.

The Advisory Committee on Equal Opportunities
for Women and Men

Secondment of civil servants is not the only means available for member states to exercise indirect influence on European equality policy. In 1981, the Commission set up an Advisory Committee on Equal Opportunities for Women and Men to 'advise the Commission on the formulation and implementation of its policy' (Commission Decision 82/43/EEC). The Commission appointed two representatives from each member state drawn from national committees or bodies responsible for equality. The composition of the committee was crucial in forming a European women's constituency and in co-ordinating the pressures exerted on political decision-makers at national level. In 1995, a Commission Decision 95/420/EC (*Official Journal of the European Communities* L 249 43-6, 17.10.95) enlarged the committee to include representatives of employers' and workers' organizations at EC level; the European Women's Lobby (described below) was invited as an observer.

The regular exchange of information and views between the specialist equality bodies of national governments, social partners and the European Commission has reinforced their roles within their respective organizations. National bodies have used positions advanced at European level and comparisons with other countries to defend their position at home, and the Equal Opportunities Unit has tested its policy and used the committee's formal opinions within the Commission. The frequency of meetings and the substance of debates has depended on the extent of the commitment of the head of the unit and the president of the Advisory Committee.

The European Parliament

The Women's Rights Committee of the European Parliament was set up in 1984, mainly by women members of the European Parliament (MEPs) from all political groups. The committee has generally been in agreement with the views and advice of the Commission's Advisory Committee on Equal Opportunities for Women and Men, and it has played an important role in promoting equality. It has supported the European Women's Lobby, often arguing against reductions in funding proposed by the European Parliament's Committee on Budgets, and opposing the positions adopted by the Council of Ministers.

The discussions (from September 1991 to March 1992) surrounding the Council Recommendation 92/241/EEC on childcare provide an example of the manoeuvring of the Commission between the European Parliament and the Council of Ministers. The Commission proposed that member states should 'ensure that public funding makes an essential contribution to the development of affordable, good quality, coherent services' (Commission Proposal 91/C 242/03, Article 3e). The European Parliament (*OJEC* C 326, 16.12.91, pp. 274–9) added that member states should fund care services and also put them under scrutiny and supervision. The Council's final text simply states they should 'encourage national, regional or local authorities, management and labour, other relevant organizations and private individuals, in accordance with their respective responsibilities, to make a financial contribution to the creation and/or operation of coherent child-care services which can be afforded by parents' (92/241/EEC, p. 18).

The European Parliament has also promoted new issues for EC action, which go beyond traditional EU competence. Reports by feminist MEPs are one outcome from the pro-equality lobby. For example, during the parliamentary session 1989–94, the Committee produced 27 reports covering issues such as women's health care and the violation of the freedom and fundamental rights of women (European Parliament, 1994, pp. 12–13). Links and co-operation between Commission services in charge of equality and the Women's Rights Committee were strengthened by activities of common interest, such as the campaigns to promote women in the European elections. In 1989, the Women's Information sector in Directorate General X launched a campaign under the slogan 'Women a trump for Europe'.[1] A second campaign was supported by the Equal Opportunities Unit and its Network on Women in Decision-making, with the slogan: 'Vote for a gender balance in the European Parliament in 1994'. Another slogan being used in the campaign for the 1999 elections was: 'Women are a winning card for Europe'.

Women's organizations

The women's movement and women's Non-Governmental Organizations (NGOs) have played a critical role in the development of EU equality policy. A European organization created in 1983, the European Network of Women (ENOW), exercised pressure for change in policy-making at Community level. The network established contacts with MEPs and requested Community funding to develop actions (for example on poverty among women). One of its founding members, Eva Eberhardt, was subsequently employed by the Commission as an expert in the Equal Opportunities Unit.

---

1. Directorate-General X is in charge of information and communication policies. The women's information sector has responsibility for informing women about European issues. Campaigns promoting women's votes for the European Parliament were undertaken within this context.

In 1989, a new policy actor entered the European equality policy arena: the European Women's Lobby was established at the initiative of the Commission. The support given by Vasso Papandreou, one of the two women commissioners appointed at the beginning of 1989, was decisive in taking forward the work of the lobby. By the late 1990s, the lobby had become an umbrella organization, covering almost 2700 member organizations and lobbies. Its two functions were to inform, link and raise awareness of women's organizations about European issues, and to ensure that women's needs and perspectives become an equal and integral part of European policies. In the context of its second mission, the lobby developed links with the Women's Rights Committee and with politicians from all parties at European level. It also operates at national level through its national co-ordinators. The general secretary, Barbara Helfferich, who took office at the end of 1992, adopted a professional approach to lobbying. The lobby came to be regarded as a serious interlocutor by both Commission officials and MEPs. Its well-documented positions on Community official texts were issued in good time and influenced decisions in the early stages of the process. Feminists in the lobby and the European Parliament have welcomed the introduction of new issues on the equality agenda, with a view to extending the scope of equality to the family and household, and as a means of challenging gender relations in areas other than the workplace, such as the sharing of domestic and childcare responsibilities between women and men.

The trade unions

The European consultative institution, the Economic and Social Committee (ECOSOC), has also played a supportive role in the promotion of equality in the Union. The committee regularly provides opinions on all major communications from the Commission. It consists of appointed representatives of trade unions, employers' organizations and other interest groups in member states, and some of its reports, which are generally drafted by external consultants familiar with equality issues, have been extremely progressive. The Women's Committee of the European Confederation of Trade Unions (ETUC) has also been supportive of equality policy. They have supplied observers on the Advisory Committee on Equal Opportunities for Women and Men, to work with representatives of employers organizations, the Union of Industrial and Employers' Confederations of Europe (UNICE) and the European Centre of Enterprises with Public Participation (CEEP).

To the extent that the Women's Committee has been involved in overall ETUC decision-making structures, women trade unionists have been able to influence the general positions adopted by the confederation. In the context of the reinforcement of the social dialogue and the Europeanization of industrial relations through the implementation of the Agreement on Social Policy, women had a better opportunity to be involved in decisions concerning equality in Europe. Cynthia Cockburn (1995) has shown, however, that structural barriers to women's participation in the European social dialogue have prevented them from reinforcing their role in negotiations.

Regular formal or informal contacts between these different policy actors make an important contribution to the political environment in which decisions are taken and policies are drawn up. The larger the number of policy actors involved in the process, the larger the number of alliances that can be formed, enabling productive negotiations to take place not only at the level of institutions, but also between politicians and officials.

A STRONG ALLIANCE FOR EQUALITY: THE THIRD ACTION PROGRAMME

The preparation of the Third Action Programme on Equal Opportunities between Women and Men (1991–1995) began in 1989 in a women-friendly environment due to the presence of key women in key positions. In addition, progress over the completion of the internal market in 1992 had led to optimism among decision-makers about the prospects for economic growth, which would create an environment conducive to the development of social policies, including equality policy. A woman, Vasso Papandreou, had been appointed as the new Commissioner for Social Affairs, and Christine Crawley, an active member of the British Labour Party, had been elected as chair of the Women's Rights Committee of the European Parliament. The Equal Opportunities Unit had a new head, Claire Mandouze, who remained in post until after the adoption of the programme. A well-informed man, Frank Boddendijk, from the Advisory Council on equal opportunities policy to the Dutch government, chaired the European Advisory Committee. Contact and co-operation between the Commission, the European Parliament and representatives of member states was strengthened, with the Commission reporting several times a year to these two bodies on its activities.

Helle Jacobsen from the Equal Status Council of Denmark was asked by the acting head of the unit, Chris Docksey, to prepare the first draft of the Third Action Programme. A Danish expert was selected for the task, because Denmark was well advanced in equality policy and familiar with policy for promoting women in decision-making, an issue which the advisory committee proposed should be included as a new element in the programme. Diana Brittan, who was connected with the Equal Opportunities Commission in Great Britain, played an active role in the preparation of the draft report and co-signed it. The report was a comprehensive 72-page document, proposing six equal opportunities programmes: women and employment, the combination of working and family life, education and vocational training, equal opportunities and the media, women in decision-making, and women and poverty. Seven tools were also recommended: legislation, research and evaluation, statistics, information and communication, mainstreaming equal opportunities policy, equal opportunities structures in the Commission and funding (Jacobsen and Brittan, 1989).

On the basis of the report, Janet Hemsley, the national expert from the United Kingdom seconded to the Unit, prepared a shorter strategic document for consultation with relevant policy actors. This document was presented in March 1990 and discussed with the co-ordinators of the expert networks operating under the second programme and the chair of the advisory committee. He gave the document his strong support, subject to a few reservations about the use of the term 'mainstreaming'. It was also presented and discussed at the Women's Rights Committee before its final adoption by the Commission in November 1990 (COM(90) 449 final, 6 November 1990).

Co-ordinators from the expert networks argued for a clearer distinction to be made between objectives and tools, for more emphasis on childcare and disadvantaged groups of women, such as ethnic minorities and women living in poverty. In addition, in its resolution (*OJEC* C 240, 16.9.91, pp. 247–50), the European Parliament requested directives on parental leave, childcare and the protection of the 'dignity' of women and men at work, implying protection against sexual harassment. Parliament also called for additional initiatives to counter possible dangers for women arising from the Single Market.

Compared to the first draft of August 1989, the final text of the programme was substantially weaker. The Community initiative under the European Structural Funds (ESF), New Opportunities for Women (NOW), hijacked a large part of the programme. Because the Greek commissioner's cabinet, which was responsible for redistributing labour, had little experience in dealing with equality issues and policies outside the scope of the ESF, it underestimated the political importance of the programme for the promotion of equality. Community initiatives were integral parts of the ESF and could not be easily associated with the implementation of other Community action programmes, in terms of either administration or funding procedures. References to migrant women were dropped during the interservice consultation, and references to informal work, home-working and atypical employment were considerably toned down.

The Third Action Programme marked an important advance in terms of the scope of its activities. It provided an opportunity for the new, highly motivated and active head of the Equal Opportunities Unit to develop innovative actions and initiate new policies. The primary concern of Agnès Hubert, who took up office in February 1992 and remained head of unit until April 1996, was to build on the existing consensus between policy-making bodies, experts and women's organizations in the EU. Eight expert networks were set up under the programme.[2] Academics, policy-makers, civil servants, equality practitioners, activists and researchers were involved in producing guides and disseminating information at national level on European equality policy. The participation of representatives from across the EU meant the Commission could form a clear idea of national developments. New ideas were tested at conferences, in a context of exchange of experience between women coming from countries with different equality traditions. The subsequent discontinuation of the networks as part of mainstreaming in 1996 under the Fourth Action Programme, therefore, provoked serious criticism by women's constituencies at national and European levels.

The strong consensus over the reconciliation objective of the programme signalled clear progress (Ross, 1998). The expert Network on Childcare and Other Measures to Reconcile Employment and Family Responsibilities, co-ordinated by a British academic, Peter Moss, provided a valuable background for studies, reports and publications, and was instrumental in alerting national governments to the importance of the quality of care services. The 1992 Council Recommendation 92/241/EEC on childcare was one of the outcomes of the network's

---

2. They cover the situation of women in the labour market, equal opportunities in broadcasting, local employment initiatives, equality law, equal opportunities in education, positive action, women in decision-making and childcare and other measures to reconcile employment and family responsibilities.

efforts. It also helped to extend interest from childcare to eldercare and care for the disabled, and to make men a target group for reconciliation measures. The childcare network coexisted with the European Positive Action Co-ordinating Group, also co-ordinated by a British official of the United Kingdom's Equal Opportunities Commission, Janet Hemsley. The network developed similar activities targeted at private and public companies, in an effort to encourage equality in human resources and total quality management programmes of enterprises. The aim was to promote positive action programmes by demonstrating their economic and social benefits for companies. The network examined the gender impact of work organization and career promotion schemes, and developed guidelines for instituting good practice in the provision of childcare.

The other six networks also contributed to policy formulation in their respective areas. Within this favourable context, in 1994, the Unit began preparing an ambitious Fourth Action Programme aimed at developing EU gender equality policy. The increased representation of women in the elections for the European Parliament the same year, and the appointment of five women as commissioners in January 1995 completed the picture. In practice, however, progress and alliances in policy-making proved to be much more complicated and very fragile.

THE BREAKDOWN OF CONSENSUS: THE KALANKE RULING

The first incidence of the emerging bureaucratic and political opposition to positive action and to the strong alliance on equality created at EU level was the ECJ judgement on Case C–450/93 Eckhard Kalanke v Freie Hansestadt Bremen [1995]. The judgement referred to a regional German law on positive action in the public sector (*Land* of Bremen), which the ECJ held was incompatible with Council Directive 76/207/EEC. The Bremen law imposed an unconditional and automatic preference for women in cases of promotion.

The judgement was made possible because of a weakness in the EC directive and due to the non-binding character of Council Recommendation 84/635/EEC on the promotion of positive action for women. It reduced the scope of the directive and seriously damaged public acceptance of positive action. The emerging movement in favour of quotas in decision-making bodies and in high status professional occupations was called into question at a moment of increasing public support following the success of the Third Action Programme. The judgement received wide publicity in the press, which took the opportunity to declare quotas and affirmative action programmes to be unlawful (Rice *et al.*, 1995). All the policy actors were mobilized to interpret and comment on the judgement. The European Parliament gave its reaction in a report on the implementation of equal opportunities for women and men in the civil service. The report, drafted by an MEP from the Women's Rights Committee, Jessica Larive, strongly reaffirmed the need for positive action (European Parliament, 1996). The European Women's Lobby identified the sex composition of the ECJ as a negative influence on the judgement. Its president, Anne Taylor, argued that the judgement might have been different had women been involved in the decision-making process. She warned that, without a firm constitutional base for equality encompassing affirmative action, European women would use their voting power to prevent further European integration (European Women's Lobby, press release, 17.10.95, p. 1). Pursuing the same line of argument, women activists at national level criticized the judgement and attacked the ECJ for holding back progress on equality matters.

In a Communication (COM(96) 88 final, 27 March 1996, p. 7) five months later, the European Commission attempted an interpretation of the judgement, arguing that 'the Court seems to condemn, in principle, the special feature of the Bremen law, that is the automaticity of the measure which gives women an unconditional right to promotion'. The text proposed a 'declaratory clarifying amendment' to the equal treatment directive authorizing all other forms of positive action (European Commission, 1996). The Council of Ministers was reluctant to adopt this amendment, considering it unnecessary. An MEP on the Women's Rights Committee called for a report (Lulling), but its formal adoption was deliberately delayed to prevent it from being adopted by the Council of Ministers.

Much less publicity was given to another case, in which the judgement went the other way. Two years later, in 1997, Case C–409/95 Hellmut Marschall v Land Nordrhein-Westfalen [1997] received a judgement in favour of positive action, which provided a certain amount of flexibility. Meanwhile, at the Intergovernmental Conference, on the initiative of some women-friendly governments, a new provision had been introduced into the draft Treaty of Amsterdam. It affirmed that 'the principle of equal treatment shall not prevent any Member State from maintaining or adopting specific advantages in order to make it easier for the under-represented sex to pursue a vocational activity or to prevent or compensate for disadvantages in professional careers' (*OJEC* C 340, 10.11.97, p. 242, Article 141 §4). The Marschall judgement was a 'political response' by the ECJ to the Kalanke judgement. The responsible Commissioner welcomed the judgement, stating in a press release that 'the ECJ had recognized that certain deep-rooted prejudices and stereotypes as to the role and capacities of women in working life still persist' (European Commission, Spokes-man Service, IP/97/973, 11.11.97, p. 1). For its part, also in the same press release, the European Women's Lobby interpreted the judgement as an encouraging sign for women.

The Kalanke judgement was not the first time the ECJ had adopted what could be described as a 'women-unfriendly' stance. In Case 96/80 Mrs J.P. Jenkins v Kingsgate (Clothing Productions) Ltd. [1981], the ECJ interpreted equality law in a way that was unfavourable to women. Differences in pay between part-time work and full-time work were allowed, if they could be objectively justified on the basis of criteria unrelated to sex. Given that the majority of part-timers are women, this judgement could be considered as unfriendly to equality. In a similar way, the judgement in Case C–408/92 Constance Christina Ellen Smith and Others v Avdel Systems Ltd [1994] enabled compliance with equal treatment over pension age by levelling down and prohibiting transitional arrangements that would favour women (Hoskyns, 1996, p. 198). The Kalanke judgement, and others that followed it, showed the importance of establishing strong binding instruments, allowing relatively limited scope for interpretations that might adversely affect equality objectives, as a means of tackling deeply rooted social problems like the unequal gender division of labour.

THE SHIFTING BALANCE OF POWER: DIRECTIVES ON PARENTAL LEAVE AND PART-TIME WORK

The Kalanke ruling illustrated the limitations of EC equal treatment law, at the same time as the general political context prioritizing economic performance in the second half of the 1990s made it almost impossible to produce new legislation in the social field. A series of proposals for directives had remained on the Council's table for years. Among them was a Commission proposal for parental leave, which had been submitted in 1983, but was considered too prescriptive, since it also aimed to change the behaviour of men through the non-transfer-ability of entitlements (Hoskyns, 1996, p. 147). In 1992, the Maastricht Treaty introduced a new procedure for law-making in the Agreement on

Social Policy (Protocol no. 14 on social policy), which helped to shift power from the Council to the social partners.

Under the Agreement on Social Policy, management and labour organizations could initiate discussions and conclude agreements on issues proposed by the Commission. The agreements could become instruments of European social policy, or even Council directives, following a proposal from the Commission. Any such directives were not applicable in the United Kingdom, which had not signed the Agreement. In political terms, the procedure consisted of a *de facto* solution to two conflicting interests with regard to the social role of the EU: it satisfied those who opposed the blocking of European social policy acts by the British government, since the United Kingdom was excluded from decisions; it also satisfied those arguing for the limitation of state control and in favour of a more active role for organizations from both sides of industry.

In the mid-1990s, after the ratification of the Treaty on European Union and at a time of economic and political upheaval in the preparation for Economic and Monetary Union, the Commission gave the social partners the opportunity to implement the Agreement on Social Policy. The Commission was being pushed by the European Parliament to develop hard law on equality, and the social partners wanted to give a new impetus to the social dialogue and legitimate their role in the EU. Parental leave was the most appropriate issue with which to begin. From a symbolic point of view, it offered the opportunity to demonstrate that the social partners could find solutions to directives blocked by the Council. The social partners were interested in the topic since it was linked with the flexibility debate. From an administrative point of view, the proposal fitted in with organizational changes in Directorate General V, which had moved the Equal Opportunities Unit from the Directorate for Employment to the Directorate for Social Dialogue. Parental leave was a familiar issue for the new Swedish Director General, who had upgraded the social dialogue and gender equality in the policy agenda. Also, for reasons related to the Scandinavian tradition in gender equality, family policy had been incorporated into the Equal Opportunities Unit in July 1997.

The negotiation procedure anticipated 'secret' discussions among the three major European organizations representing the trades unions (ETUC), employers in the private sector (UNICE), and employers in the public sector (CEEP). The differences between the Commission proposal for a directive in 1983 (COM(83) 686 final, 24 November 1983) and the directive adopted in 1997 (Council Directive 96/34/EC) were significant. Comparison between the two texts points to a policy shift. The recitals and the main body of the directive show clearly that the main purpose was to reconcile parental and professional responsibilities and not to promote equal treatment for women and men, indicating the lack of strong commitment among social partner organizations to gender equality. Their primary concern seems to have been to make it easier for women (and possibly men) to stay at home and look after their children during a period of increasing need for flexibility in the labour market. Changes whereby the right to entitlement, according to the age of the child, was extended from two years to eight years support this assumption. The participation of women in the negotiations on the parental leave agreement was, however, very limited. The proportion of women in decision-making bodies in the ETUC was lower than in most of its EU national member organizations (Braithwaite and Byrne, 1994, pp. 4, 25–6). The ETUC was the only European social partner organization to set up a women's committee, but there is no strong evidence that the leadership consulted the committee before or during negotiations on the parental leave directive.

The social partners managed to agree on parental leave as a reconciliation rather than an equality measure. The financial implications were to be minimal, since no pay or social security benefit was stipulated in the directive for the period of parental leave. This 'weak' regulation of parental leave was not expected to play an important role in promoting women's interests. Only in very few cases, as in the United Kingdom, which was not covered by the directive at that time, could it have a positive impact on women who did not previously have a right to parental leave. In most other countries, the provisions of the directive did not affect existing regulations. Its impact on equality is to be found in the provision of parental leave for both parents on a nontransferable basis, since in most member states men did not previously have the right to parental leave. The general considerations in the annex to the directive specified that 'men should be encouraged to assume an equal share of family responsibilities' by taking parental leave, but without further specification on how this could be achieved. It seemed unlikely that, even if leave were with pay, take-up by men would increase significantly (see also Chapter 3).

Within the same logic, another 'weak' directive on part-time work (Council Directive 97/81/EC) was adopted a year later, in 1997. The directive had been announced in the Fourth Action Programme for equality, under the objective of desegregation of labour markets. In the final text, no connection is made between part-time work and inequality between women and men in employment. The purpose of the frame-work agreement for the social partners was explicitly 'to provide for the removal of discrimination against part-time workers and to improve the quality of part-time work' as well as 'to facilitate the development of part-time work on a voluntary basis and to contribute to the flexible organization of working time in a manner which takes into account the needs of employers and workers'. In recital no. 5, reconciliation appears as one of the reasons why the social partners attach importance to measures facilitating access to part-time work. This interest in pro-moting reconciliation corresponded to the concern of member states to create employment and flexibility in the labour market.

The shift in power from the Council to the social partners, illustrated by the negotiation of these two framework agreements which became directives, had an ambivalent impact on gender equality. It permitted the unblocking of Community legal instruments, but provided little evidence to suggest that the social partners would show greater commitment to the promotion of women's interests. Negotiations at this level had, generally, been less favourable to equality than regulations made by governments, as illustrated in the case of gender pay differen-tials. The situation was similar at national level, where centrally negoti-ated collective agreements between the social partners allowed for smaller gender pay differentials than agreements made at company or even sector level (Rubery, 1994).

GENDER MAINSTREAMING: NEW ACTORS AND NEW RISKS

Gender mainstreaming was introduced in the first draft of the Third Action Programme as an innovative feature (COM(90) 449 final, 6 November 1990). Proposals were not taken forward during an, other-wise, very creative and pro-active period of implementation of the pro-gramme. No policy actors had requested their implementation, probably due to scepticism when the programme first appeared. Christine Crawley, on behalf of the Women's Rights Committee, had stressed the risks of mainstreaming in early discussions of the programme in April 1990. The Advisory Committee on Equal Opportunities for Women and Men also anticipated problems, and asked for more clarification of the term, which was difficult to understand and translate into Community languages. The concept was considered to be too vague and, therefore, threatened to dilute specific actions in favour of women (personal communication to the author).

The Fourth Action Programme, adopted by the Commission in July 1995 (COM(95) 381 final, 19 July 1995), shortly before the United Nations' World Conference on Women in Beijing, included only vague references to mainstreaming. Commission services became more familiar with the term during the Beijing Conference, at which the EU played an active role in promoting mainstreaming. In its decision on the programme (in December 1995), the Council upgraded mainstreaming of equality to a primary, as well as a transversal, objective of the programme. Political conditions for its implementation in EU policies were created by the operation of a new structure in the Commission: the Group of Commissioners on Equality between Women and Men and Women's Rights, which was set up in early 1995 by President Santer under pressure from certain MEPs. At a public hearing of commissioners before they took up their posts, Commissioner Flynn, who was in charge of social affairs, was questioned intensively on his plans for equality.

Jacques Santer chaired the group, which had four regular members: Commissioners Pádraig Flynn, Anita Gradin, Monika Wulf-Mathies and Erkki Liikanen. The meetings were open to other commissioners and, once a year, to representatives of the European 'women's constituency', which was composed of the presidents of the Women's Rights Committee, European Women's Lobby and Advisory Committee on Equality. All were major policy actors whose role had been reinforced during the Third Action Programme. Inviting external bodies was an unusual feature for Commissioners' groups, but proved to be very effective in upgrading the status of equality in the Commission's agenda.

Women commissioners provided the driving force in the group, promoting gender mainstreaming in their respective policy areas. Once more, the enlargement to the North was critical, as two of the members were Scandinavian (Gradin and Liikanen). The Kalanke ruling in October 1995 offered a further argument in favour of mainstreaming. The existing Inter-service Group on Equality between Women and Men continued to meet, and a new group of gender mainstreaming officials from almost all Commission services was set up in 1996. The Commission formalized the emerging interest in mainstreaming by the adoption of a Communication on incorporating equal opportunities in all community polices (COM(96) 67 final, 21 February 1996).

The relevant policy actors welcomed the communication but criticized its vague definition of mainstreaming and its declaratory form. The risks of diluting positive action in the name of gender mainstreaming were also expressed. The Kokkola Report (European Parliament, 1997) proposed a dual approach to equality (gender mainstreaming and positive action), with appropriate funding and administrative structures and emphasis on mainstreaming in the structural funds, which were under revision. The European Women's Lobby (1996) added a more concrete definition and raised the issue of women in decision-making bodies.

Before implementing mainstreaming, the Commission's Equal Opportunities Unit requested the secondment of a national expert on mainstreaming, Anne Havnör, again from a Scandinavian country, Norway.[3] The scope of mainstreaming was clarified and reinforced to ensure benefits for equality and to avoid existing equality tools being negatively affected. The implementation of gender mainstreaming in Community policies facilitated the shift from equal treatment and desegregation objectives to reconciliation of paid work and family life. Major policy documents drafted during this period included references to reconciliation as a step towards mainstreaming (European Commission, 1996, 1997b).

LESSONS FOR THE FUTURE

This chapter has highlighted the uniqueness of the equal opportunities policy process at EU level. Equality issues have been extended beyond the initial remit provided for in the Treaty of Rome. Over the years, equality policy has been promoted by a strong body of dynamic policy actors, generally mobilized by women. Their commitment has remained steadfast since the 1970s, founded on the conviction that gender inequality is present in the lives of all women in one form or another, despite their different national, economic and social backgrounds. However, the diverse obstacles they have had to face along the way, including institutional barriers and inertia, as well as hostile reactions from colleagues and collaborators, at times from other women, have reduced the impact of policies, often in ways that suited other policy priorities. At the same time, equality was being recognized not merely as a topic for social policy but as affecting all aspects of women's and

---

3. According to the Decision of the European Economic Area Joint Committee (no. 55/96) of 28 October 1996, Norway is able to participate in the Fourth Community Action Programme on Equal Opportunities for Men and Women (1996–2000).

men's lives. Equality objectives were, therefore, being integrated into other policy areas at European level. Measures to prevent the trafficking of women were, for example, included in home affairs policy, and an attempt was made to promote women and the gender dimension in science and technology research programmes.

A multiplicity of policy actors have been involved in equality issues at national level. The French introduced Article 119 in the Treaty of Rome, but also provided the heads of the Equal Opportunities Unit (until 1996) among their European officials. The British influenced equal opportunities policy through the secondment of national experts and by providing the largest proportion of external experts working for the Commission: over half the co-ordinators of the experts networks during the Third Action Programme were British. The Scandinavians brought their influence to bear on new policy areas such as those concerned with women in decision-making and gender mainstreaming. The European institutions established by the treaties have promoted equality policy, to the extent that political decision-makers and motivated individual officials have been in a position to bring forward suggestions that could be fed into policy solutions.

In the field of equality in employment, significant shifts have occurred over the period since the First Action Programme: policy objectives moved from equal treatment to reconciliation of paid work and family life, and policy measures from positive action to gender mainstreaming. However, reconciliation, as used in EU policies, has been seriously questioned as an equality objective, since it tends to neglect the sexual division of labour and gender roles (Junter-Loiseau and Tobler, 1999). Women had to negotiate at an individual level with their husbands over their use of time and not as a group of workers. They also had to negotiate with their employers over promotion and pay, in some cases protected by positive action legislation. Gender mainstreaming of employment policy has focused attention on work-time arrangements as a reconciliation measure. Such provisions are likely to contribute to gender equality only if they are also targeted at men, as in the Scandinavian tradition, where reconciliation means 'more men take care of their children', rather than 'fewer women are in full-time employment'. Effective reconciliation policy includes costly measures such as the individualization of social rights, adequate provision of good quality childcare facilities and positive action at the workplace. The Treaty of Amsterdam reinforced both the mainstreaming approach and positive action, providing the opportunity for the European women's constituency to develop policies on a firm legal basis.

Acknowledgements

The author is grateful to Catherine Hoskyns for her advice and guidance on this chapter and to Agnès Hubert for her comments on the draft, and for having shared life in the Equal Opportunities Unit from 1992 to 1996. Thanks are also due to Janet Hemsley for her useful comments.

The views expressed in this chapter are the personal opinions of the author and do not represent the official standpoint of the Commission.

3 Reconciliation Policies from a Comparative Perspective

Marlene Lohkamp-Himmighofen and Christiane Dienel

The problem of reconciling family responsibilities and employment is not peculiar to the late twentieth century. It dates back to the process of industrialization when the separation between the place of work and the home was established. However, the ensuing difficulties only became an issue for policy-makers in the 1970s, when the number of women in gainful employment began to rise continuously in most European states. The reasons for this development are well known: changing economic (and income) structures as a result of economic growth, greater equality in gender roles, and also changing family structures.

From the 1970s, the policy objective of reconciliation of employment, family life and family responsibilities gradually moved onto the political agenda in most member states in the European Union (EU). At European level, although the topic had been raised in the Council Resolution of 1974 concerning a social action programme, it was not addressed further until the 1980s (see Chapters 1 and 2). Despite considerable variations in the political impact of the issue, and also in the level and tenor of public debate from one country to another, a range of measures have, progressively, been implemented to reduce the conflicts between paid work and family life.

Reconciliation measures may be initiated by the state through its labour market and employment policies, and/or by companies. Typical measures in this context would be the reduction of weekly or annual working hours, the supply of part-time jobs, and flexible working time arrangements at company level, although the aim is not necessarily to help parents combine paid work with family life. The measures introduced by companies are usually based on economic or management considerations rather than gender equality objectives. Their purpose may be to make better use of the existing potential of labour, reduce unemployment or increase productivity and satisfaction at work. Measures to improve the compatibility of family and employment have also been initiated through policies targeting what are considered as the special needs of women as working mothers, such as the protection of pregnant women.

During the 1990s, emphasis shifted, increasingly, towards gender policy, in line with the notion that equality of opportunity can only be fully realized by an equal distribution between men and women of paid and unpaid work, implying greater access by women to positions of responsibility outside the home and greater involvement of men in family life. Typical legislation against gender discrimination would include quotas for employment and job promotion, or the guarantee of reinstatement after maternity or parental leave. Finally, certain measures, categorized in some countries as belonging to family policy, may serve to reduce conflicts between paid and unpaid work: maternity and parental leave and childcare provision. Their main goals are to encourage the development of opportunities for children, to relieve the everyday burden on families and create greater family stability.

Since primary responsibility for all these policy fields remains in the hands of individual EU member states, each country has developed its own distinctive profile of reconciliation policies, according to the main political objectives being pursued. Even in fields where European directives, for example on maternity and parental leave, do exist, they provide only a broad framework for each member state to implement specific measures or bundles of measures. In this chapter, maternity, parental and paternity leave are taken to illustrate the diversity of national reconciliation policies within the EU.[1]

The first section of the chapter gives an overview of existing measures for leave and benefits in the 15 EU member states, and also in Poland and the Czech Republic. The two countries from outside the EU when the data were collected have been included in the study because they were two of the first five Eastern European countries due to join the EU. The findings from this overview are then analysed by defining six different concepts of reconciliation policy. The last section of the chapter returns to the interactive relationship between European and national reconciliation policies.

---

1. This overview is based on a study carried out by the Gesellschaft für Familienforschung (GeFam) on behalf of the German Bundesministerium für Familie, Senioren, Frauen und Jugend (1998). The data were supplied by national experts in the relevant ministries in response to a questionnaire which they completed at the end of 1997.

LEAVE ARRANGEMENTS IN EU MEMBER STATES, POLAND AND THE CZECH REPUBLIC

The comparative analysis in this section provides an overview of the different forms of leave available to help parents reconcile family life and paid work in 17 countries, and demonstrates to what extent EU legislation has been translated into national measures. Figure 3.1 illustrates how different countries have organized the provision of leave for family reasons. Based on 1997 data, it indicates the length of mandatory leave, the period during which it can be taken, and the extent to which different periods of leave can overlap. Maternity and paternity leave are included only when they are•statutory and when all, or the great majority of, employed parents have entitlement and access to leave. The transferability of part of the leave to the other parent is not shown. The figure also indicates whether parental leave is statutory or available under collective agreements, and whether it is paid or unpaid. Entitlements are not, for example, included if leave applies only in the public sector, but they are displayed if it applies to all employees, with the exception of workers in very small firms. Where parental leave does not give entitlement to reinstatement or other forms of protection, it is excluded from the figure. Where leave is granted only to mothers, it is indicated separately. Where each parent has an individual non-transferable right to parental leave (Sweden and Austria), this is shown by a black line dividing the two parts. In the case of Finland, the black line indicates the division between parental leave and child home-care leave.

Maternity leave and pay

European legislation on the protection of pregnant women was not introduced until the 1990s and, even then, it was not presented as part of the equality agenda. Maternity leave was one component of Council Directive 92/85/EEC, which was passed in 1992 by majority voting (after having failed previously to achieve unanimity) as a measure 'to improve the health and safety at work of pregnant workers and workers who have recently given birth or are breastfeeding'. The directive prohibited dismissal of women workers for reasons of pregnancy, and their exposure to specific agents or working conditions which could endanger their health and safety; it ensured the preservation of rights derived from the employment contract and stipulated that maternity leave of at least fourteen consecutive weeks should be a statutory right.

Figure 3.1   Maternity leave, paternity leave and parental leave and allowances in EU member states, 1997

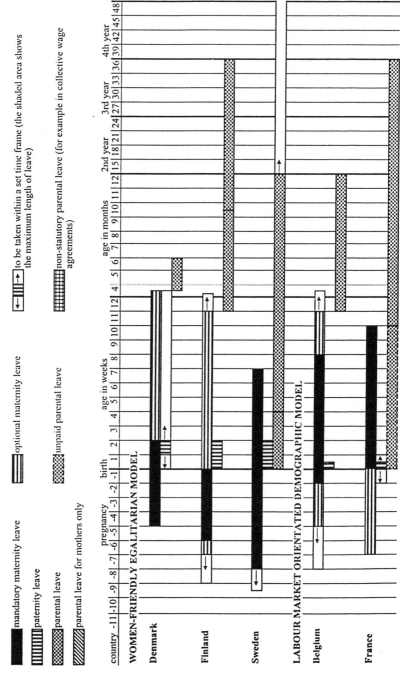

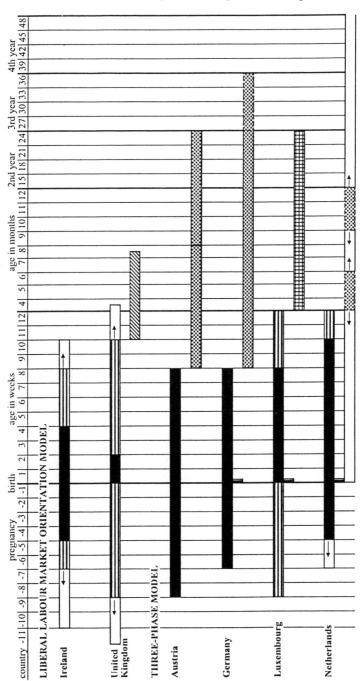

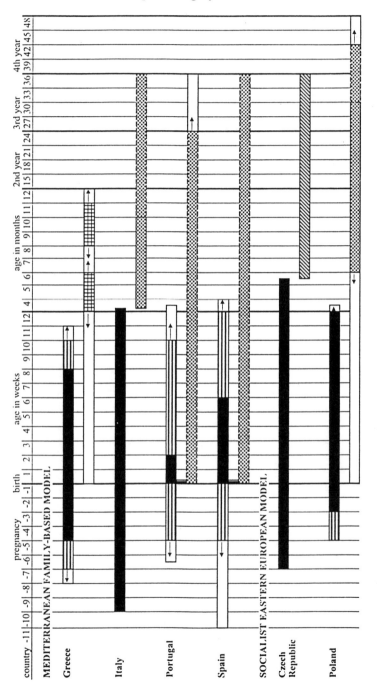

Source: Adapted from Bundesministerium für Familie, Senioren, Frauen und Jugend, 1998

It did not impose a mandatory payment during the leave period, but recommended that benefit should be paid on the same basis as sick pay.

When the directive was agreed, all member states (except Ireland and the United Kingdom) already made some form of statutory provision for maternity leave, but the conditions and arrangements varied considerably from one country to another, explaining why some governments had been reluctant to see binding legislation brought into force. In the event, the directive left member states a large degree of discretion in setting the conditions under which leave could be taken. Maternity leave was intended primarily to serve as a means of protecting the health of mothers and children, but it can also be construed as a way of preventing pregnancy and motherhood from becoming a reason for excluding or downgrading women workers and as a possible strategy to help them combine family life and employment.

By the end of 1997, when the data were collected, women workers in all EU member states, and also in the Czech Republic and Poland, were entitled to statutory maternity leave. The United Kingdom introduced statutory provision in 1992 and Ireland in 1994. In Portugal, maternity leave was extended to 14 weeks in 1995 (previously 90 days) to comply with the European directive. The duration of maternity leave in the 15 EU member states ranged from 14 weeks in Germany, Portugal and Sweden to 22 weeks in Italy, with 18 weeks in Denmark, Ireland and the United Kingdom. The Czech Republic provided for 28 weeks, with an entitlement of 37 weeks for lone mothers. In all EU member states, and also in the Czech Republic and Poland, mothers were protected against unlawful dismissal and given a guarantee of reinstatement after maternity leave, ranging from one additional month in Belgium to a total of 22 months in Italy. In most countries, fathers could only be included in maternity leave schemes in exceptional circumstances (for example due to the death of the mother), but gainfully employed fathers were entitled to claim the last four weeks of maternity leave in Spain. A similar exception existed in Portugal, where fathers could take part of maternity leave after the mandatory two weeks allocated to mothers following delivery.

Seven EU member states (Austria, France, Germany, Greece, Luxembourg, Netherlands, Portugal), and also Poland, paid full salary during maternity leave. In Denmark and Italy, a maternity benefit equal to the full salary was normally paid, but the level of payment was regulated by collective agreements not by law. In all the other countries, maternity benefit was paid at a lower rate: in Spain and Sweden at 75 per cent of salary, and in Finland on average at 66 per cent; in some cases, the rate decreased over time: in Belgium from 82 per cent to 75 per cent; and in Ireland and the United Kingdom, the level of payment depended on the employment record; the Czech Republic offered maternity benefit at 69 per cent of salary.

Parental leave and pay

A directive on parental leave was first drafted in 1983, but attempts to make it law failed for more than a decade (see Chapters 1 and 2). One of the intentions behind the directive was to encourage more equal sharing of parental responsibilities by involving fathers in childrearing. Each parent was to have a three-month non-transferable entitlement, but this was seen as too prescriptive in a climate where social attitudes were not yet ready for such momentous change (Hoskyns, 1996, p. 147). Council Directive 96/34/EC, which was eventually passed in 1996 as a 'framework agreement on parental leave concluded by UNICE, CEEP and the ETUC', stipulated that parental leave of at least three months should apply to both men and women workers as an individual right until their child reached the age of eight, and should be granted, in principle, on a non-transferable basis. The directive was to be transposed into national legislation by 1999. Member states were left to decide whether leave should be granted on a full or part-time basis, or in the form of a time credit, and whether they would make leave dependent on a service qualification. Provision was made for small undertakings to be given special consideration. During the negotiations, no agreement was reached over payment. Any benefit paid during parental leave is, therefore, a possibility rather than a mandatory requirement for member states, although they do have discretion to implement more favourable regulations at national level.

While parental leave is a relatively new family policy measure at international level, it already existed in many member states before the directive was passed. In Sweden, parental insurance was instituted in 1974, long before Sweden became a member of the EU. The objective was to enable employed mothers or fathers to stop working for a period of time, or reduce their working hours to care for a young child (see Chapter 9).

At the end of 1997, before implementation of the directive was due to be completed, 11 EU member states (Austria, Belgium, Denmark, Finland, France, Germany, Italy, Netherlands, Portugal, Spain, Sweden), and also Poland, already offered statutory parental leave. With the exception of Italy, all gainfully employed mothers and fathers covered by social insurance were entitled to take parental leave, in some cases subject to a service requirement (in France after employment of one year). In Italy, only mothers were entitled to parental leave, although the whole or part of the entitlement could be transferred to the father. In most of these countries, parents were covered for health insurance during leave and were guaranteed reinstatement afterwards in a similar job.

Parental leave arrangements applied under more limited conditions in Greece, Ireland, Luxembourg, the United Kingdom and the Czech Republic. In Luxembourg, only mothers and fathers in the public sector and in firms with collective agreements had the right to take parental leave. The situation was similar in Greece: civil servants and workers in companies with more than 100 employees were entitled to take leave. In Ireland, parental leave existed only under some collective agreements. In the United Kingdom, under the 1992 Social Security Act, mothers who had been in employment for more than two years were entitled to take 'maternity absence' after the end of maternity leave, which could be seen as a first step towards parental leave. In 1998, the British government, under New Labour, announced its intention to implement the parental leave directive (see also Chapter 7). In the Czech Republic, only mothers had the right to parental leave in 1997; fathers were entitled to take part of the leave only in the event of the death or illness of the mother.

The duration of parental leave varied considerably from one country to another: with a minimum of 2.5 months basic entitlement in Denmark and a maximum up to the time of the child's third birthday in the Czech Republic, Finland (including legislation on child home-care leave), France, Germany, Italy, Poland and Spain. In the Netherlands and Sweden, parents were, in addition, entitled to take parental leave up to the time when the child reached the age of eight years, and in Poland up to the age of four years. Furthermore, in Sweden the form of leave was very flexible; it could be taken as a block or in short periods.

The possibility of working part-time during parental leave is important as a reconciliation strategy not only for financial reasons but also because it enables continuity of employment. In 1997, in Austria, Belgium, the Czech Republic, Finland, France, Germany, Luxembourg, the Netherlands, Poland and Sweden, parents were allowed to pursue part-time employment while on parental leave. Only in Denmark, Greece, Italy, Portugal and Spain was parental leave offered solely on a full-time basis. In five countries (Austria, Belgium, Luxembourg, Netherlands, Sweden), if leave was taken on a part-time basis, its total length could be extended in proportion to working hours. In France, Luxembourg and Austria, both mother and father could take a part-time job and be on parental leave at the same time.[2]

Most countries made it possible for parental leave to alternate between the two parents at least once: in Germany, parents can exchange three times, in Poland four times, in Sweden up to three times a year, and in Luxembourg as often as they wish. Austria and Sweden also offer special incentives for fathers to take parental leave: in Austria, six months of the parental leave cannot be transferred from one parent to the other, and are lost if one of the parents does not take the allocation; in Sweden a minimum of one month must be taken by the mother and also by the father (the so-called 'daddy month'). Also in Greece each parent has an individual right to three months of the non-statutory parental leave.

The attractiveness of parental leave regulations depends on the payment offered during the period of leave. If leave is unpaid, or paid at a very low level, take-up is likely to be low. The participation of fathers and better paid women would seem to depend very much on the level of pay, because the reduction of family income is usually greater when fathers (or well-paid women) take leave, and is only partly compensated if payment is made at a fixed rate or pro rata. Parental leave was without pay in three countries in 1997: Greece, Portugal and Spain. In the Netherlands, as well, paid leave was not guaranteed by law, but it was available under some collective arrangements. Also, 'maternity absence' in the United Kingdom was unpaid, and neither national legislation nor collective provision existed on paid parental leave in Ireland.

Paternity leave and pay

At European level, the 1996 parental leave directive made some provision for parents to take leave for urgent family reasons (*force majeure*). By late 1997, apart from the provisions for fathers under parental leave, only a few EU member states had introduced strong incentives to

---

2. The most flexible model of part-time work during parental leave is offered in the non-EU member state of Norway. Parental leave can be taken in the form of a time-credit arrangement, whereby parents can reduce their working hours to 50, 40, 25 or 10 per cent of their standard hours. In this way, the duration of parental leave can, for example, be extended to 5 years by reducing working hours to 10 per cent of the standard length of working time.

encourage fathers to devote time to their children. By the late 1990s, only the Nordic states granted a special paternity leave in the form of paid time off work reserved for gainfully employed fathers on the occasion of the birth of a child. Denmark, Finland and Sweden provided paternity leave of two weeks, paid at 65–75 per cent of salary out of social or parental insurance.

By contrast, in Belgium, Germany, France, Luxembourg, the Netherlands, Portugal and Spain, employed fathers had the right to take only one to three days of special leave for childbirth, in most case with pay (except in the Netherlands and Portugal). In the United Kingdom, some collective agreements made provision for time off work for childbirth, but fathers in Austria, the Czech Republic, Greece, Ireland, Italy and Poland had no such statutory right or collective agreements.

In sum, it could be said that, by the end of 1997, leave arrangements in nearly all EU member states conformed to the EU directive as far as maternity was concerned, but to a lesser extent for parental leave. As already intimated, the minimum provisions stipulated in the European directives represent a lowest common denominator, leaving member states to make higher levels of provision in accordance with their own national preferences.

RECONCILIATION POLICY MODELS IN EUROPE

Periods of leave, particularly parental leave, and the ways in which fathers are integrated into the parenting process are conceptualized very differently from one country to another. Each country appears to have developed its own specific arrangements, which are co-ordinated and harmonized with other aspects of the national system (Wingen, 1995, p. 30), depending on dominant family and gender policy issues and objectives, cultural traditions, legislative frameworks, social policy concepts and the state of the economy (Garhammer, 1997, p. 49). The countries examined in this chapter can be divided into six basic models or 'ideal types' of reconciliation policies located in relation to their socio-economic and political backgrounds (Schunter-Kleemann, 1994). At one end of a continuum is the women-friendly or egalitarian model characteristic of the Nordic states, followed by the labour market orientated or demographic model of Belgium and France. Ireland and the United Kingdom can be described as belonging to the liberal labour market orientation model. A three-phase model is found in several of the member states in the geographical centre of continental Europe. At the other end of the continuum are the family-based model of the four Mediterranean member states, and the contrasting socialist model characteristic of Eastern European countries.

The women-friendly egalitarian model

In the Scandinavian countries, where women-friendly policies were a priority for governments long before European integration, a concept of reconciliation has developed, based on equal parenthood and a dual-breadwinner family. This model ensures individual rights and duties for both men and women: for example individual taxation and the absence of protective labour regulations, such as the prohibition of night work for women. Policy has been focused on how to achieve egalitarian structures in all aspects of social and economic life, including a more equal distribution of both paid and unpaid work, on the one hand by enabling women to participate more fully in labour market activity, and on the other by offering specific measures to ensure greater take-up of parental leave by men and greater involvement of fathers in family responsibilities. Such measures include an independent entitlement to paternity leave, and the father-month as part of parental leave. In addition, the Nordic countries have tried to modify the continuous, long working hours model, generally adopted by men, and replace it by more flexible work-time models, so that men's working patterns are also more compatible with family life. They have established generous care arrangements for children of all age groups and, in addition, part-time work is a widespread practice in Denmark and Sweden.

In the Nordic countries, parental leave is considered as a short but relatively well-paid break in employment. In Sweden, it takes the form of a parental insurance scheme, created in 1974 out of the traditional maternity insurance. The basic principles of parental insurance are that the benefit received during parental leave is conceptualized as a compensation for loss of salary, and parental insurance is seen as an important form of support for parents, enabling them to devote their full attention to young children, but without endangering their opportunities in the labour market; time-credit schemes, for example, allow parental leave to be organized on a flexible basis.

The approach of the Nordic states towards gender policies, as illustrated in arrangements for different forms of leave and other reconciliation strategies, is not homogeneous and may not always work to the advantage of women. Finland, for example, operates a mixed system of parental leave and child home-care leave and allowances. After a parental leave of more than 6.5 months, gainfully employed parents are entitled to take child home-care leave until their children reach the age of three. This means they can choose between public day care for their children or child home-care leave, including an allowance financed by the state and local government. Finland is also distinguished from the other two Nordic EU member states by its relatively low level of part-time work among women. The greater flexibility afforded through the arrangements made for parental leave would not appear to have opened many new opportunities for women in Finland, however, and the effect of reconciliation measures may have been to reinforce the traditional division of labour (Ilmakunnas, 1997, p. 191). The same could be said of policies in Denmark and Sweden to encourage part-time work among women or to create public sector jobs, since workers who take such forms of employment generally receive lower rates of pay and tend to be considered as less committed to paid work.

Notwithstanding these reservations about the possible negative side-effects of reconciliation policies, the Nordic states would appear to have gone furthest in achieving gender equality, long before the topic moved on to the EU agenda, as can be illustrated by their high ratings for women's participation in the labour force, women's access to decision-making positions, their high percentage of elected representatives at regional level, and the greater sharing of household tasks and family responsibilities, compared to other EU member states (see Chapter 1). The same reasons help to explain why women in the Nordic states have also been the strongest opponents to European integration: they feared a levelling down towards the least advanced member states (see Chapter 9).

The labour market orientated demographic model

Women-friendly policies have also been developed in France and, to a lesser degree, in Belgium, but the underlying objectives differ from the Scandinavian model. Both countries have recognized the importance of women's contribution to the economy. Their participation in the labour force has traditionally been supported by the state, especially during periods of economic growth and reconstruction, when it was in the national interest for women to be both workers and mothers. Policy was, consequently, aimed less at promoting equality of opportunity than at exploiting the full potential of the labour force, while at the same time maintaining a satisfactory demographic balance (Fagnani, 1998b, p. 58). Parental leave has, therefore, been conceptualized as a relatively short interruption to what can otherwise be described as continuous, predominantly full-time, employment pattern (see also Chapter 4). Before statutory parental leave was enacted in 1997 in Belgium, only civil servants were entitled to leave. In France, women and men are eligible to take parental leave only after one year of employment, and the childrearing allowance is paid only from the second child. Specific measures to integrate fathers into unpaid family work have not been developed (Veil, 1997, p. 31). Evidence from France shows that parental leave is also unattractive for well-paid women. When entitlement to paid leave was extended to women with two children in 1994 (previously it applied from the third child), uptake was found to be high among unemployed and low-paid women (Afsa, 1996).

In addition, both these countries have a long tradition of publicly funded childcare, which is seen not only as beneficial for mothers and as a means of reconciling paid work and family life, but also as important for the development and socialization of children. In sum, by the late 1990s, this reconciliation concept could be described as a 'modified' breadwinner model (Lewis, 1992). Parental leave provision was reinforced by well-established policies for family benefits and childcare, although a more equal sharing of leave and domestic tasks had not been achieved.

The liberal labour market orientation model

In the United Kingdom and Ireland, as in most other EU member states, the issue of reconciling paid work and family life has not rated high on the political agenda but, in contrast to other countries, the state has not attempted to promote the compatibility of family life with paid work through legal statutes. Rather, particularly in the United Kingdom, market forces have operated, and regulations have been based mainly on negotiated schemes between employers and workers. Employers have been left to take the initiative by providing childcare support and working arrangements designed to retain a skilled workforce. Families in these countries are expected to make their own arrangements without help from the state, except insofar as the state has intervened to protect children, if necessary by ensuring that mothers remain at home to look after very young offspring, as in Ireland. Gender role segregation has thus developed as a largely unquestioned assumption: women have been considered primarily as homemakers and as secondary earners, ideally suited for part-time and flexible jobs, enabling them to combine family life and paid work (see Chapters 1 and 7).

Although the United Kingdom has long practised career break schemes, in the absence of statutory arrangements, they have been introduced at the discretion of employers. Since the 1992 Social Security Act, employed mothers – but not fathers – have been entitled to take unpaid leave at the end of maternity leave, but only when they have an employment record of more than two years. Following the Labour government's undertaking to sign up to the Agreement on Social Policy, the United Kingdom was required to introduce a stronger form of legislation (including leave entitlement for fathers) (see Chapter 7). When the directive was agreed, Ireland did not have any provision for parental leave either. In the Irish case, EU equality legislation, and the parental leave directive is no exception, has served as a strong impetus for policy innovation in areas where change might not otherwise have been realized (Conroy Jackson, 1993, p. 91).

The three-phase model

Four EU member states – Austria, Germany, Luxembourg and the Netherlands – share a certain similarity of approach to the distribution of employment and family responsibilities between women and men, in that they all represent a model which, for a long time, favoured the labour force participation of the male breadwinner, while women were encouraged to leave employment altogether when they had children. The chronological ordering of the different phases in family and working life has followed a pattern whereby the first phase, prior to family formation, involves full-time employment, the second phase withdrawal from the labour market during family building, and the third phase a gradual return, if at all, to the labour market, often on a part-time basis, particularly for mothers with school-age children. In most cases, this concept is associated with a non-individualized taxation system, which gives advantages to single-earner couples or discriminates against working wives (Germany, Netherlands) and, therefore, serves as a work disincentive for women, keeping them out of the labour force. In Austria, Germany and Luxembourg, the model is characterized by a long and relatively low-paid parental leave, and a parental allowance. In Germany and Luxembourg, it is also paid to parents who were previously not economically active. In both countries, parental allowance is paid exclusively out of tax-financed transfers from the state, and is seen as recognition of the contribution made by parents – essentially women – to childcare (see Chapter 5). Paid parental leave can thus be described as, primarily, family-policy orientated As a result, women's policy, or the implementation of specific measures designed to involve fathers in family responsibilities, plays only a minor role.

In all four countries, family policy has long been dominated by the idea that young children need a high degree of continuity of care and that the mother is the person best able to provide it. Motherhood is, therefore, generally not considered to be compatible with economic activity outside the home. If mothers with young children must go out to work, they are expected to do so on a part-time basis. The conviction that mothers cannot be replaced without posing a threat to the child's development has resulted in poor provision of childcare facilities and kindergarten places, and half-day schooling, on the assumption that the mother is at home to prepare lunch and supervise homework.

The four countries share several of the broad characteristics of the three-phase model, but the statutory arrangements for parental leave are far from being uniform. For example, some aspects of the Scandinavian system have been adopted in Austria, where part of parental leave must be taken as an individual right, or in the Netherlands, where parents are entitled to a short period of parental leave but can take it at any time before the child reaches the age of eight. Although the traditional breadwinner model has continued to be widely practised, family and gender policy-makers appear, increasingly, to be moving in the same direction as in the Nordic states (Bundesministerium für Familie, Senioren, Frauen und Jugend, 1998, pp. 37, 40).

The Mediterranean family-based model

In most Mediterranean states (with the exception of Italy), compatibility of family and employment only became a policy objective in the 1990s, under pressure from the EU. The increasing participation of women in the labour force and the steep fall in fertility rates were, undoubtedly, precipitating factors (see Chapters 6 and 8). In these societies, traditionally, families, and often the multigenerational family, have been responsible for the care of their own children without support from the state, while gender role divisions have gone unquestioned. Even in the mid-1990s, conventional patterns of family building (institutionalized family forms, large family size) were more characteristic of the Mediterranean countries, compared to other EU member states. Women's labour market participation rates remained below the European average, except in Portugal, and women were able to combine paid work with family building, largely due to the help received from the extended family, and above all from grandparents.

All four countries make statutory provision for parental leave, but regulations are often poorly developed and implemented. Leave is without pay, except in Italy, which means that parents have little incentive to take it. In the absence of a guarantee of reinstatement and adequate provision of public childcare facilities, women often remain as homemakers after maternity leave. Although EU membership has moved reconciliation issues onto national agendas, by the late 1990s the need to comply with European directives did not appear to have brought about any significant improvements in arrangements for combining paid and unpaid work.

The socialist Eastern European model

The reconciliation of family life with employment has been approached very differently in the Czech Republic and Poland, compared to the other groupings of counties. As former socialist countries, their policy-making framework was very similar to that of the German Democratic Republic (GDR) before unification, and bears some resemblance to the labour market demographic orientated model in France and Belgium. Women's economic activity was supported by the state as a means of making full use of their labour force potential, and also to underpin the economic and demographic development of the country.

In contrast to the three-phase-model in West Germany, the GDR provided generous childcare arrangements for children of all ages, free of charge and with long opening hours, as well as the so-called 'baby-year' for mothers (and fathers). As a result, labour force participation rates for women were very high, close to those for men (Lohkamp-Himmighofen, 1993, pp. 103, 116, 120). However, after unification, many West German policies and practices were transposed to the new *Länder*; regulations concerning maternity, parental and paternity leave and allowances were brought into line with those in West Germany. The outcome was far-reaching change in the lifestyles and employment prospects for women in East Germany. The birthrate fell dramatically, and unemployment reached unprecedented levels.

Neither the Czech Republic nor Poland offered such generous childcare facilities as in the former GDR. In Poland, in particular, with its strong Catholic tradition, women's primary role was as homemaker. The closing down of childcare facilities in the 1990s in both countries led to serious problems for women's employment (Holmes, 1997, p. 262). In the post-communist era, a number of changes were made to their social provisions. For example, in 1995 the Czech Republic implemented non-earnings related paid parental leave, covering the whole period of leave (36 months), financed by the state, but indexed to the cost of living. Also in Poland in 1996, the duration of parental allowance was extended to 24 months, paid for out of social insurance, but again at a low rate. These countries had, thus, developed regulations for parental leave independently from membership of the EU.

NATIONAL CONCEPTS AND EUROPEAN REGULATIONS

An analysis of the ways in which measures for reconciling paid work and family life have been formulated and implemented affords a useful tool for understanding the impact on policy of different socio-cultural, economic and political environments. Reconciliation policies illustrate how national priorities vary from one member state to another and provide an indication of the interactive relationship between policy-making at national and European level.

As the standards set at international level are the outcome of a negotiated compromise between member states, European directives, particularly in the social field, tend to represent minimal standards and to provide only a broad framework within which each member state is required to implement national measures (see Chapter 1). In most EU member states, national reconciliation policies have developed gradually over a long period of time. As illustrated by the French case (see Chapter 4), they are situated at the juncture of employment and family policy, and may be designed to achieve very different, often conflicting, policy objectives. The extent to which individual member states have influenced the direction of EU policy with regard to the reconciliation of employment and family policy is illustrated by the contributions to this volume. Although the topic was on the agenda from the mid-1990s, the strongest pressure for policy to shift away from equal pay and equal treatment and protective measures for women as workers, initiated by the French, towards the concept of more equal sharing of both paid and unpaid work roles, undoubtedly came from the new Nordic member states in the early 1990s (see Chapter 9).

British membership tended to slow down the process, whereas the impact of the Mediterranean states was minimal, except insofar as they were likely to oppose any measures that would strain their limited resources. The overview provided in this chapter of the implementation of selected reconciliation measures suggests that, by the late 1990s, the full impact of European legislation was yet to be felt in countries, such as Ireland or the Mediterranean states, which might not otherwise have created public policies to support mothers in their role as paid workers outside the home.

The former socialist countries, as exemplified by East Germany, had probably gone furthest in bringing women's labour force participation rates close to those of men, and had done so with strong state support for childcare. The overthrow of communism and German unification would seem to have forced a re-alignment of the East German socialist model with the three-phase model of West Germany.

Although, since the early 1990s, governments in the Nordic states, as elsewhere, have been attempting to roll back the state and reduce public spending, Denmark, Finland and Sweden are generally considered to have come closest to achieving more equal sharing between men and women in their dual roles as workers and parents, largely as a result of women and family-friendly policies. Again, this development took place mainly outside the EU (with the exception of Denmark). The extent to which the implementation of the reconciliation measures formulated at European level will bring about greater integration between national social policies is likely to continue to depend upon the national socio-cultural factors determining how policies to help parents combine employment and family life are conceptualized and how the policy process operates at national level.

4 From Equality to Reconciliation in France?

Marie-Thérèse Lanquetin,
Jacqueline Laufer and
Marie-Thérèse Letablier

When the European Economic Community (EEC) was established in 1957, France was responsible for the inclusion of Article 119 on equal pay between women and men within the social policy section of the founding treaty. Unlike other EEC countries, France had ratified the International Labour Organization's (ILO) Convention no. 100, 'concerning equal remuneration for men and women workers for work of equal value'. The French, therefore, argued the case not on the grounds that provision for equal pay was necessary to promote social integration, but rather because it would prevent unfair economic competition. Unlike the ILO convention, Article 119 in the Treaty of Rome did not, however, refer to work of 'equal value', and the interpretation given to Article 119 by the European Court of Justice (ECJ) after 1976 revealed the gap that existed between the paternalistic conception of equal rights observed by the French and the approach adopted by the EEC.

In France, state intervention with regard to equal opportunities between men and women is embedded in a conception of universal rights developed from the 1789 Declaration of Human Rights. Although the universal rights of citizens to freedom and equality were recognized in the declaration, women were not included in the 'revolution'. Their place was primarily in the home and, according to the Civil Code of 1804, married women were not allowed to take paid jobs without their husbands' permission. This conception left its mark on French equality law up to the Second World War.

When, during the nineteenth century, the state intervened to regulate the labour contract and the terms and conditions of employment, the aim was, initially, to protect the health of children and young people, and later of women. At that time, the reasons for state intervention were ambiguous, since governments were also concerned with demographic

68

problems and wanted to encourage family building. It was not until after the Second World War that a more egalitarian conception of rights was to develop. The first section of the chapter examines in more detail how equality has been conceptualized in France.

An important feature of the French legal system is the emphasis it places on the 'majesty' of law. In France, a strictly hierarchical system is observed in the implementation of international and national standards: the Constitution has supremacy over international treaties and laws, while administrative regulations and collective agreements carry much less weight. Legal texts thus play a major role in regulating human relationships and in administering a system of public order designed to protect individual citizens by guaranteeing universal rights. Negotiation, by contrast, has a minor place in the organization of social relationships. Equal opportunities strategies have, therefore, had to overcome two obstacles in France. On the one hand, the way in which equality has been conceptualized makes it difficult for the social partners to deal with what are often conflicting principles in the context of labour law. On the other, the relatively weak bargaining power of the unions, despite the incentives provided by the law, discourages them from tackling questions of equality at work. The second section of the chapter analyses the development of gender equality policy in employment and the role played by the social partners in the process of policy formation and implementation.

The question of how to reconcile employment with family life and the debate about the role the state can and should play in helping families find reconciliation strategies have been pursued separately from issues concerning equal pay and equal treatment policies. Reconciliation was already on the policy agenda in France when the European Community (EC) began to address the topic in the mid-1970s. The importance the state in France accords to the family as the site for demographic reproduction and as a fundamental social unit has underpinned government action to promote greater equality of opportunity for women as working mothers (Haut conseil de la population et de la famille, 1987). Since women's employment has been identified as a major cause of the fall in the birthrate, demographic issues have provided a link between employment and family policy. In its efforts to support families, the state has legislated to control women's working conditions. For more than a century, public policy has sought, simultaneously, to protect both the family and women at work, by considering women as workers and as mothers, although consensus is far from having been achieved over the way in which policy should take account of women's dual roles. Public policy is thus characterized by a series of compromises between the need to protect the family as a unit by encouraging women to withdraw from employment, and the desire to preserve freedom of choice for women over whether or not to engage in paid work.

Women began entering the labour market in large numbers in the late 1960s in France, and their full-time economic activity rates were among the highest in the European Union (EU) by the late 1990s, even when they had young children (see Chapter 1). Compared to other EU member states, French women are also less likely to work part-time and to do so voluntarily. Since fertility rates in France have remained above the EU average, it could be argued that state intervention may have gone further in making paid work compatible with family life than in other member states. The third section of the chapter looks more closely at the relationship between employment and family life in France and also assesses the effectiveness of measures to reconcile paid work and family life.

THE EQUALITY PRINCIPLE IN FRENCH LAW

The first article of the 1789 Declaration of Human Rights states that 'all men are born and remain free and equal in rights'. Article 6 specifies that

> the law must be the same for all, whether it be to protect or punish them. Since all citizens are equal in law, they all have the same access to human dignity, to positions in public life and employment, in accordance with their abilities and without distinction other than that which is determined by their own talents.

However, not all people were citizens: all men gained citizenship rights in 1848, but women had to wait for another century.

The conception of equal rights in law and before law has continued to underpin the legal system in France. In 1982, for example, the Constitutional Council rejected as anticonstitutional a proposal to set a limit of 75 per cent on the proportion from either sex for the lists of candidates at local elections. In its ruling, the Council referred to the 1789 Declaration of Human Rights, which still has constitutional force. For the Council, any distinction based on sex is illegal, since it is not dependent on the capacities of the individual. It follows that any constitutional texts that have not been drawn up specifically with reference to women – their special treatment being justified on the grounds of their biological difference – continue to be interpreted as if they applied to both men and women, in line with the principle of universal rights.

Progressively, in the course of the nineteenth century, state intervention in economic and social life to correct *de facto* inequality came to be accepted as legitimate. The concept of equality based on difference replaced the notion that 'all men are born free and equal in rights'. The state afforded special protection to children and young people in 1841 and 1874, for example, and extended it to adult women in 1892, through legislation restricting the length of the working day and prohibiting night work in manufacturing industry. The same reasons were invoked to support the 1892 bill as had been used to exclude women from the universal rights of freedom and equality on grounds of sex: legally, they were considered as minors; the state, therefore, owed them protection; and their primary place was in the home. Women were also considered to be in competition with men for jobs. The impact of the law was to place women under the protection of the state and to characterize them as a workforce with interests that were different from those of men. Women were thus excluded from some areas of economic activity because of measures to protect them (Scott, 1991; Lanquetin, 1998a). In the parliamentary debates surrounding the bill, supporters of the welfare state, unlike the liberals, were in favour of protecting women and children. At trade union congresses, women's work was on the agenda. It was argued that women should be excluded on the grounds that, because they were paid less, they cost employers less and were, therefore, in unfair competition with men for jobs.

The argument changed after the Second World War, when women were belatedly given the vote in 1944, in recognition of their contribution to the Resistance. The Senate had opposed the vote for women because they were considered to be too close to the Church and under its power. On the grounds that it was appropriate at that time, the preamble to the 1946 Constitution laid down the principle of equality between men and women in the following terms: 'the law guarantees women equal rights to those of men in all areas'. It marked a departure from existing legislation, and opened the way for a complete overhaul of French law. This was to be a lengthy process. Family law was revised before labour law. In the late 1990s, the individual, man or woman, was still not the basic unit for assessment in fiscal and social security law because of the family-oriented conception of rights.

Two laws were passed in the 1970s with regard to equality in employment, but without affecting rights in other areas. The first in

December 1972 was intended to facilitate implementation of the ILO Convention no. 100 on equal remuneration. The second, in 1975, concerned non-discrimination in recruitment on grounds of sex. The Comité du travail féminin, which had been set up in 1971 and continued to operate until 1981 under the auspices of the Ministry for Labour, was responsible for raising the issue. In the 1970s, the committee became a major actor in promoting equality between women and men. It played a consultative role for all issues concerning women's economic activity and was responsible for examining all the points to be covered in Council Directive 76/207/EEC on equal treatment. Significantly, the person in charge of the European Commission's Equal Opportunities Unit at the time was a French woman, Jacqueline Nonon, who played a major role in taking forward the equal treatment directive. In 1983, the Haut comité à l'égalité professionnelle took over the functions of the earlier committee.

In 1980, Marguerite Thibert, who had previously worked for the ILO, helped to prepare a report on the right to work in France. The report identified measures promoting or impeding equality. A distinction was made between measures that were protective and legitimate and those that were no longer deemed to be appropriate, and thus provided a useful framework for transposing the equal treatment directive into national law. At the time, France was strongly opposed to quotas, but the report considered that any measures intended to compensate women for the disadvantages associated with childbearing were inevitable and would, ultimately, have to be accepted. The idea of positive action, developed in the United States, was also examined and was found to be more flexible than quotas. Following the change of government in 1981, when the Left came to power, and the upgrading from a junior ministry to a full ministerial position for women's rights, two laws were enacted in 1983, one for the private and the other for the public sector. However, they were not fully debated in parliament, since nobody was prepared to argue the case against the principle of equality.

Some doubts were expressed about the conformity between French and European law. France was condemned by the ECJ on two occasions for non-conformity. The prohibition on women's night work in the Code du travail (Labour Code) was also ruled to be illegal, since it did not conform to the directive. The ECJ rulings focused attention on the way in which equality was conceptualized in France. In the public sector, a number of exceptions to the principle of equal treatment had been maintained, with the intention of progressively feminizing the sector, including the police force. On 30 June 1988, France was condemned by the ECJ for not being sufficiently transparent in setting out the criteria to be used (Case C–318/86 Commission of the European Communities v French Republic [1988]) (Bonichot, 1988).

The French trade unions, and in particular the Confédération générale du travail (CGT), wanted to maintain the special provisions for women that had been written into collective agreements. They were very critical of the ECJ's ruling, firstly because they considered that it represented an attack on acquired social rights, and secondly on the grounds that women's paid work should be dissociated from their family roles. In the debate in parliament, Yvette Roudy, the Minister for Women's Rights, had acceded to the unions' demand that special provisions should be retained in collective agreements. The social actors were invited to renegotiate such provisions, but no deadline was fixed for the negotiations. In the same year, France was again condemned by the ECJ (Case C–312/86 Commission of the European Communities v French Republic [1988]) (Lanquetin and Masse-Dessen, 1989). Parliament also criticized the judgement in 1989, when a time limit of two years was set for the negotiations. One member of parliament, who supported night work for women, claimed that: 'France is far ahead of most other EC member states in terms of its social policy and should be proud of the fact'.

Although a judgement by the ECJ (25 July 1991) relating to the discriminatory nature of the prohibition on night work (Case C–345/89 Criminal proceedings against Alfred Stoeckel, Preliminary ruling [1991]) provoked strong reactions in some quarters,[1] it did not cause France to ratify ILO Convention no. 171, which regulated night work for both men and women. Nor did France amend its Labour Code, and the French government was, therefore, again condemned by the ECJ on 13 March 1997, on the grounds that 'any incompatibility with national legislation can only be entirely removed if measures are introduced that are equally binding in law to those they replace', which means that they

---

1.   Force ouvrière (FO) argued that night work should be outlawed for all workers. The CGT opposed the ruling on the grounds that it represented a form of economic liberalism that was unacceptable and paid insufficient attention to social rights. The Confédération française des travailleurs chrétiens (CFTC), for its part, denounced the capitulation before the heads of industry and technocrats in Brussels. The Confédération française démocratique du travail (CFDT), by contrast, supported lifting the prohibition on women's night work on the grounds that it ran counter to the principle of equality and excluded women from some types of employment.

must be adequately publicized (Case C–197/96 Commission of the European Communities v French Republic [1997]).

The authorities in France had not foreseen how the ECJ would interpret Article 119 in the Treaty of Rome. Nor had it predicted how European directives would be used to enforce the principle of equal treatment between men and women at work. Not only the lawyers but also policy-makers in France firmly believed that harmony reigned between French law and the requirements of the Community. Indeed, some of the rules in French labour law reduced the likelihood of cases being brought for indirect discrimination: for example, the French Labour Code stipulated that full and part-time workers must be employed under the same conditions (Lanquetin, 1994).

Men were the first to contest the ruling, following the second judgement by the ECJ. They began demanding the same advantages as those accorded to women, such as allowances for childcare and leave for family reasons,[2] and they won their cases. They also claimed the right to workplace benefits offered only to women as a result of positive action to protect them at childbirth and in cases of adoption. Again, they succeeded on the grounds that they were seeking an increase in salary designed to compensate parents for the additional costs incurred due to the presence of children (Lanquetin, 1997).

In November 1994, following a conference providing in-service training for magistrates on the question of discrimination at work (Guerder, 1995; Lanquetin, 1995b; Masse-Dessen, 1995), the court of appeal in Riom applied ECJ case law on proof of discrimination. For the first time, a group of women working as warehouses attendants were compared to a group of men with the same job qualifications, thereby revealing wage discrimination.[3]

Similarly, the Social Chamber of the Court of Cassation raised a legal point in 1995 over a worker who claimed that she had been discriminated against because she had not been accredited for maternity leave and had, therefore, lost the chance of gaining promotion. The ECJ rendered its judgement on 30 April 1998 in Case C-136/95 Caisse nationale d'assurance vieillesse des travailleurs salariés (CNAVTS) v Evelyne Thibault [1988], and the French court adopted its interpretation

---

2. Cass. soc. 27 février 1991, Cahiers sociaux du Barreau de Paris, p. 93; Cass. soc. 9 avril 1986, Bulletin civil, vol. V no. 144; Cass. soc. 8 octobre 1996, Bulletin civil, vol. V no. 311.

3. Cass. soc. 12 février 1997, *Bulletin civil*, vol. V no. 58, *Droit social* 1997, no. 7, p. 526, obs. M-T. Lanquetin.

in a ruling on 16 July 1998.[4] Hitherto, and in similar cases, the Court of Cassation had treated absence from work for reasons of maternity as sick leave and had discounted it in grading employees.

These examples show how European case law has helped change thinking in France and has made implementation of the equality principle more effective, while at the same time having an impact on other areas of social law. The Court of Cassation has stated that equal pay for men and women falls within the more general provisions of equal pay for equal work and has applied it to workers of the same sex in identical situations, the burden of proof resting on the employer.[5] In the late 1990s, the notion of indirect discrimination was invoked by trade union organizations to combat discrimination among their militants.

Whereas equality in employment is an area of concern for trade union organizations, even though they have had difficulty in dealing with the issues it raises, women's movements have been slow to take up the question. They have paid more attention to social issues such as abortion or rape. Only sexual harassment at work has been seized upon as a cause by an association, the Association contre la violence au travail, which is sufficiently well established to bring cases to court.

The equality debate was relaunched by feminist movements in the 1990s over the question of women in politics. Under-representation of women has been a constant feature of political life in a country that was one of the last to grant women the vote. The refusal by the Constitutional Court in 1982 to allow quotas to be introduced led, ultimately, to the Council of Ministers in France adopting a proposal in 1998 to amend the constitution. The intention was 'to enable the law to encourage equal access by women and men to political positions and appointments'. The Jospin government was behind the move, with support from women's associations, such as the Conseil national des femmes françaises, or the Association parité, and from women journalists and militants in political parties. Parity in political representation was one of the themes in the presidential election campaign in 1995. Most of the candidates committed themselves to introducing measures designed to promote greater parity between men and women, although they did not agree over what the most appropriate and effective measures might be.

---

4. CJCE 30 avril 1998, aff. C–136/95, CNAVTS c/E. Thibault D. 98 som. 246, obs. M-T. Lanquetin; Cass. soc. 16 juillet 1998, CNAVTS c/E. Thibault, *Droit social*, no. 11, p. 947, obs. M-T. Lanquetin.
5. Cass. soc. 29 octobre 1996, *Bulletin civil*, vol. V no. 359, *Droit social*, 1996, pp. 1013–15, obs. A. Lyon-Caen; Dalloz, 1998, som. 259, obs. M-T. Lanquetin.

Even if it is widely accepted that action is necessary to resolve the problem of political representation, it is questionable whether the Constitution needs to be changed to achieve that end. Critics of the bill argued that changing the Constitution would mean that women would be granted rights as women and not as free individuals. Supporters of the bill feared a return to the notion of biological difference, which would call into question the long and gradual emancipation of women. They also pointed out that political power has not been monopolized by men in the name of universal rights but rather at the expense of such rights (Rapport public 1996 du Conseil d'État, 1997).

PUTTING THE EQUALITY PRINCIPLE INTO PRACTICE AT WORK

While parity in political life had moved onto the national agenda in the early 1980s, equality of opportunity in employment was the priority of the Ministre des Droits des femmes (Minister for Women's Rights), Yvette Roudy, under the new leftwing government. As a result of the 1983 act, known as the *loi Roudy*, Council Directive 76/207/EEC on equal treatment was implemented in the private sector in France. Unlike previous legislation, the act covered all aspects of equality in employment between men and women. It brought some improvements as far as equal rights were concerned. Measures introducing positive action as a means of reducing *de facto* inequality challenged the French conception of universal rights, which prioritizes equal treatment rather than equality of opportunity, and the individual rather than the group.

The 1983 act had a number of objectives (Laufer, 1984). On the one hand, it reinforced and improved equal rights for women at work with regard to recruitment, promotion, training, qualifications and classification systems, and specified that work of equal value implied equivalent skills, experience and responsibilities. In the case of wage discrimination, in practice the burden of proof was reversed: while employers are not obliged to prove that they are not discriminating, they must justify any differences in pay (Lanquetin, 1998b). With regard to equal treatment, the act abolished the notion of legitimate cause, used previously to justify not employing women, and replaced it by a list of jobs where a specified sex is a necessary condition. Objective criteria were adopted in the list rather than the subjective notion of legitimate cause. The law also stipulates that the special provisions for women written into collective agreements should be removed unless they specifically concern the protection of maternity. However, no deadline was set for renegotiating those special provisions that were included in collective agreements.

A second objective was to introduce a more coherent approach to equality in employment in the Labour Code. Collective bargaining, which takes place every year at the level of branches or firms on issues such as wages, hours worked and the organization of working time and training, and every five years at branch level on classification systems, must now include information on the comparative situation of women and men in these areas, with the goal of ensuring equal treatment. A possible outcome might also have been greater equality of pay, through the re-evaluation of women's skills in the professional classification system. However, trade unions have not engaged much with the subject (Jobert, 1994; Silvera, 1996). Moreover, when the issue of equal pay and classification systems was brought before the court, the freedom of firms to determine the level of pay, beyond the minimum defined by the law and in branch classificatory systems, was given precedence by the judge (Lanquetin, 1995a).

A third objective of the 1983 act was to promote equal opportunities between women and men and to introduce the principle of positive action as a means of overcoming *de facto* inequalities at work, as provided for in the 1976 directive. These positive actions covered issues, such as working conditions and training, which could be introduced through collective bargaining at the level of either the branch or the firm. At the level of the firm, two instruments were created by the law for this purpose (Laufer, 1992). The first was the obligation placed on companies with more than 50 employees to prepare an annual report comparing the general conditions of employment of women and men, regarding recruitment, promotion, training and working conditions. The report is also expected to list actions taken during the year to promote equality as well as those planned for the following year. *Comités d'entreprise* (works councils) are required to receive and discuss the reports each year, and the reports are intended to form a basis for discussion, although this aim has not usually been achieved (Laufer, 1986). The second instrument took the form of incentives to encourage negotiations over equal opportunities schemes, including temporary measures to be implemented at company level to improve training, recruitment, promotion and working conditions for women. The state provides financial support for schemes, or equality programmes, considered to be exemplary, leading to equality contracts being signed by the state and the company. It will fund up to 50 per cent of the costs of a scheme and, for schemes involving training, it funds 50 per cent of the cost of training and 30 per cent of women's wages. Since 1994, companies can also obtain financial assistance for audits carried out by an external consultant on the situation regarding equality at work. The audit must propose measures expected to improve equality of opportunity and has to be submitted to the works council for an opinion on the audit itself and on any measures recommended. However, few companies have arranged for audits to be carried out.

In 1987, a third instrument was introduced to promote greater equality at work through *contrats pour la mixité des emplois* (desegregation contracts). These contracts are designed to encourage the diversification of jobs occupied by women and their promotion. They enable companies with fewer than 600 workers to receive funding from the state to cover 50 per cent of the costs of the action and, when it involves training, 50 per cent of the training costs and 30 per cent of the women's wages.

Despite the 1989 agreement encouraging sectoral collective agreements on positive action, at the branch level the practical outcome has been disappointing, since many agreements simply refer to the principles contained in the law, and make no attempt to introduce positive actions. Only a few of the new branch agreements mention consultation with workers' representatives over the implementation of equal opportunities.

At the firm level, some 34 equal opportunities schemes had been negotiated between 1983 and 1998, 22 of which benefited from state funding; and 1500 desegregation contracts were signed between 1987 and 1998, generally for training programmes, allowing women to enter jobs where men were previously in the majority. While some equal opportunities schemes have covered issues of pay discrimination, recruitment and career development, training has usually been targeted as the main area for action. Training programmes have been directed at poorly qualified workers in factories and employees in firms that introduce new technologies, requiring upgrading of the skills of their female workforce.

Relatively few companies in France have been interested in introducing positive action strategies in employment and human resource management policies. Many of them have seen the requirement to produce an annual report as an administrative constraint rather than as an opportunity to carry out a proper audit of the situation concerning women's employment. The information contained in these reports is often insufficiently detailed to allow a full analysis of any differences between women and men, with regard either to the jobs they are doing or to pay and indirect discrimination. Employers tend to use labour market constraints, or the nature of jobs occupied by women and their skills and qualifications, rather than company policies, as a means of explaining any differences that are noted in their reports (Laufer, 1986).

Nor has the annual reporting requirement on companies, as might have been hoped, given rise to a proper debate between management and workers, leading to widespread development of equal opportunities schemes. In some cases, the opposite has occurred: the desire to establish an action plan has led firms to become aware of the need to monitor the situation of women at the workplace and improve their diagnosis of the reasons for gender inequality (Groupe de recherche sur l'activité des femmes, 1989). However, some firms have conducted studies on the situation of women. Electricité et gaz de France is often cited as a company that has carried out an in-depth analysis of the question, resulting in changes to its business culture and alerting management to issues they need to take into account in the recruitment and career development of women (Laufer, 1996).

A second reason for the small number of equality projects negotiated by social partners may be the lack of political will on the part of the government to promote the act once it had been passed. The act relies on voluntary compliance by companies. To be effective, it would have required an active communication strategy and properly trained specialists to support individual companies. The available information suggests that it is essential for the information flow to be regular and continuous, both towards and within companies, if awareness is to be promoted among the different actors (Mazur, 1995). In the years immediately following the passing of the act, public companies were encouraged to play a leading role and to innovate in the area of equality at work. However, only four companies negotiated equality schemes, and the public sector has not, therefore, played the role expected of it, as was the case in some other EU member states (Grandin *et al.*, 1989).

A third reason why the act has not been more successful is that the unions have had difficulty in knowing how to position themselves in relation to questions of equality at work. With the notable exception of the CFDT, management have generally taken the initiative and have decided on how action plans should be formulated and what their content should be. They have been operating in an economic context where the main need was to invest in working arrangements and human resource management. The mobilization and training of women workers, therefore, afforded a way of coping with change. In many cases, trade unions have had problems developing their own strategies on equality issues, while they have also been reluctant to accept proposals made by management. The weak bargaining power of the unions in France is, undoubtedly, a factor affecting their involvement, particularly in small firms, which are often not covered by sectoral agreements (Jobert, 1994). In addition, the steep rise in unemployment during the 1980s diverted the attention of the unions away from equality issues.

A fourth reason explaining the reluctance of management and trade unions to engage with equality issues may be that many of them believe they are already meeting their commitments through existing labour law and do not need to take further action. A minimum wage is in force in France; companies are obliged to negotiate over pay; they are compelled to fund in-service training; and they are entitled to receive financial support to train unskilled workers. Even though these measures do not make explicit reference to equality between women and men, they could be considered to subsume gender equality issues (Laufer, 1998). In practice, a much more explicit commitment to equality objectives seems to be needed. For example, although the minimum wage has, undoubtedly, played an important part in reducing differences between low wages for women and men, the way in which jobs are evaluated continues to undervalue what are seen as women's jobs and female qualities (Lanquetin, 1995a; Sofer, 1995; Silvera, 1996). Analysis of the progress made since the early 1980s suggests that equality issues have been only gradually taken into account in collective bargaining. Despite the improvements achieved in some areas, less importance has been attributed to equality than other issues concerning employment, such as working time and training (Jobert, 1994; Junter-Loiseau, 1997).

THE PROTECTION OF WOMEN AS WORKING MOTHERS

Underlying state intervention in what has come to be called 'reconciliation' between paid work and family obligations is a conception of the welfare state according to which women should not be prevented from engaging in economic activity because of their family obligations. But nor should paid work be allowed to have an adverse effect on family life. The theme was already present in debates in the nineteenth century, such as those leading up to the 1892 act prohibiting night work for children and women. The poor working conditions in the textile industry, in particular, were denounced by members of parliament and some industrialists as harmful for family life (Combette, 1976). Although maternity leave of eight weeks was introduced in the Labour Code in 1909, paid leave was not granted until 1928, and then only for public sector employees. Parental leave came much later in 1977, though well before the European directive. Since 1966, the law has been changed to ensure greater protection under the labour contract.

On the one hand, the state has been seeking to protect women within the family and to safeguard their reproductive function. On the other, it has acted to encourage women to engage in an economic activity which will provide them not only with an income and, hence, financial autonomy, but also with the social rights associated with employment. Public policy has thus been caught between two socio-political currents, representing different interest groups. The family is supported as a fundamental social institution by powerful family associations; women's groups are seeking to free women from their economic dependence on a male breadwinner and to help them acquire their own social citizenship rights.

The protection of women at the workplace rests on three pillars: child protection policy, family policy and employment policy. The first pillar is based on the way in which childhood and motherhood have been socially constructed in France: children are considered as both private and public 'goods'. The responsibility for children is, therefore, shared between the state and the family. The state intervenes not only to help families but also to protect children. The development of public childcare facilities and nursery schools has two objectives: to assist mothers who are economically active, and to give all children equal opportunities, irrespective of their social background. The interests of children thus coincide with those of their mothers.

The second pillar concerns the place of the family within public policy. Important policy developments have occurred reflecting changes in the social construction of women's roles. Under pressure from feminists, a more egalitarian view has progressively replaced the strong family orientation contained in family policy, with its focus on women as homemakers. As early as 1920, women had obtained the right to belong to a trade union without the permission of their husbands; in 1938, they gained the right to take paid work, but their husbands could oppose their decision, in the 'family interest'. Between 1965 and 1975, a series of laws were enacted that affected the rights of family members, marking an important turning point in the conceptualization of the place of women within the family, and calling into question the male-breadwinner model. Instead, the image projected was of women as working mothers (Prost, 1984). The reforms confirmed recognition of women's rights as individuals, the ending of the legal subordination of women to their partners in marriage, and more equal sharing of obligations and responsibilities between parents with regard to children. They also ensured greater equality within families as fathers lost their legal right to parental authority. The reform of matrimonial rights in 1965 had introduced greater equality between spouses. Divorce by mutual consent, granted in 1975, also weakened conjugal ties. Developments in contraceptive methods and the liberalization of the law on abortion in the same year helped further to give women a sense of power and responsibility.

Under the third pillar, policies were developed during the 1950s, 1960s and 1970s in response to the need to recruit women. Women were entering the labour market under the same conditions as men as full-time workers, although many of them left employment when they had children. Progressively, as family size declined and public provision of childcare was extended, more women were remaining in employment. The developing dual-earner family weakened the traditional family. The male-breadwinner model, which was dependent on women being homemakers, and was reinforced when the social security system was established in 1947, has been progressively eroded under pressure from women seeking greater autonomy. At the same time, a single wage has become insufficient to support a family (Strobel, 1997). The centrality of work and of the family–state relationship in this arrangement is confirmed by the way in which the state supports lone parents, generally the mother. The *allocation de parent isolé* (lone-parent benefit) is paid to parents until their children reach the age of three, which is when young children are guaranteed a place in nursery school. Mothers are obliged to seek work at this stage, which explains why lone mothers in France have relatively high economic activity rates compared to countries such as the United Kingdom, where, until the late 1990s, benefits were paid until children reached the age of 16 (Bradshaw *et al.*, 1996).

The coming together of these three pillars meant that the question of equality between women and men had to be linked with that of the support afforded by the state to the family and to women as workers (Hantrais and Letablier, 1996). Under the presidency of Valéry Giscard d'Estaing, the shift in the model was confirmed, symbolically, by the creation of a Secrétaire d'État à la Condition féminine (Junior Minister for Women's Condition) in 1974. The first appointee to the position was Françoise Giroud. The Women's Movement[6] was exerting pressure to promote individual rights, which brought it into conflict with public policy centred on the family as a unit rather than its individual members. The pressure for change came, to a large extent, from social movements, particularly women's movements and from women trade unionists. The Comité du travail féminin played an important role in providing institutional support, in launching the debate and in bringing forward proposals for reform. Women such as the feminist labour sociologists, Madeleine Guilbert, Andrée Michel and Evelyne Sullerot, played a major role in promoting the debate. The Ligue des droits des femmes (1976), for its part, aimed to denounce all forms of sex discrimination in law and politics and to promote a new right for women.

It was at this point in the 1970s that the concept of the reconciliation of paid work and family life first appeared in political discourse and moved onto the political agenda. One of the aims of the Comité du travail féminin had been to reflect on the question of how to harmonize paid work and family life. It brought forward proposals to the government for improving the relationship between the two spheres. In parallel with the progression of equal treatment between men and women, in particular with reference to pay, the question of women's access to employment was clearly set out in terms of the responsibility they bear for family life. The way was open in France for considering equal opportunities not only with reference to paid work, but also by taking account of the conditions under which women gain access to employment and pursue an occupation. Implementation of the principle of equal treatment involved abolishing a number of measures designed specifically to protect women in employment, but which had the effect of preventing them from taking some types of work. At the end of the 1970s, very few specific measures remained, with the exception of the protection of motherhood, or the protection of women in their domestic and family roles (length of working time, work organization, retirement age) (Deveaud and Lévy, 1980).

By the late 1970s, the model of the woman in the home was an accurate description of only a minority of women in French society. Most couples had two earners, and most children had a mother who was economically active. Marriage was being postponed, women were

---

6. After 1968, the feminist movement in France was renewed, and by the 1970s mobilized to promote women's rights, including civic and legal rights, the right to employment and the right for women to decide how they use their own bodies.

having fewer children, and their employment patterns were becoming more continuous. National consensus over the aims of family policy was being diluted, as the wage-earner society developed. Women's earnings were no longer seen as a supplement but as an essential component of household income. The legal framework had also been evolving in parallel with the changes in individual and social behaviour.

By the early 1980s, the programme of the successful socialist candidate, François Mitterrand, in the campaign leading up to the presidential elections took these changes into account. It suggested replacing family policy by measures to support children. They were not intended to have an impact on family forms, the number of children or the economic activity of women.[7] The programme proved difficult to implement. It created the impression that public policy lacked coherence, and this weakness resulted in disillusionment among women voters (Jenson and Sineau, 1995). The shift between right and leftwing governments during the 1980s reinforced the impression of incoherence. When the Right returned to power, policy with regard to the 'choices' offered to women and mothers between family life and paid work was projected as neutral and non-prescriptive (Haut conseil de la population et de la famille, 1987). The reconciliation measures introduced were intended to apply to both men and women and were not solely targeted at women as in the postwar period. A lively debate took place over the new measures to help parents combine paid and unpaid work, to a large extent because some political groups have always suspected the state of trying to encourage women to withdraw from the labour market for pronatalist reasons, particularly in a context of high unemployment and falling birthrates (Lebras, 1992). Although a broad consensus was reached over the need to develop public services and childcare facilities, measures designed to reduce working time, or the childrearing allowance paid to parents who took leave to look after young children, were much more contentious. The promotion of part-time work was seen as a retrograde and anti-egalitarian step, imposing constraints on opportunities for women (Bouillaguet-Bernard *et al.*, 1986).

---

7.   President Mitterrand was elected in 1981. He presented his programme for women's rights on 8 March 1982, at a ceremony held at the Elysée Palace, commemorating International Women's Day, with the slogan 'autonomy, equality, dignity'. The aim was to promote women's autonomy, democracy within the family, at work and in civic life, the right to employment and equality at work. The programme was intended to mark the shift towards a more modern approach after 20 years of traditional policy.

During the 1980s, support for public childcare became the weak link in policy for reconciling paid work and family life. In a report submitted in 1975 to the Conseil économique et social on the problems associated with women's work and employment,[8] Evelyne Sullerot (1981) had recommended that the state should develop facilities for young children and make them available as a public service, and that motherhood should be seen as a social function justifying direct state support. Nursery provision was, however, progressively being replaced by more diversified and individualized forms of childminding. Public funding shifted from the provision of collective facilities for young children to more individualized support in the form of childcare allowances and parental leave. The shift was justified on grounds of cost and because of the constraints imposed by greater variation in work-time schedules. Despite the relatively long opening hours of nurseries and after-school provision for young children compared to other countries, many parents in France were looking for more flexible ways of co-ordinating their own working hours with arrangements for their children.

Proposals from the Right to introduce paid parental leave were justified on the grounds that parents should have the opportunity to choose the most appropriate form of reconciliation to suit their own needs. Leftwing politicians opposed paid parental leave, arguing that such measures were intended to remove women from the labour market and send them back into the home with a substitute income. The Right feared that family policy would be weakened if women were encouraged to subcontract their homemaker roles to an even greater extent. Unpaid parental leave was first introduced in 1977 as a right for workers enshrined in the Labour Code. Paid leave, by contrast, in the form of an *allocation parentale d'éducation* (childrearing allowance), which was not proposed until 1985 by Georgina Dufoix, the minister in charge of family affairs, was presented as a family policy measure, and applied initially only to parents with three children. Subsequently, it was extended to women with two children in 1994. In the case of parental leave, the employment contract is suspended, and at the end of the period of leave, parents have the right to return to their previous position or to similar work with an equivalent level of pay.

The reasons for the controversy over childrearing allowance are that the benefit serves to meet what may be conflicting objectives. When parental leave was created, the intention was to help parents combine

---

8.   'Avis adopté par le Conseil économique et social sur le rapport Sullerot', Droit social, no. 1, pp. 117–23.

family life and employment and to create an environment conducive to raising children (Jenson and Sineau, 1997). When the Right returned to power in 1986, childrearing allowance was used as a benefit designed to encourage family building. The debate over the nature of the allowance and its objectives was relaunched on the initiative of rightwing members of parliament. They attempted to gain support for the idea of a salary for mothers at home, which had always been promoted by some family associations. A proposal from the Union nationale des associations familiales had been adopted in 1973 by the Conseil consultatif sur la famille and had been transposed into a bill brought forward by 112 rightwing members of parliament in December 1974. The two main trade union confederations and the leftwing parties resolutely opposed the measure, as did feminist movements and associations. Although the bill never became law, the debate continues to resonate since it gives expression to a strongly held conviction among family associations that an allowance should be paid to women who leave employment to look after their children (Vernaz, 1976). The same period saw the development of the notion of domestic labour and domestic production and attempts to quantify and evaluate their economic value.

EQUALITY, SHARING AND RECONCILIATION

In France, the equality debate has not been confined to employment. For a long time, efforts have been made to deal with other sources of inequality, particularly with reference to the conditions under which women gain access to the labour market as mothers. The support provided by the state for child and eldercare is based on the notion that inequality is rooted in the unequal sharing of family obligations and domestic work. As far as children are concerned, the state and local government operate in active partnership with families through public provision of facilities. However, in the 1990s, when priority was given to fighting unemployment and social exclusion, governments changed their stance, and a number of contradictions emerged (Fagnani, 1998a). Responsibility for child and eldercare became a policy issue because of its job creation potential, and not because of its importance from an equality perspective.

   While measures such as the childrearing allowance and part-time working arrangements ostensibly promote equal treatment between women and men, they can have perverse effects, unless inducements are also given to men to encourage them to take parental leave and to adopt part-time working patterns. Policies to create and develop domestic service jobs increase the demand for labour and enable parents to subcontract their family obligations towards dependants. The aim is to achieve a more equitable sharing of jobs while also helping parents reconcile paid and unpaid work. Family and employment policy overlap. The two benefits paid to parents – childminding allowances for children cared for in their own home and in that of an approved child-minder – together with tax deductions enable the state to reinforce the value of women's paid work and their occupational skills. The effect of these policies is, however, to confirm labour market segregation, since childminders are almost exclusively women. The domestic services sector is increasingly feminized, thereby reinforcing some forms of ine-quality in the labour market. Another effect could be to discriminate between the various types of childminding used by different social categories: the upper middle classes have recourse to individualized forms of childcare, the lower middle classes opt for nurseries, and the lower income groups rely heavily on family support.

Within the framework of family law, the immediate and unexpected effect of the amendments made to childrearing allowance in 1994 was to produce a fall in the number of economically active women with two children (Afsa, 1996). Mothers who were in insecure jobs or were unemployed seized the opportunity to withdraw from the labour force. The childrearing allowance thus serves as a minimum social benefit, and women who take it are likely to have problems re-entering the labour force. In addition, the fact that 98 per cent of parents who take parental leave are women shows the measure is far from being neutral in terms of encouraging a redistribution of roles between women and men. No incentives are provided to encourage men to take part of the leave allocation, as in some EU member states. Despite the declared aim of trying to make it easier for parents to combine paid work and family life, the measure may have the effect of reinforcing the tradi-tional division of roles between women and men. Some forms of labour market discrimination and segregation have, undoubtedly, increased because of the asymmetric patterns of employment between women and men. Many of the domestic service jobs created are low paid and have, therefore, accentuated pay differentials. The fact that women can take long periods of leave has reinforced prejudices among employers concerning the commitment of women to the labour market.

Since the 1970s, employment policy has been extended to cover other areas of public policy, including the family, which has tradition-ally been a priority for governments in France. As a result, parents have greater choice in the way they care for their children, which can be seen as a form of recognition of women's contribution to economic activity. At the same time, market forces have come to play a larger part in the arrangements made by families. The 'republican' model of equality between women and men has thus been weakened in favour of a more liberal conception closer to that adopted in European legislation. The protection of mothers at work, which was at the basis of the French model, has given way to a more formalized conception of equality. Parents are offered a choice among different reconciliation strategies to help them combine employment and family life, which opens the door to market forces and reduces the role played by the state in childcare. Freedom of choice, however, conflicts with the republican ideal of equality, and is constrained by new regulations governing flexibility at work and in labour markets, which are likely to produce other forms of inequality not only between the sexes but also between different social categories.

5 Equal Opportunities Policies and the Management of Care in Germany

Kirsten Scheiwe

At European level, debate over measures to assist couples in reconciling employment and family life has focused mainly on issues of childcare. Policies concerned with caring for people of all ages are, however, of central importance for equal opportunities politics for a number of interacting reasons. Firstly, women perform most informal caring activities – childcare, care for disabled or older people – both within the family and for other close relatives. Secondly, the way in which society conceptualizes caring activities affects the status, income and social security rights of women. If informal care is unpaid, as is generally the case, it has a negative impact on women's earnings and makes them dependent on financial support from a spouse or partner, other family members, or the state. If women invest long hours in informal care, their labour market participation is adversely affected. If they spend several years carrying out informal caring activities, they have problems re-establishing themselves in the labour market. If they have specialized in caring activities and family work while their partner was the main income earner, they may suffer disproportionately in the case of divorce. If no, or only limited, social rights are granted to informal carers, they are at a disadvantage in terms of entitlements to social security compared to people in paid employment.

The rights of people who specialize in unpaid caring activities or housework within the family are not only an issue for social security regulations, but also for family law, and especially marriage and divorce law. Women's and men's asymmetric specialization in paid and unpaid work raises the question of how the two types of work are shared between partners and within marriage. The advantages as well as the disadvantages of using family law to address care-related issues and to counteract sex discrimination are important components in the debate about equal opportunities strategies. The professionalization of caring activities and the extension of the service sector to cover caring (childcare, education, care for sick, disabled or older people and long-term care) may help increase female employment and create new job opportunities. The creation of service sector jobs and the upgrading of female care activities to the status of skilled and properly paid jobs and occupations are, therefore, relevant to equal opportunities policies. At the same time, the provision of adequate and high-quality care services – afterschool care for children, childcare services, 'meals on wheels' or home help and long-term care for older people – is important if women are to be economically active and reconcile employment and care duties.

Feminists have long emphasized the importance of caring issues for equal opportunities between women and men (Finch and Groves, 1983; Waerness, 1984; Holtmaat, 1992; Leira, 1992). Although views about possible strategies and policy reforms to overcome the problems faced by women are by no means unanimous, it is widely agreed that informal care activities, mainly performed by women, should be upgraded and properly acknowledged by society, and that the provision of care services needs to be improved if economic activity and family responsibilities are to become more compatible.

Germany affords an interesting example of shifts in the way in which caring is treated in politics, as recorded in changes in family and marriage law, in social security regulations and through the provision of public care services. Change has at times been contradictory and unco-ordinated, and many care-related policy issues have been highly contested, not only between different political actors, but also between different strands of the women's movement, as shown, for example, by the introduction and extension of parental leave arrangements. The reforms implemented have sometimes involved a complex set of political compromises between different political actors. Equal opportunities issues have represented only a small component in the packages agreed, although the impact of changes in legislation may be far-reaching for gender equality. The lack of political consensus about the direction which equal opportunities policies should take and the way in which care-related issues should be integrated has been a serious impediment to any improvement in women's status and social rights as formal and informal carers, and to the development of a modern, non-discriminatory service culture and welfare mix. As far as the gender dimension of the management of care is concerned, the policy instruments of the European Community (EC) were not of major importance for women.

Since they are employment related the legal instruments created since the 1970s by the EC, especially the equality directives (see Figure 1.2), have had very little impact in Germany on care politics. Even where some scope may exist for a broader legal interpretation, for example when applying Council Directive 79/7/EEC on equal treatment in social security, the case law of the European Court of Justice (ECJ) narrows down the scope of application (Sohrab, 1996; Hervey and Shaw, 1998), and interprets the concept of indirect discrimination in a restricted way to avoid interference in family affairs and in spheres where national governments claim they possess unrestricted competencies. At the European level, access to non-employment related social rights, benefits or services has been dealt with mainly in the context of equal treatment for intra-European migrant workers and their family members, where discrimination based on nationality has been banned, rather than in a gender context (Scheiwe 1994a).

In this chapter, the aim is twofold. Firstly, the management of policy on caring in Germany is examined from the 1950s to 1990s within the context of antidiscrimination legislation, with particular reference to the most influential legal actor, the Bundesverfassungsgericht (Federal Constitutional Court). This example is used to illustrate the changing approaches of hegemonic political forces and institutions towards care issues as part of the equality problem, and as a central feature of gender relations and equal opportunities policies in society.

Secondly, the impact of power relations between political actors and legal actors and the relevance of structural constraints for political reforms in the area of equal opportunities are analysed. Two examples are discussed: the introduction of a legal right to a place in a kindergarten for all children over three (as part of the abortion law reform package in 1992), and the introduction of the *Pflegeversicherung* (Long-Term Care Insurance) established in 1994 as the fifth branch of social insurance.

CARING AND THE EQUAL OPPORTUNITIES AGENDA

The period from the late 1940s to the late 1960s in Germany can be characterized in terms of the development of the constitutional principle of sex equality, the reluctance of the legislator to act and the prominent role played by the Federal Constitutional Court in setting the framework for equal opportunities policies.

Equality and the upgrading of family work

The first wave of reforms designed to abolish legal rules discriminating directly against women took place before the establishment of the European Economic Community (EEC) and was strongly influenced by the case law of the Federal Constitutional Court, which was founded in 1951. Since it has far-reaching competencies to overthrow legislation considered to be in breach of German *Grundgesetz* (Basic Law), even if its interpretation runs counter to the views of the majority in parliament, the court plays a central role in the system of checks and balances and has influenced the strongly legalized political culture of the Federal Republic of Germany (FRG) (Lepsius, 1990). The court has an ultimate decision-making power and can force the legislator to comply with certain requirements based on its interpretation of constitutional rights. This was the case with the principle of equality between men and women, especially in the 1950s: according to Article 117 of German Basic Law, all former legal rules infringing the principle of sex equality guaranteed in Article 3 section 2 became invalid on the 31 March 1953. However, parliament was reluctant to enact new statutory rules. Thus the court outlawed various discriminatory rules, stating that the sex equality clause of the constitution had direct effect.[1] It put parliament under pressure to act, until the *Gleichberechtigungsgesetz* (Equal Rights Act) of 1957 was finally made law by the reluctant legislator, and enforced in 1958. The main changes brought about concerned the rights of married women: parental rights were equalized, with the exception of the husband's prerogative to decide in conflicts over the education of children, which was later abolished by the court. The marital property regime changed from separate property to a deferred community of property (based on the Swedish model of the 1920s). The intention was to give a share to the wife for her unpaid contribution to family welfare during marriage. However, with regard to the division of labour and the choice of roles, the marriage model remained the traditional breadwinner/housewife marriage, and the explicitly stated right of the wife to engage in paid work was subordinated to family interests.

In the 1950s and 1960s, the case law of the Federal Constitutional Court challenged the unequal treatment of women, especially in family law. Its interpretation rejected more traditional views which were

---

1. Decisions of the Federal Constitutional Court, Bundesverfassungs-gerichtsentscheidungen, subsequently abbreviated to BVerfGE, 1953, vol. 3, p. 225.

dominant in the family law literature, and counteracted attempts to integrate the principle of sex equality under the constitutional clause of Article 6, which protects marriage and the family as institutions (Simitis, 1994). In 1957, the court abolished compulsory joint taxation of a married couple's income, which punished a wife's employment by imposing higher progressive tax rates (BVerfGE, 1957, vol. 6, p. 55). It rejected the intended effect of the regulation – to keep the wife out of employment and at home – in the name of sex equality. The prerogative of the father to decide in educational matters in the case of conflict between parents, introduced by the Equal Rights Act, was declared to be in breach of the sex equality principle in 1959 (BVerfGE, 1959, vol. 10, p. 59), and case law of 1964 abolished the prerogative of a younger son over an older daughter to inherit a family farm (BVerfGE, 1964, vol. 15, p. 337). The court was also more progressive than the legislator in another question that was highly relevant for unmarried mothers shouldering the main burden of care for children, when it challenged discrimination against children born out of wedlock (BVerfGE, 1969, vol. 25, p. 167), which was already banned by Article 6 section 5 of German Basic Law, but not implemented until 1969 through a statute in conformity with the constitutional claim by the legislator.

These examples underline a particular trait of the (West) German equal opportunities culture: it is strongly legalized, due not only to the hierarchy of norms and the predominance of German Basic Law, but also to the particular position occupied by the Federal Constitutional Court and its competence to overrule even the legislator. In this first period, the interpretation of the equality principle focused strongly upon family law and marriage, and these historical imprints can be found in later developments regarding the management of care.

The first wave of legislation to abolish direct sex discrimination, especially within the family, came to an end in 1969, when the statute providing for equal rights for children born out of wedlock was implemented. The dominant interpretation of the principle of sex equality in this period could be characterized as 'equality of the sexes despite objective biological and functional differences',[2] as expressed by the

---

2. This argument was first developed in 1953 (see BVerfGE, 1953, vol. 3, p. 242) and used in various cases by the Federal Constitutional Court up to the 1980s. The court assumed that objective biological and functional (related to the division of labour) differences between the sexes existed, which called for different treatment according to the specific nature of the life situation concerned, but these differences did not allow discrimination against women and disadvantageous

Federal Constitutional Court through case law since 1953. During this period, the special role of women as (house)wives and mothers and their responsibility to provide for the home and children were not seriously questioned by the dominant political forces, and equal rights for women were claimed despite these differences. The constitutional ban on sex discrimination in law was interpreted mainly as a prohibition against different treatment in law, based on differences in sex. The 1950s and 1960s were the years when the ideas of the traditional nuclear family, the housewife and the caring mother were booming, and a traditional division of labour within the family remained largely unquestioned.

In this context, some changes in the legal treatment of women's family work, housework and caring activities were taking place. Caring for the home and for children by the wife was considered to be a maintenance contribution on an equal footing with maintenance in cash (the traditional duty of the husband and father). This was explicitly stated in the Equal Rights Act. Previously, the provision of care and housework by the wife had been considered as an unpaid service which she was obliged to perform as a marital duty (Scheiwe, 1999). In 1963, the Federal Constitutional Court declared that the equal value of different maintenance contributions, including unpaid care activities under family law, was a direct consequence of the constitutional sex equality principle (BVerfGE, 1964, vol. 17, p.1). This idea of 'different but equal contributions' by husband and father and wife and mother became an important interpretation of the principle of sex equality. It also served to justify the constitutionality of legal claims by the wife to an equal share in property acquired during marriage in the case of divorce, as introduced by the *Erstes Ehereformgesetz* (First Marriage Reform Act) of 1976. In addition, it justified the legal principle that a mother is fulfilling her maintenance duty towards children sufficiently through care work. Therefore, her income is not taken into consideration when the absent father's maintenance contribution is calculated. The topic continues to be debated in legal argumentation: the legal regulation of the economic duties of the former husband after divorce and the rules providing for pension splitting and for the sharing of other jointly acquired assets between the former spouses in case of divorce have been declared to be constitutional (BVerfGE, vol. 53, p. 224; vol. 55, p. 134;

---

treatment. The argument disappeared gradually and was not explicitly rejected until the 1990s. What was formerly seen as objective (functional) difference was now treated as a result of a traditional division of labour, which should not be perpetuated by legal rules (for example BVerfGE 1991, vol. 84, p. 9, concerning the wife's name).

vol. 57, p. 361; vol. 66, p. 84), since they acknowledge the different but equal contribution made by the wife, whose duty it is to run the household and care for the children during marriage.

This interpretation of the equality principle resulted in a certain upgrading of family work within marriage, but its impact was limited to the private sphere, since it was concerned only with sharing within the (married) couple. The management of care remained a private issue, but was given recognition through the compensatory rules introduced within marriage. The traditional division of labour was not challenged; rather, it was compensated for by the limited upgrading of women's activities as wife and mother. While some unequal treatment of women in the public sphere was seen as a compensatory measure for their 'double burden' and their special role as mothers and wives, the exclusion of men from such rights (for example in widow's pensions, the right to a monthly day off for housework duties, or the prohibition of night work for women) continued to be upheld by the Federal Constitutional Court into the 1970s. The court denied that they were an infringement of the sex equality principle and did not consider that these measures might also reinforce ideological stereotypes, or work to the disadvantage of women and exclude them from access to certain segments of the job market. Such measures were considered to compensate for 'objective biological and functional differences' between the sexes.

The limitations of formal equality for care-related issues

While most forms of direct discrimination based on sex had been eliminated, in the following period on several occasions men claimed an infringement of the equality principle, in an attempt to challenge their exclusion from the few remaining 'privileges' granted to women, such as the monthly day off (BVerfGE, 1979, vol. 52, p. 369), the exclusion of the unmarried father from custody (BVerfGE, 1981, vol. 56, p. 363), and the unequal pension age for women and men (BVerfGE, 1986, vol. 74, p. 163). However, men's claims were not always successful. The Federal Constitutional Court never adopted a purely formal interpretation of the sex equality principle; it maintained a position which allowed for some unequal treatment of certain differences.

During the 1970s, the ideal of the housewife marriage lost ground. Women's participation in the labour market, especially that of married women, increased considerably, as elsewhere in Western Europe, while marriage and fertility rates began to fall, and divorce rates increased. The family law reforms of the 1970s brought about the overdue implementation of equal rights for spouses with regard to the division of roles and easier access to divorce, as well as a far-reaching reform of the economic consequences of divorce. Marital breakdown as the reason for divorce replaced the former fault-based grounds for divorce. The claim to postmarital rights was no longer reserved for the innocent partner, and the regulation of the consequences of divorce (maintenance provisions, separation of marital property and assets, pension rights and child custody), irrespective of the guilt of a partner, can be considered as an acknowledgement of the caring activities and the family work of the partner (the wife), who assumed the main burden for carrying out such duties. This way of managing the problem of caring within marriage is ambivalent: it secures a share of family assets for the caring partner, who is at a disadvantage because of the responsibilities borne, but it also reinforces a traditional division of labour.

Although divorce law reforms are usually not discussed in terms of equal opportunities policies, these developments are instructive in indicating some of the particular features of managing the problem of care in (West) Germany, notably with reference to the privatized approach: the centrality of the marriage institution as a social security valve has been strengthened through divorce law reform, since the carer may claim postmarital maintenance due to her former or ongoing care obligations. Pension splitting in the case of divorce provides her with some compensation for the loss of personal pension rights during marriage. Since the financial resources of divorcing couples are generally limited, often the law cannot live up to its own promises (Caesar-Wolf and Eidmann, 1987; Willenbacher *et al.*, 1987). The centrality of marriage in providing social security and compensation for a (married) carer is further strengthened through tax provisions and the regulation of survivor's pensions (Scheiwe, 1994b), which excludes unmarried lone parents from access to various measures that may compensate partially for care-related disadvantages.

In the 1980s, the focus shifted towards the implementation of equal treatment in employment and in access to training and jobs. The equality directives of the 1970s and 1980s led to further change in German labour and social security law. In 1980, a statute was enacted translating the EC directives into national labour law rules (Pfarr and Bertelsmann, 1989). Most forms of direct discrimination had been abolished, and attention centred upon problems of indirect discrimination. The concept of indirect discrimination, as developed by the ECJ, turned out to be innovative and challenging, especially with regard to the treatment of part-time workers. However, care-related issues have hardly been affected by these developments. The employment focus of the European directives has avoided intervention in the regulation of family-related issues; social security regulations that are not concerned with employment or social policies in general have largely been a taboo area touched upon only occasionally, and not generally in the context of the European Union's (EU) equal opportunities policies (Ostner and Lewis, 1995; Sohrab, 1996; Hervey and Shaw, 1998). Rather, they have been drawn up as measures providing for equal treatment of migrant workers and their families (Scheiwe, 1994a). Another reason for the lack of impact of European equal opportunities legislation upon care-related policy measures in Germany is that the concept of indirect discrimination, developed mainly by the ECJ, has barely been taken up by the German Federal Constitutional Court (Bieback, 1997, pp. 45–50), even though this legal concept might have some further potential for combating the disadvantages of women under social security regulations, due to their greater involvement in care activities and their role as mothers. At the national level, case law of the Federal Constitutional Court did undergo some changes in interpreting the equality principle: the formula of 'objective biological and functional differences' between the sexes was no longer used.

Combining employment and care activities

In terms of national social policies, the 1980s and 1990s have been characterized by contested policy measures in an attempt to make employment more compatible with family responsibilities, which has become a central issue in equal opportunities policies. The parental leave package and the introduction of pension credits for childcare periods, enacted in 1986 under the Christian Democrat/Liberal coalition (against opposition from the Social Democrats), brought into operation a policy model that favoured long employment interruptions for mothers and private childcare by the mother for children under three in their own home, by providing some social guarantees (job protection during the leave period, pension rights, allowances). At the same time, the path towards more extensive childcare services for children under three was blocked; and the level of financial support for carers reinforced dependence on a (male) partner with a higher income, and acted as a disincentive for men to take up parental leave. Again, the management of care in this context is characterized by a social policy model which, through a few limited social rights, confirms the primacy of (women's) private responsibility to provide care, reinforces dependency upon a partner and incites long employment interruptions. Feminists (Landenberger, 1990; Götting, 1992; Ostner, 1993, p. 102; Scheiwe, 1994b, p. 216) have criticized such a model as a modern version of the old male-breadwinner model: in the one-and-a-half-earners couple, the wife follows a patchwork career with long employment interruptions to cover the care needs of the family. The relatively high wage level of the German economy, supported by tax law provisions which favour the single-earner marriage, and subsidized through the means-tested parental allowance, make such strategies economically viable. In the absence of feasible alternatives, most mothers take the whole period of parental leave (36 months); only 10 per cent interrupt employment for less than 6 months; and fewer than 50 per cent return to their workplace after parental leave. More than 30 per cent of returning mothers reduce working hours and work part-time (Regierungsbericht, 1990, p. 15).

PUBLIC CARE PROVISION

One reason why so few mothers remain in full-time employment is the lack of public support services. From a comparative perspective, the scarcity of public care services for children and for older people is a distinguishing characteristic of the (West) German service culture. Disparities in the level of provision in East and West Germany reflect two very different traditions. Before unification, only 2 per cent of children aged 0–3 years had places in crèches in West Germany, compared to 50 per cent in the eastern *Länder*; 78 per cent of children aged 3–6 were in nursery schools in West Germany, compared to 100 per cent in the East; 5 per cent of children under 10 had places in afterschool care in West Germany and 85 per cent in the East; elementary schooling lasted 4 hours a day in the West and 8 hours a day in the East, from 08.00–16.00 (Colberg-Schrader, 1991; European Commission Network on Childcare and Other Measures to Reconcile Family and Employment Responsibilities, 1996, p. 46).

The low level of public provision of childcare facilities in West Germany poses major problems for mothers who do not want to interrupt employment for three years after childbirth. When parental leave was introduced in 1986, the duration was 12 months; progressively it has been extended to three years. A means-tested allowance is paid to the caring parent for up to a maximum of two years; the amount has not been changed since 1986 (Schiersmann, 1991; European Commission Network on Childcare and Other Measures to Reconcile Family and

Employment Responsibilities, 1994). For mothers of children below school age, opening hours of kindergartens are a problem. Although places are available for most children (but not for all), the full implementation of a right to a kindergarten place, due to be introduced in 1994, was postponed until 1999, because of the financial problems in the *Länder* and municipalities. Even part-time employment is very difficult to organise, since most kindergartens are open only until 12.00 or 13.00. Short and irregular school hours in elementary school are another obstacle for mothers, and places in afterschool care are nearly as scarce as places in crèches for under-threes. In the old *Länder*, the lack of childcare has been a serious impediment for the compatibility of employment and family obligations. Childcare provision in the new *Länder* was still extensive (although shrinking) in the years following unification, but large numbers of mothers lost their jobs, and some families were no longer able to afford to pay the increasing fees. In East Germany, places in publicly funded *Krippen* for children under three fell by 27 per cent between 1990 and 1991 (98 000 places were lost); and places in kindergartens decreased by 17 per cent (185 000 places were lost); places in afterschool care (*Hort*) fell by 17 per cent between 1989 and 1990 (European Commission Network on Childcare and Other Measures to Reconcile Family and Employment Responsibilities, 1996, p. 46). As a consequence, staff working in childcare facilities in the new *Länder* had to be reduced, and many more women lost their jobs.

The underdevelopment of childcare services in the old *Länder* runs counter to the goal of equal opportunities for women and to the constitutional principle of equality for women and men, which requires that 'the State promotes the factual realization of equality of women and men and works for the elimination of all existing disadvantages'. This clause, which calls for positive action, was added to Article 3 section II of German Basic Law in 1994 after German unification.

Traute Meyer (1994) discusses possible reasons for the poor provision of childcare services. As personal services, they are labour intensive, difficult to standardize and mechanize, and thus tend to be relatively more expensive than other forms of production. Since adequate provision of childcare services cannot be left to market dynamics, and they cannot be sold for profit, they are costly to maintain and accessible only for the better-off categories of the population. The welfare state is forced to take over the task (a genuine equal opportunities policy), but fiscal considerations constrain even state agencies that try to reduce public provision of personal services and shift them to the private sector. Another explanation for the poor public childcare services can be found in the tradition of the German welfare state. The Bismarckian reforms introduced social insurance as the building block of the welfare state, and paved the way for a monetarization of social policies, emphasizing wage replacement through benefits that had specific stratifying and status-maintaining effects. The relatively high level of social insurance benefits was intended to provide for (male) workers within families. Following in this tradition, relatively little value was placed on social policy instruments with potentially more egalitarian effects, such as benefits in kind, provision of welfare-state services or universal benefits. Side by side with this conservative model of social security, social-catholic ideas had a strong impact on family policy and the service culture, and have been enshrined in enduring structures of social service provision, such as the subsidiarity principle. In this context, subsidiarity means that the state provides welfare services only in cases where the independent welfare organization (mainly the churches and other non-profit organizations and charities) are unable to satisfy the demand. The principle was introduced during the 1920s under the influence of the Catholic Zentrumspartei, which opposed more state intervention. Once established, it came to be considered as an irreversible principle guiding social service provision.

In the area of childcare services, the subsidiarity principle was confirmed by the *Kinder- und Jugendhilfegesetz* (Children and Youth Support Act) of 1990. The state intervenes only if voluntary organizations, as primary providers, are not meeting the demand for childcare provision. In 1992, two-thirds of all childcare facilities in the FRG were run by independent welfare organizations, with the churches accounting for over 90 per cent of provision. They employed 61 per cent of all educational staff in childcare facilities, while 35 per cent were employed by local government, and 5 per cent by private providers. The small number of crèches for under-threes, which are particularly cost intensive, are mainly run by public authorities. Some big municipalities (Berlin, Hamburg, Frankfurt, Munich, Stuttgart) provide 75 per cent of all places in crèches in the old *Länder*. Although social service provision is dominated by the churches, it is publicly financed and, therefore, semi-public: public subsidies generally cover about 75 per cent of the costs. The dominance of independent welfare organisations does not mean that the state has no control, since the *Länder* have legal competence to regulate the provision of childcare services and can, therefore, also implement rules about opening hours, as some have done. However, the *Länder* are generally reluctant to introduce longer opening hours, or to intervene if this would incur additional costs. While local government is responsible for delivery, the financing of childcare facilities is shared between the local communities and the *Länder*, but without any federal subsidies.

Split competencies with regard to financing and the subsidiarity principle governing service provision are strong impediments to social reform in this area. International comparisons suggest that the extension of childcare facilities may be easier if competencies and finances are centralized, or at least unified at one level of decision-making, especially if childcare institutions are integrated into the educational system, as with preschool provision. Split competencies and financing make it more difficult to exercise political pressure, which is already difficult enough since women's lobbies are quite weak. The decentralization of social service provision and the complicated financial competencies, as well as the subsidiarity principle, which put private organizations and charities in a strong position, lead to a multiplicity of political actors with very divergent interests, who are often in conflict. Political actors prefer low-cost reforms. If reforms are costly, attempts are made to shift the financial burden away from government. The bifurcated system of social protection also hinders a co-ordinated policy of social innovation. It is split between the provision of monetary benefits, mainly financed and provided by social insurance, and social services, mainly financed and provided by local government and the *Länder*, and then delegated to churches and private organizations according to the subsidiarity principle.

The history of the introduction of a legal right to a kindergarten place for each child above the age of three illustrates the problems that arise (Meyer, 1996). A first attempt in 1989 by the minister for family affairs, Ursula Lehr, to introduce such a right to a place failed, due to the veto from the *Länder* on the grounds of cost. Even the *Länder* governed by the Sozialdemokratische Partei Deutschlands (SPD) opposed reform until the Federal State agreed to provide subsidies. A second attempt to implement the right was successful in 1992 in the context of the reform of abortion law. This was due to the political pressures resulting from a major disruptive event, German unification, and the need to find a parliamentary compromise to harmonize the different abortion laws in the old and new *Länder*. The former socialist abortion law, allowing the unrestricted right to interrupt pregnancy in the first three months, continued to exist for a transitional period and was supported by a majority of the population in the new *Länder*, as opinion polls demonstrated. The resulting need for the harmonization of abortion law, and for conservative forces to find allies and to legitimate their anti-abortionist claims, gave rise to some new coalitions crossing traditional party boundaries and to political compromise and deals. The conservative forces that voted for more restrictive abortion law had to demonstrate some moral coherence not only in protecting unborn life, but also in assisting children already born. A majority in parliament voted in favour of the right, but the opposition of the *Länder* (and the Federal Minister of Finances) had to be overcome. The compromise found involved a gradual postponement of the full implementation of the right to a kindergarten place from 1996 to 1999, and some redistribution of the tax burden between the Federal State and the *Länder*. Financial considerations meant that local government had to increase fees for parents, or make group size larger. Disputes over funding were, once again, an important driving force in social policy-making. They resulted in postponement of the reforms, and political consensus among the actors was reached only under the strong pressure resulting from German unification. Although the right to a kindergarten place is a very useful reconciliation strategy, it is not sufficient, since the short opening hours of kindergartens are not affected. In some cases, full-day places in public childcare facilities have even been transformed into normal (short-hours) places to comply with the need to offer more places. Equal opportunities considerations have been given a low profile.

LONG-TERM CARE INSURANCE

The introduction of the Long-Term Care Insurance brought about some improvement for women as the main informal carers, although the compensatory measures provided are limited and institutionalized within the traditional parameters of social policy. The main driving force behind the reform was financial considerations, particularly for local government and the *Länder*, which were paying steadily increasing amounts to cover social assistance for people in need of long-term care in institutions, and who could not afford to pay privately. Before the introduction of long-term care insurance, 70 per cent of all costs for institutional care for the elderly were financed through social assistance paid for by local government and the *Länder*. Social assistance expenditure on long-term care trebled between 1970 and 1976 and more than doubled during the subsequent decade (Statistisches Bundesamt, 1995, p. 20). At the beginning of the 1990s, more than one-third of social assistance payments were for people in need of long-term care, and 90 per cent went to nursing homes. Financial relief for local government was one of the main incentives for change. Equal opportunities policies were only a secondary consideration. They turned out to be a useful public relations argument in selling the less popular aspects of the reform package, such as the redistribution of resources to the better-off and their potential heirs, or the minimalist financial design of payments for professional care services provided for people cared for at home.

As elsewhere in the EU, in Germany, most people needing long-term care are looked after by women as informal carers at home. About 1.65 million people are estimated to need long-term care, and 75 per cent of them are living at home. Women are the main care-providers in the home: as partners (24 per cent of all carers), daughters (26 per cent) or daughters-in-law (9 per cent) or mothers (14 per cent). Men are involved as husbands (13 per cent of all carers) or sons (3 per cent). The remaining 11 per cent are other relatives, friends or neighbours (*Bundesarbeitsblatt*, 1994, no. 7, p. 9). Most female carers are already above pension age (60 per cent), while 10 per cent of women in gainful employment give up their job to look after a person in need of care. At the beginning of the 1990s, 20 per cent of the people requiring care in their own home received partial support through local out-patient care services (Bäcker, 1991, p. 92). Only 4 per cent of people over the age of 65 were in institutional care, a figure that is relatively low by international standards. For the population over the age of 80, the proportion in institutional care was 20 per cent in the late 1980s (Bäcker *et al.*, 1989, p. 130). Services for older people and for those in need of long-term care are relatively scarce in Germany, as comparative studies have shown (Jamieson, 1991; Alber, 1992, 1995).

Some of the basic arguments already developed with reference to the scarcity of childcare facilities may also help to explain the underdevelopment of services for older people. In a comparative study of social service provision for the elderly, Jens Alber (1995) has argued that three factors have a major impact upon differences between countries: financial controls, competencies and responsibilities of providers. They would help to explain the relatively low level of provision in the FRG. The decision to introduce the Long-Term Care Insurance in Germany, after many years of bargaining, can be seen as a move to expand social insurance at a time of welfare retrenchment. Analysis of the difficulties faced in reaching an agreement shows that they resulted mainly from the complexity of the decision-making process (Götting *et al.*, 1994). The negotiations over care insurance are also relevant to the analysis of the potential of equal opportunities policies with regard to care, which was an item, albeit a secondary one, on the policy agenda. The position of informal carers did improve to some extent as a by-product of the reform, but equal opportunities considerations were of minor importance compared to other political goals.

In 1994, a broad majority in parliament voted in favour of the Long-Term Care Insurance (*Bundesgesetzblatt*, Part I, no. 30, 1994), uniting to form a grand coalition embracing the governing Christian Democrat/Liberal coalition and the Social Democrat opposition party; the Bundesrat was unanimous. The political system of power balances, represented by bicameralism and federalism, means strong pressure is exerted to form a grand coalition if major issues of social policy are at stake, since otherwise the parliamentary majority can be vetoed by the Bundesrat, the second chamber representing the *Länder*, which has to confirm legislation in important social policy areas. Since 1990, the *Länder* governed by the Social Democrats had a majority in the Bundesrat, which gave them a strong bargaining position. The federal system is not conducive to active reform policy; incrementalism is the dominant policy style (Benz, 1995). The structural barriers to majority rule within the German political system (especially bicameralism) demand a high degree of co-ordination and co-operation between parliamentary parties. The enactment of the Long-Term Care Insurance was only possible as the result of such a grand coalition, involving lengthy bargaining, complicated compromises and deals among the various actors. The low profile of equal opportunities considerations in this context and the irrelevance of women's lobbies as strategic actors have been identified in the bargaining process (Götting *et al.*, 1994). In the past, other major reforms, such as the *Arbeitsförderungsgesetz* (Employment Promotion Act) of 1969, or the *Gesundheitsreformgesetz* (Health Reform Act) of 1988 had gone through parliament in a consensual manner. One particular feature of the Long-Term Care Insurance was that this was a political compromise between diverse actors, which allowed them to pursue multiple goals simultaneously (Landenberger, 1994, p. 324), covering diverging policy aims.

Benefits and services provided under the Long-Term Care Insurance encompass benefits in kind and in cash: the use of professional at-home care, a care allowance paid to the person in need of care (who can pass it on to an informal carer), subsidies for institutional care, and additional benefits, for example for short-term care. One major concern is to promote the provision of long-term care in the home. Benefit levels are not designed to cover the total costs or provide the full range of services needed: rather, the limits imposed imply that additional support by the family (in cash or kind) and the investment of personal resources, or means-tested assistance, are still necessary, especially in the case of institutional care, since the maximum subsidies available are already below average costs. Cost containment considerations influenced the decision that no state funding should be provided to cover possible deficits in Long-Term Care Insurance (in contrast to the principles governing other branches of social insurance). This more minimalist design departs from the relatively high level of wage replacement benefits under other social insurance schemes.

The scheme contains some provisions for improving the social rights of informal care-givers. Pension contributions to a maximum of 75 per cent of average pension points can be paid for carers if their employment does not exceed 30 hours a week; pension credits are not time-limited and can be combined with personal employment-related pension credits. Registered carers are insured against accident and injury, and care periods of up to five years can be taken into account in calculating benefit during retraining. This part of the package improves the social rights of informal care-givers. The care allowance paid to the person in need of care can be transferred to the carer, enabling women to benefit from the new care insurance as informal carers.

However, women's interests are manifold and may be contradictory due to their involvement in care relationships as formal and informal carers, as clients and as recipients of care. The minimalist financial design of the Long-Term Care Insurance also affects pay rates for professional care services in the home and, thus, indirectly, the quality of care services, which has an impact on the employment conditions of care-providers. The rates for care in institutions are higher. In this case, the Long-Term Care Insurance relieves municipalities of the means-tested benefits that they paid previously for people in institutionalized care. If the person in need of care opts for a professional carer in their own home (benefit in kind), which applies to fewer than 20 per cent of all persons in need of long-term care living at home, the maximum rate paid by the Long-Term Care Insurance agency to the care-providers is too low to cover the costs of minimal care as laid down in the statute. The hourly rate of pay falls below the real costs of professional, trained care staff, which also adversely affects the working conditions of formal carers, many of whom are women. Together with the introduction of a new system for paying care-providers, based on a Taylorist-style time evaluation scheme, the low rates of pay and the mode of calculation act as an incentive to perform professional care in the shortest possible time. The fact that the Long-Term Care Insurance agencies who 'buy' the marketed services are also forced to generate competition and bargain for low prices[3] means the quality of professional care services may be endangered. Increasingly, important questions are, therefore, being raised about how to secure adequate standards of provision, control the quality of services and represent the interests of clients (consumer protection) (Wienand, 1996).

INSTITUTIONAL CONSTRAINTS ON POLICY REFORMS

The chances of the social rights and coverage of new risks related to unpaid work and care activities being extended are limited in Germany, due to the particular constraints which result from the political system and power balances, and also from internal features of the institutions themselves. Some innovation has taken place, resulting in a limited coverage of childcare-related risks and greater social rights for informal carers. However, these developments occurred mostly within the traditional boundaries set by two separate, but interconnected, institutional circuits of distribution and redistribution: that institutionalized through marriage and family law; and that created by social security institutions, representing a fragmented system of strongly employment-related social insurance, with stratifying and status-maintaining effects, weak universal rights and relatively underdeveloped public services and infrastructures for children, families and persons in need of care.

Path dependency means that institutional change remains within the parameters of the institutional frames established as long ago as the last century, and that the main path of development is smooth adaptation, minor change at the microlevel, but no radical overhaul. More fundamental change and a break with existing principles will come about only under extreme conditions and, with time, if the dysfunctionalities of the

---

3. The intention was to establish a 'care market' through the statute regulating care insurance. Private care providers are to be enticed to compete with the (non-profit oriented) welfare organisations who traditionally dominated in this sector. This limits the traditional prerogative of welfare organisations to a guarantee via the subsidiarity principle, since private providers can compete on equal terms. The Long-Term Care Insurance agencies (Pflegekassen) are obliged to accept even more providers to this market beyond the limits of real need. One consequence is that the non-profit oriented independent welfare organisations are becoming more 'market-oriented', or transform their institutions into private firms in order to be more competitive.

existing institutional structures become overwhelming. Institutions, including institutionalized lobbies, bureaucracies and interest groups, create their own needs and push the path of reform in certain directions, limiting it within given systemic boundaries. In this chapter, attention has been devoted to identifying the constraints in the German system which limit the degree of change, and may, therefore, also block more radical and far-reaching equal opportunities strategies.

These institutional constraints contribute to the strong path dependency of the German social security system, which allows for only limited upgrading of care-related social rights for women and constrains the extension of social coverage of needs within the traditional boundaries of the fragmented system of social protection. However, the emergence of new risks, many of them predominantly female (such as lone parenthood or the economic consequences of divorce) would require a comprehensive and broad approach to co-ordinated reform, encompassing the complementary regulation of the welfare state and family law provision, in terms not only of rights and benefits but also of social service provision.

The concept of social care services, borrowed from the Scandinavian debate, is useful in overcoming the dichotomy between public and private service provision and, therefore, in analysing it from a gender perspective (Rauhala *et al.*, 1997). The prospects for such a co-ordinated path of reform, as opposed to a piecemeal strategy where reform takes place at the level of single institutions, look rather gloomy, because of the complexity of such an endeavour, the multiplicity of actors involved, the power relations and split competencies in the German political and legal system. In addition, equal opportunities policies remain only a secondary policy goal. Nonetheless, some improvement has taken place under exceptional circumstances, namely German unification, or as a result of Long-Term Care Insurance, despite welfare retrenchment and budgetary constraints. In the future, a prominent actor in the German institutional system may have an important role to play in advancing gender equality. If the German Federal Constitutional Court were to interpret the clause added to the constitutional principle of sex equality (German Basic Law, Article 3 II) after German unification on the responsibility of the state to promote gender equality and institute positive action as an obligation to pursue care policies which enhance the compatibility of family obligations and employment and extend social services, some incentive for change might emerge. Such an interpretation could, as in the past, put the legislator under pressure to act to implement more effective reconciliation policies.

6 The Paradoxes of Italian Law and Practice

Alisa Del Re

In Italy, gender equality law and practice are characterized by a number of paradoxes. An important body of legislation has been enacted to ensure greater equality of opportunity for women, but the legal instruments put in place are often contradictory and ineffective. Institutions have been created to promote equality, but they are often working in opposition to one another. As in all the member states in the European Union (EU), more women have been joining the labour market, but in the mid-1990s their participation rates remained below the European average, and their primary role was still expected to be that of homemaker. Opportunities for women are, in addition, very different between the North and South and from one generation to another. In the North, economic activity rates for young women (between the ages of 14 and 24) were, for example, very close to those for men in the same age group, whereas in the South, they were much lower (ISTAT, 1997, pp. 44–5).

As elsewhere in Europe, in Italy the notion of equality between women and men has developed over time at a varying rate and with different degrees of intensity (Beccalli, 1993, pp. 64–5). During the postwar period, emphasis was, initially, on the relationship between equality and the protection of women as workers, which at times provoked ideological conflict between Catholics and laity. The social doctrine of the Christian Democrats and the Catholic Church centred on the maintenance of the family unit with a male breadwinner and the mother as homemaker. Following the openly discriminatory and exclusionary protectionist policies previously pursued by the Fascists, different currents of opinion were able to coexist from the Second World War to the 1960s, as women fought simultaneously for equal pay legislation and for the protection of women as pregnant workers.

In the 1970s, equal rights were given precedence over equality of opportunity, although the debate shifted from the emancipation of women at the workplace to the family sphere, social reproduction and the redefinition of gender roles. Efforts to harmonize the rights of women and men were pursued in the face of scepticism on the part of the Christian Democrats, who were more interested in promoting positive action as a means of preserving gender differences.

By the 1980s, the problem was being raised of how to transform the sexual division of labour by tackling the dialectical relationship between equality and difference. Two types of differences were distinguished: exclusion, which had to be eliminated, and was being addressed by equality policy; and specificity, or gender identity, which had to be preserved or promoted. The debate involved both protective measures, set this time within a more philosophical framework, and a raft of policies aimed at transforming waged work and the production of goods in accordance with the reproductive needs of men as well as women. Such policies had to be handled carefully: if they could be seen as targeting women, they ran the risk of creating sources of discrimination and of reinforcing the exploitation of women and their segregation at work. The objective was to transform work for both men and women by making working arrangements and conditions less rigid, and by forcing men to participate in reproductive work. The case was still being argued in parliament in 1998, when the Minister for Social Affairs, Livia Turco, proposed a bill introducing parental leave.[1]

The economic recessions of the 1980s and 1990s, combined with political instability, have affected the approach to equality issues in a number of ways: the flexibility sought by women was translated into a lack of guarantees over the conditions of employment. Non-standard work contracts have become widespread, with shorter working hours and lower wages as a result. The outcome has been that women have had to find their own ways of combining paid and unpaid work. Retrenchment of welfare since the early 1980s, reinforced by the need to implement EU equal treatment legislation, has meant that some of the privileges previously afforded to women have been abolished, such as the earlier age of retirement. The most obvious impact of European directives on national legislation was the 1977 act regulating parity in employment, but its only effect was to enable women to take mining jobs in Sardinia, or to carry out dangerous industrial work, which they were previously prohibited from doing. The Italian government, for its part, exerted pressure at European level for legislation to be introduced

---

1. Italy already had a form of parental leave, introduced in 1977 under Act 903/77, according to which either the father or the mother was entitled to take six months' leave during the child's first year, paid at 30 per cent of salary. The proposal in 1998 was for non-transferable paid leave.

to protect working mothers. They gave strong support to Council Directive 92/85/EEC in an attempt to align other EU member states with Italian law and practice (Del Re, 1993, p. 52). As confirmed in an annual report of the European Commission (1998) on equal opportunities for women and men in the EU, Italy has reacted to European directives by providing ample evidence of good intentions but very few practical measures.

By the mid-1990s, despite a strong body of equality legislation, the concentration of women in some areas of activity had increased markedly, particularly in the service sector. Banking, insurance and, more especially, food retailing and public administration, accounted for 61 per cent of women in employment, compared to 41 per cent of men. Only 9 per cent of women occupied management positions, compared to 17 per cent of men. In education, which is traditionally a strongly feminized sector, women accounted for 90 per cent of teachers in primary schools, 62 per cent in upper secondary schools and 31 per cent in higher education (ISTAT, 1997).

This chapter reviews the different phases in the policy process whereby interest has shifted between the concepts of equality of opportunity, positive action and the utopian ideal of combining equality and difference, making it possible for policies promoting individual differences to coexist with measures aimed at universal equal rights, at least for women in employment. The shift is examined with reference to the development of policies to help parents and, more especially, mothers combine employment and family life, under pressure from European legislation. The chapter assesses critically the role played by different policy actors in promoting or resisting change.

CHANGING GENDER RELATIONS

The history of gender relations in Italy has been shaped by conflicting ideologies, with the result that the development of equality policy has been pulled in different directions. The Italian Constitution of 1947 set out the contradictory principles on which the Republic was founded. Article 37 §1 stated that 'Working women have the same rights as working men, and for equal work they receive the same remuneration as men.' But it went on to say: 'Their working conditions should allow them to carry out their essential role within the home and should ensure special and adequate protection for women and children.' Article 29 defined the relationships between men and women, confirming the importance of family unity and the subordination of women within the family. The constitution thus embodied the principles of equal pay and protection, while emphasizing the centrality of women's place in the home. The paradoxes that have developed over the postwar period were rooted in the constitution, which was strongly influenced by the conservative doctrine of the Catholics and the emancipatory ideology of the Socialists and Communists.

Equal pay and protection for women as workers

When Article 119 of the Treaty of Rome was being negotiated, the Italian trade unions were claiming that all workers should receive equal pay for equal work. While direct recourse has not been made in law to Article 119, over time it has had more impact on equality policy than any of the European directives (Ballestrero, 1990, p. 11). Although the Italian government signed the International Labour Organization's (ILO) Convention no. 100 on equal remuneration in 1956, and supported Article 119 in the Treaty of Rome, little action was taken in the 1950s to implement equal pay. From the 1960s, however, at the height of the postwar economic recovery, the Italian trade unions became an important policy actor through their struggle for equal pay. Previously, women had been considered separately in collective agreements; they did not have the right to equal pay for equal work on the grounds that they produced less than men. Paradoxically, egalitarian policies were gaining momentum in the 1960s as a consequence of the expansion in social insurance cover (health, old age, invalidity). The Christian Democrats had pushed for an improvement in social security provisions, and were supported by the Church. The primary aim was to safeguard the family unit by protecting a single source of income: that of the husband and father. Equal pay, by contrast, involved treating women in the same way as men rather than as a special case, if discrimination was to be avoided. The debate over work of equal value, which was intended to correct the undervaluing of work done by women, focused attention on the concept of indirect discrimination (Jones, 1995, pp. 46–7). It raised questions about who should determine what is meant by equal value: the market, employers or trade unions. Once a working definition of equal value has been agreed, the question is then whether it is the quantity or quality of the product, or the social value of the work that has to be taken into account. Does bringing up a child, for example, have the same value as producing a software programme? (Donaggio, 1994, p. 86)

Between 1960 and 1963, a number of agreements were reached over equal pay between women and men, confirming that substantial differences existed between female and male earnings. The agreements signed in the early 1960s did not take account of equality of opportunity and were concerned only with equal rights. No evidence can be found of any attempt to interfere with sources of inequality, segregation and discrimination. Over the years, labour market policies providing for equal pay tended to give better guarantees to low-paid workers, and wages were index-linked to inflation from the 1970s until 1993. By the mid-1990s, however, women's earnings continued to represent, on average, 75 per cent of men's among manual workers and only 56 per cent among managers. Even in public administration, which is reputed to be more egalitarian, women's earnings were 17 per cent lower than those of men, and the difference increased to 29 per cent among managers (Altieri, 1994, p. 110). The disparity can be explained by the fact that women tend to be concentrated in areas where average salaries are particularly low. They are segregated into low-skilled jobs, and when they do have the same skills and qualifications as men, they tend to be employed in less well-paid jobs. Women are also frequently excluded from schemes involving bonus payments or allowances, and they tend to work shorter hours than do men and to avoid overtime because of their family responsibilities. More than two-thirds of the women employed in the service sector, for example, work reduced hours, even though part-time work is poorly developed in Italy. Women are still usually alone in bearing the burden of domestic and caring tasks, in the absence of publicly provided child and eldercare services.

At the same time as equal pay moved onto the agenda, social policies were being developed to protect mothers as workers. The Christian Democrats, including Catholic Communists, were the driving force. They held the majority in parliament for 50 years. Measures introducing statutory maternity leave under the *legge di protezione della maternità* (Maternity Protection Act) 1204/71 of 1971 were strongly supported, even by women who were Christian Democrats (Ascoli, 1984). Women gained entitlement to two months' paid leave before the birth and three months following it, with the right to free medical care and reinstatement in the same job, making the Italian scheme the most generous in the European Community (EC). The reaction among employers was to refuse to recruit women, since their guaranteed absence made them too costly compared to men. Overprotection therefore resulted in unemployment or informal work. In both cases, it meant that women lost social protection rights. The clear aim of the legislator was to ensure that women were sent back to the home.

Despite their ideological differences, the two main political parties (Communists and Christian Democrats) were in agreement over the way in which the family should be conceptualized. Socialists and Communists shared with Catholics and Marxists a conception of the family dominated by an authoritarian male breadwinner. Any differences between Catholics and Marxists concerned the participation of women in the labour market. For the Marxists, labour market activity was to be safeguarded as a means of emancipating women. For the Catholics, it was an inescapable economic necessity against which wives and mothers had to be protected. During the postwar period and into the 1960s, the secular parties had been the vehicles for two strands of policy. The Communists were pressing for women workers to be guaranteed the right to continue working, while the Socialists were seeking to offset the influence of the Church over the process of socialization. The outcome of these conflicting pressures was that several pieces of legislation were passed, which recognized the importance for society of the dual roles of women as workers and mothers. In 1963, the marriage ban was lifted, and a pension was introduced for women who had been housewives, acknowledging the economic value of housework; state nursery schools were instituted in 1968, and crèches operated by local government in 1971.

From equal rights to positive action

The specificity of the Italian situation can be found in the fact that legislation on equal pay was enacted much earlier than in other EU member states (in the early 1960s), but the culture of equal opportunities came much later (1991). The Community directives on equal treatment opened up new perspectives: equal treatment in recruitment, training, promotion and working conditions. Equality measures had to be implemented to outlaw direct and indirect discrimination, particularly with regard to family obligations.

The 1970s were characterized in Italy by the activity of strong social movements, which exerted pressure to develop education and health provision and to invest in the family. Institutional care in psychiatric hospitals, asylums and prisons was called into question, but the educational system was expanded, and healthcare became part of a universal health service. More women were entering and remaining in education. Services for the protection of women's health were developed, and women entered public administration in large numbers. Over the period, emphasis shifted progressively from initiatives concerned with women as workers to ways of supporting reproduction and family life. Women's movements were the main driving force behind the change. Between 1970 and 1978, protest movements had a decisive influence over the political agenda: divorce, abortion, contraception and family planning were all actively promoted by women's groups (Del Re, 1993, pp. 44–6).

Feminism undoubtedly played an important role in the political conflict, which set three different groups of actors against one another: the Catholics, represented by the Church and Christian Democrats; the Communists, represented by the Italian Communist Party; and the secular parties (Socialist, Radical and Liberal). The Italian feminist movement contained two intermeshing strands. The first was of secular origin (radical-liberal), and defined women's liberation on the basis of the right to self-determination with regard to sexuality and family life. The second was associated with an antagonistic conception, more typical of Marxist culture, which focused on the economic value of domestic labour, the need for legislative change and for women to gain control over areas of public life concerned with reproduction (social and medical services) (Memoria, 1983). Social services, schools and universities became the site for the intellectual development of feminism, which was able to expand and grow both within and outside political institutions. In the 1980s, however, the feminist movement lost much of its grassroots support and seemed to disappear from the political scene. The 1978 act (184) on abortion, and its approval in 1981 in a referendum, brought to an end the demonstrations and removed the main objective that had united the movement. Equality was not, in any case, a central plank for the movement. It was more interested in positive action focusing on difference.

The promotion of the distinctiveness of women involved a number of different approaches. According to the conservative interpretation, because of their biological identity, women preferred to devote themselves to reproductive tasks and carry out 'women's' work. Policies were, therefore, needed to ensure that domestic tasks were recognized and valued by society. Arguments such as these have been used to exonerate companies that completely avoid confronting issues concerned with equal opportunities. The more progressive rendering adopted by feminists in the 1970s and 1980s called for a different policy stance. They argued for positive action to promote work of equal value. Feminist trade unionists had been responsible for bringing equal opportunities issues onto the policy agenda, but they were interested in legal and institutional rights. Later, the same themes were taken up by women in political parties. Act 903/77, the *legge di parità* (Law on Parity) of 1977, which abolished existing discrimination at work, was the product of the symbiosis of feminist culture and the sexually neutral culture of the worker's movement. It can be seen as legitimizing the presence of women in the labour market. The act was confined, however, to outlawing all forms of sex discrimination. Equality was to be achieved essentially by levelling down: women began working in the mines in Sardinia and on the production line in Fiat, where the male labour supply was declining (Becalli, 1985, p. 97).

Since the early 1970s, feminism has infiltrated the Communist Party, providing the movement with an institutional base. By the end of the 1970s, due to the debate over abortion (1978) and the referendum in 1981, women in the Communist Party became feminists. Gradually, their presence made the party and the trade unions more aware of women's issues. The feminist movement also had to adapt to overcome the difficulties experienced when it was trying to negotiate as an actor outside the political system. The law against sexual violence affords an example of the way in which the process has operated. Although the feminist movement was divided, when the bill was brought before parliament in 1979, it gained the support of the Communist and Socialist Parties. However, the process of negotiation was protracted, and revealed not only the conflicts between the parties but also between women within the parties. It was eventually passed in 1996, and a cross-party task force was set up, composed of women members of parliament from the Alleanza nazionale to rifondazione comunista, which no longer represented a motivating force for the movement, due to the highly differentiated positions it was adopting. At the most, it could be seen as playing a mediating role between the different ideologies of members of parliament, driven by its strong desire to see the bill enacted.

While the debate was raging in parliament, the institutionalized women's movement was developing its activities out in the field, inspired by a vision of structural change that would improve the organization of everyday life. The feminists had gained valuable experience from programmes for restructuring opening times in the social services, in shops and in urban living that had been put into practice in a number of towns and provinces (Emilie-Romagna, Toscany, Venice, Catanes, Genoa and Turin). The programmes had taken women's needs as a central plank for developing urban policy. Although time policies may have helped to make paid and unpaid work more compatible, they did little to change the balance between the two. The measures implemented reflected the position adopted by the Communist and Socialist Parties towards women's work and, more especially, their reproductive work. The lay parties have always believed that women will achieve emancipation (which is not the same as the individual rights and freedoms demanded by women) in paid work. To be able to work outside the home, women had to find their own way of reconciling paid with domestic work, but they also retained full responsibility for reproductive work, and there was no question of them being able to share or delegate it.

On 10 April 1991, the *leggi sulle azioni positive per la realizzazione dell'uguaglianza tra uomini e donne nel lavoro* (Positive Action for Achieving Equality between Women and Men at Work) 125/91 was passed (Del Re, 1993, pp. 52–3). The act can be seen as embodying the ambivalence and compromise that have developed between two cultures of equality in Italy. The one, founded on the recognition of gender difference and of women's specificity, interpreted even protective laws as precursors of policies supporting women's distinctiveness. The other, premised on societal change for both men and women, demanded the abolition of discrimination as a prerequisite for constructing new forms of equality in paid and unpaid work.

The declared aim of the act was to adopt specific measures to eliminate discrimination against women, in response to the European Council's Recommendation 84/635/EEC on the promotion of positive action for women. The opening paragraph of the act sets out a list of positive actions, covering training, recruitment, promotion, and mobility. In areas where women are under-represented, or in cases where working time and working conditions are being restructured, recommendations are made to enhance women's opportunities and to promote greater sharing of family responsibilities between the sexes. Article 4 of the act was innovative in that it referred to the notion of indirect discrimination, recommended the use of statistics to prove that discrimination had occurred, and set out the principle that the burden of proof should fall on employers, who would have to demonstrate that discrimination had not taken place. Articles 5 and 6 recommended that the remit of the Comitato nazionale di parità, attached to the Ministry of Labour, should be extended through an equality advisory service operating at regional and local level. Under Article 9, public administration and private companies with more than 100 employees are obliged to prepare a report every two years on the situation regarding men's and women's employment, covering both quantitative and qualitative aspects. They are also required to report on the progress of any positive action carried out, although the act does not specify what form such action should take. For the private sector, positive action is voluntary, but it is compulsory in the public sector.

Compared to the equality act of 1977 (903/77), the 1991 act did represent a theoretical advance towards the notion of equality of opportunity through the concept of indirect discrimination. Positive action was conceived as a way of changing working patterns and altering the relationship between productive and reproductive work for both women and men. The acceptance of the notion of differences (disparities) between workers represents a shift away from the principle of non-differentiation incorporated in labour law. The concept of indirect discrimination is of wider interest, in that it applies not only to individuals but also to groups of workers, and could, therefore, be used in cases of racial discrimination. In this context, discrimination means not simply the outward signs of discriminatory practices but also, importantly, the possible effects of actions, behaviour and practices for particular categories of workers (Ballestrero, 1995).

The act has been criticized on two counts by feminist lawyers like Maria Vittoria Ballestrero, and by trade unionists such as Franca Donaggio of the Confederazione generale italiana lavoro: firstly for its failure to promote positive action outside the workplace and to extend it to other areas of social life; secondly for the lack of measures that might encourage social partners to consider how the productive system could be changed to accommodate the special needs of women. In most cases, the proposals put forward by companies for positive action, often with the approval of trade unions, have been designed to make savings on training costs. Although the act was very advanced in terms of the standards it was seeking to set, it was ineffective in terms of outcomes. It brought no real improvement as far as discrimination was concerned. The obligation placed on employers in the public sector, and the financial inducements offered in the private sector, to encourage them to introduce positive action programmes produced very few initiatives: 500 in the six years between 1991 and 1997. Nor were any new agreements signed between the social partners. Many of the positive actions implemented were those traditionally used in collective bargaining to reduce segregation in training, human resource management and negotiating structures, but they did little to bring about any radical change. The sanctions imposed for failure to submit a report on positive action undertaken were completely ineffectual, and no provision was made for penalties to be applied if reports were inaccurate or misleading.

The shortcomings of the act raise a number of questions about the efficacy of measures aimed at achieving equality of opportunity by outlawing all forms of discrimination. Clearly, legislation on its own is not enough, if no sanctions are available to ensure that legal provisions are implemented. Another problem with the act was that it focused on inequality between the sexes only at the workplace and did not take sufficient account of inequalities in reproductive work, which has continued to be seen essentially as the responsibility of women. The aim of trying to make paid work compatible with reproductive work only for women entraps them because it increases their everyday burden, thereby also preventing greater equality in paid work.

INSTITUTIONAL ACTORS

The Italian government has set up several organizations to help bring national equality legislation into line with the standards set by international organizations, such as the United Nations and the ILO, and to ensure compliance with European directives. Although the organizations established are impressive in terms of their size, they have not been very effective in their operations.

In 1983, the Comitato nazionale di parità was established under the auspices of the Ministry for Labour, with the aim of removing discrimination and the obstacles preventing effective equality between citizens in access to work and in employment. The 1991 act (125/91) set out more clearly the structure the committee was to have, and instituted an advisory service on parity at regional level: Consigliere di parità. Of the 40 committee members only 24 have the right to vote. Because of its size and composition,[2] the committee cannot intervene rapidly and effectively to solve the problems brought to its attention. The members

---

2. In addition to the Minister of Labour and the national adviser on parity, the committee has 22 members, of whom 50 per cent are appointed by trade unions associations, managers and co-operatives, and 50 per cent by feminist associations and movements from representatives at national level concerned with parity and equal opportunities. A further 6 legal, economic and social experts are included, together with 5 representatives from different ministries – education, justice, foreign affairs, industry, civil service – and also 5 civil servants from the Ministry of Labour.

represent a number of different constituencies with widely differing interests, resulting in protracted discussions, and making it difficult to strike a balance between conflicting demands.

The Commissione nazionale per le pari opportunità tra uomo et donna was set up under the direction of the Council of Ministers in 1984, although its structure and remit were not properly defined by law until 1990 (act 164/90). The commission is permanent, although its membership is renewed every three years by order from the chair of the Council of Ministers.[3] Its terms of reference are to receive and disseminate information and data relating to the situation of women in society, to study and develop amendments to legislation to ensure parity between the sexes and to improve the representation of women in public life. The functions of the committee on parity and of the commission for equal opportunities overlap, and this has frequently produced conflicts between them.

In the 1990s, several Italian regions used the act to set up regional commissions for equal opportunities, and many local authorities followed suit. The commissions' work has focused on the collection of information about women's rights, on efforts to alert policy-makers to women's issues and on the provision of support for training programmes for women. In 1993, committees for equal opportunities were established in public administration, with the aim of carrying through policies to promote parity and equal opportunities. The same year saw the creation of committees to promote women to management positions, as provided under act 215/1992. They sought to initiate positive actions, supported by national funds, although the necessary funding was not released until 1997 because the measures received parliamentary approval only in December 1996.

Over a ten-year period, parity organizations were swiftly put in place across the country. The speed with which the movement developed can be interpreted as a sign of the strong desire to improve the situation of women through measures to promote personal and professional development. It is difficult to judge whether the proliferation of organizations had any real effect on parity. The evidence from trends in the labour market activity of women is not encouraging, and it seems unlikely that the setting up of committees is in itself sufficient to resolve deep-seated problems.

---

3. The Comitato nazionale di parità is composed of 29 women, 7 of whom represent women's associations, 11 political parties, 3 trade union organizations, 4 management and co-operatives and 4 the cultural scene.

From 1996, Italy had a minister responsible for equal opportunities,[4] which was a completely new departure. In her first official statement, the minister made reference to 'mainstreaming' and 'empowerment'. She claimed that it was pointless simply to continue to argue that women were a socially disadvantaged group, since that would not solve the problem. She went to great lengths to have the 215/92 act on women in management implemented, after being on the statute book for five years. She succeeded in obtaining funds from central and local government to create agencies throughout the country to improve access to training for women. The agencies are charged with providing information and also tools for measuring and evaluating the viability and validity of projects. Previously, government training schemes for women had been directed towards traditional female activities such as seamstress or hairdresser. The minister attempted to introduce change by using the network of commissions set up across the country to iden- tify labour market needs. Regional training programmes were launched, with support from management, unions and state schools. The schemes were designed to change the normative imagery associated with women's jobs and to create observatories capable of tracking demand in a specific area.

The power of the minister to promote change was constrained by the limited financial resources made available. The minister was without portfolio and could only have access to funds to support initiatives with the approval of the president of the council. On many occasions, she found her hands were tied and, in some instances, was unable even to make the case for women's interests to be taken into account, as for example when an employment pact was being discussed under the Prodi government. She also met with opposition from the committees and commissions set up to promote parity and equal opportunities. In October 1997, she attempted to relaunch the parity issue by bringing all the organizations concerned with parity within the orbit of the ministry. Her purpose was to try and transform them from being institutions defending women against exclusionary practices into units able to express an opinion about the possible impact on women of all legisla- tion. They were to assume a co-ordinating role which would extend beyond consultation (Giammarinaro, 1997). The national commission for equal opportunities lost no time in responding that it refused to be

---

4.　The first appointee was Anna Finocchiaro under the Prodi government. In October 1998, the second minister appointed under the D'Alema government was the sociologist Laura Balbo.

transformed into an organization at the service of the government. On the contrary, it argued that the support functions previously developed should be removed so that it would have greater freedom of action and independence.

The issue demonstrates the continuing conflict between two opposing ideologies. On the one hand, the Catholic, conservative ideology, associated with the idea that women are primarily mothers and wives, supports the coexistence of paid work and family life. Its proponents seek to promote policy measures designed to tackle inequality of opportunity, but they do little to change social structures and, at most, tinker at the edges of everyday life. On the other hand, advocates of a secular ideology, supported by the Left, are intent on changing society, but in a deterministic way, which sometimes makes them seem remote from the concerns of everyday life and the quality of life that women are seeking to achieve. The emphasis they place on ideological victories sometimes makes them oblivious of what remains to be done in practical terms to achieve greater parity.

THE POLITICS OF RECONCILIATION

The ideological divide between Right and Left over the place of women in society reflects and reinforces the paradoxes that characterize the development of gender policy in Italy. Article 37 of the Constitution juxtaposed two inherently conflicting notions: equality and difference. Postwar legislation has oscillated between these two principles. Under act 1204/71, the state afforded protection to working mothers, providing generous leave arrangements before and after confinement, and the possibility of extending leave of absence, far ahead of most other EU member states. Act 903/77 on equality of treatment introduced the notion of intentional discrimination and took account of existing inequalities. Again, the act was one of the most advanced in the EC, and also one of the most complete in terms of the requirements of EC legislation. However, with regard to implementation, the outcomes have been negligible. Advisers on equality have no power to impose penalties for any breaches of the law. According to the Minister of Labour, very few women have recourse to the law: only in 1.1 per cent of dismissals do women bring cases for discrimination. Those implementing the law have no resources, and no real social awareness has developed of women's rights.

As far as the political parties are concerned, in the 1950s and 1960s, political action on behalf of women was confined to dealing with what were seen as women's problems as working mothers. In the 1970s and 1980s, the private sphere moved into the political arena, and the political parties had to face an antagonistic movement, which cut across the traditional cleavages of the class struggle on the Left, the interclass interests of the Centre, and the liberal individualism of the Right. The referendum on divorce in 1981 united women, enabled them to overcome ideological differences and opened opportunities to tackle problems from new perspectives. The 1990s have been characterized by the heavy investment by women in social organizations and also by the recognition of the institutional vacuum that exists. The Left have been fighting for quotas, while the Right deny there is a problem. Since parity has been achieved in law, it is, they argue, only a matter of time and good will before women are fairly represented in political life. The cleavage does not precisely match the political divide, since some positions cut across the two policy stances, signalling the difficulties that political parties have in engaging with women's issues.

The institutional solution of creating a plethora of committees, commissions and even a ministry for equal opportunities would seem to have complicated the issues rather than providing solutions to problems. Despite the strength of the feminist movement in Italy, the cultural background continues to be conservative with regard to gender relations on both sides of the political divide. Until the 1970s, parity was no more than a word, even for the progressive Left. The Catholics, including the Communist Catholics, preached and practised the difference and distinctiveness of women's roles in society. The constitution had established that women were, first and foremost, mothers and that reproductive work was a private matter concerning women within the family. The effect on policy was that measures were instituted to protect (or overprotect) women as working mothers. The outcome was to exclude women from well-paid jobs, because they were not in a position to compete on equal terms with male breadwinners.

Despite the fact that the laws protecting women as mothers are among the most far-reaching in Europe, the solution adopted by many women to enable them to undertake paid work is not to have children, or to have so few that the fertility rate in Italy was the lowest in the EU by the mid-1990s. Even then, female economic activity rates have remained very low. Population ageing has meant that older women, in particular, are paying the price for interrupted employment patterns, and low earned incomes, with the result that gender inequalities during working life are being accentuated in old age, and older women are the poorest social category in Italy. The situation is unlikely to change unless, and until, men are persuaded to share domestic tasks, until enlightened politicians push for measures to be implemented that would make paid and unpaid work more compatible, and until society recognizes that reproductive work is not necessarily gendered and is an essential component of both work organization and social relationships.

7 From Hard to Soft Law and from Equality to Reconciliation in the United Kingdom

Barbara Bagilhole and Paul Byrne

In the United Kingdom, equal pay was made law in 1970 before British accession to the European Community (EC) in 1973. Although the Sex Discrimination Act of 1975 came after EC membership, it was inspired by domestic political factors rather than any prompting from Europe; the British government was firmly committed to the goal of ending sex discrimination, at least in the workplace, before becoming a member of the EC. In terms of policy outputs and outcomes, rather than just policy aims, the United Kingdom's political culture and policy delivery mechanisms have often placed it at variance with the European approach. Successive British governments adopted their own conception of what is meant by equal opportunities and their own methods of tackling the problem. As in many other policy areas, the result has often been conflict with Brussels. The United Kingdom has been characterized by a cautious, if not negative, approach to European legislation. Between 1989–97, governments showed a repeated reluctance to bring the United Kingdom into line with other member states. In this chapter, the origins and on-going causes of these difficulties are examined by analysing developments in two stages: hard law largely during the 1970s associated with equal opportunities policies; and soft law from the 1980s on, as reconciliation policies moved onto the agenda.

HARD LAW AND EQUAL OPPORTUNITIES

As at European level, state involvement in equal opportunities began in the United Kingdom with substantial legislation. In the 1970s, a significant degree of congruence was achieved between British and EC objectives and methods, despite the United Kingdom's resistance to Euro-

124

pean jurisdiction. Each was concerned primarily with securing equal opportunities in the workplace, rather than with reconciling paid work and family life. Each turned to 'hard law', in the form of statute law in the United Kingdom and directives at the European level. Although the Equal Pay Act and the Sex Discrimination Act, particularly the latter, provided the potential for radical change in the United Kingdom, and EC directives extended this potential, actual policy outcomes were modest.

The Equal Pay Act

The principle of equal pay for work of equal value, developed in Council Directive 75/117/EEC, seemed at first sight unproblematic for the United Kingdom, since it already had an Equal Pay Act, introduced in 1970. Pressure for equal pay between men and women had been exerted over a very long period. Women active in trade unions had forced the Trade Union Congress to pass a resolution in favour of the principle as far back as 1888, but it was not until almost a hundred years later that the first legislation in this area was enacted in Britain, and the legislation did not become fully operational until December 1975. The Equal Pay Act allows women to claim equal pay with men if they are engaged on like work or work of equal value on an individual case basis. The act applies to both women and men, but a man is less likely to make a claim for equal pay with a woman, given the disparity in women's wages. This can be seen as an indictment of the act itself, since it has not significantly narrowed the gap between the average earnings of men and women.

Pressure came from the EC in July 1982 for the United Kingdom to comply fully with the 1975 directive on equal pay. The British Equal Pay Act was considered deficient by the European Court of Justice (ECJ) because a woman could only obtain equal pay in respect of work which had an equal value to that of her male counterpart if a job evaluation scheme or study had been implemented. The British government disagreed with the judgement, and the media opposed what was seen as meddling by the EC in national legislation. Eventually, with additional pressure for change from the Equal Opportunities Commission, which was set up under the Sex Discrimination Act in 1975 to help enforce the legislation and to promote equal opportunities generally, the government finally changed the law on 1 January 1983. Therefore, as the Employment Department Group (1995) guide to equal opportunities for business explains, even two different jobs can have 'equal value' if they place equal demands on workers in terms of effort, skill and decision-making. It is important too, under the act, that traditional male abilities such as physical strength are not given greater weight than what are considered to be typical female skills such as manual dexterity. The guide cites the following example:

> A female cook was held by an industrial tribunal to be employed on work of equal value with that of male painters, thermal insulation engineers and joiners working for the same employer. The jobs were assessed under five headings: physical demands; environmental demands; planning and decision making; skills and knowledge; and responsibility. The overall scores of the jobs were found to be equal. (Employment Department Group, 1995, p. 4)

The Sex Discrimination Act

Similar problems were to arise with the United Kingdom's other major piece of equal opportunities legislation, the 1983 Sex Discrimination Act. Hailed as a radical law at the time (Byrne and Lovenduski, 1978), it makes discrimination on the grounds of sex or marital status unlawful in employment, training and related matters, education, the provision of goods, facilities and services, and the disposal and management of premises. Although the act is drafted in terms of women being the object of discrimination, men can, and have, successfully brought claims under its provisions. For example, men have gained cheaper admission to swimming pools for retired people on an equal age basis to women by bringing a case to an industrial tribunal on the grounds of indirect discrimination. Even though the conditions for cheaper entrance were applied equally to both women and men, in that they had to be retired, disproportionately fewer men could comply with the condition because of their later retirement age.

The act recognizes three kinds of discrimination: direct, indirect, and victimization. Direct discrimination arises where a person treats another less favourably on sexual or marital grounds than they treat, or would treat, someone else. An example of direct discrimination would be not interviewing or appointing a woman because it was felt that, because of her sex, she would not fit into the organization (Employment Department Group, 1995). Indirect discrimination is an important aspect of British equal opportunities law. It covers treatment that can be described as equal in a formal sense between sexes, but discriminatory in its effect on one particular sex. To establish indirect discrimination it must be shown that the requirement/condition was applied equally to persons of either sex; a considerably smaller proportion of a particular sex can comply with it; the requirement is to the person's detriment because they suffer as a result; and it cannot be shown to be justifiable for particular employment. Examples of indirect discrimination include insisting on an unnecessary height requirement, requiring a person to work evenings when this is not operationally necessary, and refusing training or promotion to part-timers, if most part-time jobs are held by women and most full-time ones by men (Employment Department Group, 1995). Indirect discrimination against a married person is similar conceptually to indirect sex discrimination, and may arise where a condition or requirement is applied equally to married and unmarried people of the same sex but is discriminatory in its effect on married people. A requirement to be mobile for a job might be detrimental for more married than single people. In practice, very little use has been made of the category of indirect discrimination. Finally, victimization counts as discrimination under the act when a person who has asserted their rights, either by bringing proceedings or giving evidence, is treated less favourably.

One dimension missing from the British approach is that of positive discrimination. The Sex Discrimination Act does permit employers to take positive action to overcome the effects of past discrimination, but only in a very limited way, the most important being additional training opportunities. Where an imbalance exists in the numbers of one sex doing particular work for an employer in the preceding 12 months, the employer may provide training for that sex for that work and/or encourage members of the minority sex to apply through advertising. Moreover, positive action is not to be confused with positive discrimination: discrimination at the point of selection for work because of under-representation of a particular sex is not permitted.

As with the Equal Pay Act, pressure from the EC meant that the Sex Discrimination Act subsequently had to be amended in the light of the EC directive on equal treatment, which ruled out sex discrimination in access to employment, selection criteria, access to all jobs and all levels of the hierarchy, opportunities for training and vocational guidance, promotion procedures and other terms and conditions of employment. However, because of protracted resistance and opposition from the British government, the act was not amended until 1986. Then, to bring it into line with the directive, the employment provisions of the act were extended to include private households, firms with five or fewer employees, and collective agreements relating to pay, which had previously been excluded.

Council Directive 76/207/EEC on equal treatment has also been very influential in the area of pensions. Action programmes during the 1980s and later decisions by the ECJ made it unavoidable for the United Kingdom to equalize retirement age for women and men. Retirement age and subsequent pension entitlements for women and men have always been treated differently in the United Kingdom. A frequently cited case in this respect is C–271/91 Marshall v Southampton and South West Hampshire Area Health Authority [1993]. Marshall's compulsory retirement at 62 was tested, within the United Kingdom, as less favourable treatment under the Sex Discrimination Act. The complaint was rejected by the industrial tribunal on the grounds that the act excluded retirement issues. Marshall then claimed that her forced retirement was contrary to the EC directive on equal treatment, and her case was upheld by the ECJ. The decision was based on the concept that compulsory early retirement constituted unfair dismissal rather than differences in pensionable age between men and women. A second case often referred to is C–188/89 Foster and Others v British Gas plc. [1990], where the ECJ decided that, because of the EC directive, female employees forced to retire at the age of 60, whereas men could continue until they were 65, must be entitled to compensation for loss of earnings (Meehan, 1993b).

The Equal Opportunities Commission

As an independent body set up under the Sex Discrimination Act, the Equal Opportunities Commission has both duties and powers. It has come to be recognized as an important equal opportunities actor at national and international level. Its duties are to work towards the elimination of discrimination, to promote equality of opportunity, to keep the workings of the act under review and propose amendments. It can make grants to organizations to help promote their aims, and also allocate money to research and educational activities, with the approval of the Secretary of State. The commission may conduct formal investigations, on its own initiative or as required by the Secretary of State, where sex discrimination is suspected. It is also empowered to serve non-discrimination notices where discriminatory practices are detected, and it can help, advise and represent individuals taking cases under the legislation. In practice, complainants supported by the commission are found to be more successful than those who do not receive any assistance, but such support is limited by budget constraints. The commission is also empowered to issue codes of practice, which are not legally binding but are admissible when presented in evidence to tribunals (Department of Education and Employment, 1997).

Even though it is funded by the government, the Equal Opportunities Commission appears to have been able to maintain a considerable degree of independence. It has concentrated its efforts and resources on supporting individuals in cases considered key in clarifying or changing the law. However, the commission has been more conservative in its demands than its counterpart, the Commission for Racial Equality. The two commissions have in common that their budgets have been gradually reduced in real terms. Unlike the Commission for Racial Equality, the Equal Opportunities Commission has not called for legal aid in discrimination cases, nor has it argued for employers to keep records relating to the sexual composition of the workforce.

Despite the best efforts of the Conservative governments to minimize the scope of European legislation, EC sex discrimination law has been evoked on more occasions in the courts in the United Kingdom than in any other member state (European Commission, 1998, p. 122). The EC itself has brought proceedings against the United Kingdom to force their compliance, but the main protagonist has been the Equal Opportunities Commission, invoking European law on behalf of individuals to win sex discrimination cases against the British government. Many of these cases brought about changes to British law (Meehan, 1993a). The changes that have been introduced by the British government, because of EC pressure, appear to have been carried out grudgingly, at the last possible moment, in the narrowest possible way and in a piecemeal fashion (Meehan, 1993b). Nevertheless, it has been argued that EC influence has been a major benefit for women (Crawley and Slowey, 1995), and that, unlike other member states such as France, the United Kingdom has actively developed the right to equal pay for work of equal value (Kilpatrick, 1997, p. 25).

While recognizing that substantial gains have been made, the Equal Opportunities Commission would prefer to see a 'fresh start' in terms of legislation. It wants a sweeping reform of the Equal Pay Act, described as a 'paradise for lawyers, but hell for women' (Equal Opportunities Commission, 1990, p. 2). The commission has recommended that the Equal Pay Act and the Sex Discrimination Act should be abolished and replaced with an Equal Treatment Act, which would prompt speedier tribunals and protect women from being sacked for becoming pregnant. Such an act would, they argue, give tribunals the power to recommend reinstatement and higher compensation awards. The only significant legislative response from the Conservative governments was the

Employment Rights Act of 1996, which applies to all employees, but holds particular interest in equal opportunities terms for women in relation to maternity provisions. The act provides that women may claim maternity leave, maternity pay, and the right to return to work, if they give due notification of their intention to exercise their rights under the act. It also provides that a woman cannot unreasonably be refused time off for antenatal care and has the right to be paid for any time taken for this purpose. None of the other recommendations from the commission were implemented.

Implementing hard law in the United Kingdom

Until the change in the voting system in 1986, with the introduction of qualified majority voting in the Single European Act, the United Kingdom had blocked many of the proposed European equal opportunities directives, including parental leave, part-time work, the shifting of the burden of proof of discrimination from the complainant to the employer, and atypical work. Council Directive 92/85/EEC governing the protection of pregnant women at work came into force in 1992. However, the objections raised by the British government meant that it was seriously neutralized and prescribes only the minimum norms. Over the years, the United Kingdom opposed the directive and attempted to water it down, and then finally implemented it in a minimalist way in the Trade Union and Employment Rights Act of 1993 (Crawley and Slowey, 1995). The effect, it is claimed, is that about 60 per cent of women in the United Kingdom do not have automatic entitlement to maternity leave (Roelofs, 1995).

The impact of 'hard law' in the United Kingdom has been limited largely because of the uncodified nature of the British constitution and the implementation machinery available. Three particular factors can be identified: the way in which British law takes an individualistic approach with very little recall to group justice or class actions; the fact that it is protective rather than proactive; and legal complexity producing a situation in which the success rate for those using both British and European law is relatively poor (Bagilhole, 1997).

Firstly, unlike most other member states in the European Union (EU) that make provision for the distinctive nature of public as opposed to private law, the British system accords no special status to public law. The traditional British legal convention is that people appear before the courts as individuals. The approach is fundamentally individualistic rather than collective, despite individuals having to belong to a particular group to be eligible to invoke the law. In other words, to use the Sex Discrimination Act a complainant must be either a woman or man who is being treated differently from the other sex, but recourse under the law is only as an individual. Therefore, individuals have to take cases on their own and, where equal opportunities remedies are applied by industrial tribunals, they are restricted to the individuals concerned. Thus, the Sex Discrimination Act requires complainants to find someone who is a member of the other sex in an identical situation, with which to compare themselves to prove that discrimination has taken place, regardless of the fact that most women rarely find themselves in directly comparable situations with men. Women have usually already been filtered into an occupational or skills-based ghetto where different standards prevail. Very few parts of the British equal opportunities legislation are based on group justice or class actions. An exception is the work of the Equal Opportunities Commission, which covers everyone who belongs to an appropriate group as defined by the legislation. Also, indirect discrimination, which is rarely used by complainants, does allow account to be taken of the effect of treatment on one particular sex. Finally, the positive action aspects of the legislation in advertising and training can be seen as based on group justice by giving employers scope to help members of the under-represented sex compete for jobs on an equal footing with the other sex.

Secondly, equal opportunities legislation in the United Kingdom is protective. It involves the creation of rights, which the weaker party can assert by means of litigation, in the traditional mode of private law. It is not a proactive or preventative law. It tells people what they must not do and punishes them for wrongdoing, rather than setting up environments that would be conducive to equal opportunities. For the law to work, the protected person must invoke the legal process or the penalties must be so credible that the very existence of the law is a goad or deterrent in itself; the *in terrorem* effect. However, this has not been the case for equal opportunities legislation. In the United Kingdom, employers only have to pay an individual, and compensation levels are generally low so that 'by making discrimination cheap [the law] virtually ensures the ineffectiveness of the rights approach' (Lustgarten and Edwards, 1992, p. 274). The success rate of cases has been very poor. The situation regarding penalties may change with the lifting of the upper limit for compensation resulting from rulings by the ECJ, such as C–271/91 Marshall v Southampton and South West Hampshire Area Health Authority [1993] and also C–180/95 Nils Draehmpaehl v Urania Immobilienservice OHG [1997].

The underlying assumption behind both the individualistic and protective approach to equal opportunities legislation is that the prevailing system is essentially a fair one, although isolated cases may arise where a particular individual is treated unfairly. The implication is that the situation can be put right simply by a policy of treating individual women as though they were men. It is argued (Lustgarten and Edwards, 1992) that the law is weakened because of this adherence to individualism. The effect is to leave existing structures substantially intact. While it is agreed that women may be unfairly distributed within the labour market, the suggestion is that the situation can be redressed by a degree of redistribution; for example, by appointing a few women to senior posts or into 'male' jobs. What is not questioned is the nature of the structures themselves. The division of labour which they embody and the values that are used to decide the rewards assigned to the different sexes are not seen in any way to be inherently sexist.

Jeanne Gregory (1987) has presented a penetrating analysis of such legislation. She suggests that:

> [although] anti-discrimination legislation can be seen as a response to the demands of oppressed groups for the removal of historical barriers to the achievement of full equality ... [the] state ... assumes a conformative role, using the legislation to control those employers whose practices fall short of acceptable notions of equal opportunity, and to evolve institutional structures for channelling the conflicts.

She goes on to argue that:

> it is important to disperse the cloud of mystification surrounding the legislation, so that it is clearly recognized as part of the processes of containment. It is on the statute book in order to protect, not threaten, the fundamental structures of capitalist society, and therefore cannot by itself constitute the vehicle for achieving a nonracist, non-sexist society. (Gregory, 1987, pp. 24–5)

Equal treatment, which is clearly the guiding principle of equal opportunities legislation, merely ensures that all may, theoretically, enter the competition. It does nothing to recognize the handicaps carried by certain entrants, some of which may be so severe as to prevent them from even reaching the starting line. In contrast, special treatment for women, in the form of additional rights, positive action or even positive discrimination, might be said to advance the cause of equal opportunities, but at the cost of equal treatment. In such circumstances, the argument that according special treatment to women implies discrimination against men has to be faced. In the late 1990s, women in the United Kingdom only had special additional rights that relate to biology in the case of pregnancy and childbirth. The measures provided were designed to recognize and compensate for this disadvantage. Any additional positive discrimination which set out to treat women more favourably was inconceivable and faced difficulty at both the theoretical and practical levels.

Thirdly, the Sex Discrimination Act gives individuals direct access to industrial tribunals, which can be a problem because anti-discrimination laws are specifically designed to challenge many commonly held assumptions They, therefore, call for a sensitive and enlightened approach from panel members, a good grasp of complex legal principles and a readiness to criticize established employment practices. As a result, many complainants have experienced difficulty in getting the employer to pay compensation; some have never received the money they had been awarded. Also, victimization of the applicant and a deterioration of relationships in the workplace have often occurred.[1] In 1996, for example, the Equal Opportunities Commission reported that, for the first time, a larger number of men than women had made formal complaints against sex discrimination, often due to men's failed attempts to get low-paid jobs, which employers considered to be 'women's jobs'. In the past, men would not be considering such posts but, with the reduction in traditional male occupations, they were trying to compete with women for 'women's work' (Equal Opportunities Commission, 1996).

With more than one piece of legislation to deal with sex discrimination, difficulties have arisen when cases fall through the legislative net, as for example in the case of Meeks v National Union of Agricultural and Allied Workers (IRLR 198, 1976), brought before an industrial tribunal in the United Kingdom. A part-time secretary took a case under the Sex Discrimination Act because she was paid less per hour than full-timers. The Equal Pay Act, which was intended to cover such circumstances, was of no use because all the secretaries were women, and no

---

1. Two reports have been published by the commission on the victories and defeats of applicants in sex discrimination and equal pay cases at industrial tribunals. The titles of the reports were illustrative of the problems incurred. The report on successful cases was called 'Pyrrhic Victories' (Leonard, 1987). Pyrrhus was a leader of an army who won a battle in Greek mythology, but only at the cost of the death of most of his troops. The report on unsuccessful cases was called 'Trial by Ordeal' (Gregory, 1989).

male comparator was available. The industrial tribunal considered that a requirement making it necessary for an employee to work for 35 hours per week in order to qualify for the higher hourly rate was indirectly discriminatory. It constituted a condition with which proportionately fewer women than men could comply and which the employer could not justify. However, the industrial tribunal went on to say that the discrimination in question was not unlawful since it concerned a payment which is excluded from the scope of the act (Morris and Nott, 1991).

None of these difficulties disappeared in the 1980s and 1990s, but new and different problems arose. From the mid-1980s on, while the EU concentrated its efforts on action programmes designed to allow for subsidiarity and exhorted member states to take their own initiatives to realize common goals, in the United Kingdom the policy environment was unusually hostile to calls for state or public intervention to secure equal opportunities. The New Right philosophy, enthusiastically endorsed by the Thatcher governments, preached a creed of competition within a largely unregulated market as the only way forward in both pragmatic and idealistic terms. As Ian Forbes (1996, p. 147) has argued, this led to the emergence of a conservative view of equal opportunities which celebrates inequality and claims that the free market produces outcomes that cannot, technically, be found to be unjust. The Thatcher government's distaste for social engineering went largely unchallenged by other political forces after the mid-1980s. The Conservatives were electorally dominant. Labour was preoccupied with its internal debate over modernization. Although the situation provided scope for women to organize effectively within the party, their gains were largely symbolic, given Labour's distance from power. Other areas in which women successfully mobilized, such as the trade unions and local government, were themselves stripped of power or influence by a virtually hegemonic New Right central government.

SOFT LAW AND RECONCILIATION POLICIES

The Conservative governments in power from 1970 to 1997 in the United Kingdom were opposed to any extension of EC control, especially in the field of social policy. Ellie Roelofs (1995) has argued the case in the following terms:

> EU law has given women more legal instruments with which to insist on an improvement in their position. But the restricted scope of the equal opportunities policy is largely a result of the decisive

role which the member states themselves play in the Union's decision-making process. (Roelofs, 1995, p. 139)

Successive Conservative governments, determined to maintain a minimum level of regulation in the labour market, opted out of two notable developments of European legislation: the Community Charter of the Fundamental Social Rights of Workers, approved by the European Council in December 1989, and the Agreement on Social Policy appended to the Maastricht Treaty of 1992. Their preference for non-state action, or 'soft law', remained intact.

A characteristic example of the Conservative strategy was the Opportunity 2000 initiative, launched in 1991. Aimed at improving the proportion of women in middle and top management posts, the initiative received the public backing of the then Prime Minister, John Major, but the government was not the instigator, and the measure did not have legislative force. It was, rather, an exhortatory proposal, calling upon major private sector companies and public sector organizations voluntarily to prepare programmes of organized reform providing a full range of equal opportunities measures and, subsequently, monitor their progress towards their targets publicly (Forbes, 1996). Perhaps predictably, progress was slow. A 1997 survey by the Labour Research Department (Johnston, 1997) showed that women accounted for only 1.7 per cent of executives and 4.2 per cent of all directors among the top 100 companies listed on the Stock Exchange; even among the 305 organizations that backed Opportunity 2000, only 11 per cent of directors were women in 1997. This contrasts with modest success for women in the public sector: they constituted 28 per cent of National Health Service executives, 9 per cent of the top three grades in the Civil Service, 8 per cent of local government chief executives and 6 per cent of university chancellors and vice-chancellors.

John Major's governments may have been more sympathetic to the idea of publicly endorsing equal opportunities, but if the EU was calling on the British government for action, Major's governments in turn only called for action, rather than initiating any legislation themselves. Opportunity 2000 encouraged, but did not compel, employers to take appropriate steps, typifying the Major governments' approach. Even the body with primary responsibility for promoting equality of opportunity, the Equal Opportunities Commission, was speculating by the early 1990s whether a better response from employers would be forthcoming if the emphasis was placed on how equal opportunities policies could improve employee initiative, effectiveness and productivity. Employees needed to be persuaded to take action because equal opportunities policies were 'of direct benefit to themselves' (Ollerearnshaw and Waldreck, 1995, p. 24). 'Soft law' in the British context meant some employees responded positively; others simply disregarded the issue.

The advent of a New Labour government should have signalled a decisive change. It came to power in 1997 with a huge 179-seat majority in the legislature, and with women comprising around a quarter of all its members of parliament, which gave rise to some optimism that the United Kingdom would be more receptive to EU initiatives in this area and might even produce some of its own. Labour had a long tradition of endorsing social engineering, and talked openly of the need to reconcile work and family life as well as equal opportunities.

The new government reversed Britain's opt-outs from the Agreement on Social Policy as part of an explicit commitment to pursue a more 'constructive' relationship with the EU. After a year in power, the record was more mixed, not because any serious ideological doubts were raised about the desirability of equal opportunities, but simply because other objectives took priority. Much positive rhetoric was introduced on such issues as parental leave and conditions for part-time workers, but it was always accompanied by an explicit commitment to the overriding priority of maintaining the United Kingdom as a relatively low-tax, low-cost, unregulated labour market. New Labour's 'third way' might be interpreted by cynics as support in principle for family-friendly measures such as flexible working time and childcare, but only if they do not cost too much. Crucially, cost in this context is seen by Labour as not just public expenditure, but also the labour costs of private sector employers. It could be argued that, as long as Labour is convinced that stringent limits must be placed upon any increases in non-wage labour costs in the private sector, its ability to deliver all its family-friendly aspirations are likely to be significantly curtailed. Moreover, a system like that of the United Kingdom, with strong single-party unitary government, offers relatively little scope for interest and pressure groups to question this position. Nor can it be assumed that, just because Labour's government and parliamentary party contain significant numbers of women, the equality agenda will be pursued with vigour. Labour did make significant changes to its own policy-making machinery, and to relations between the extra-parliamentary party and members of parliament, and between members of parliament and the government. The effect was to strengthen considerably the power of the leadership. While the weight of women's opinion should keep equality issues firmly on the agenda, little possibility exists for a successful challenge to a leadership committed to prioritizing other issues.

Some steps had been taken to bring the United Kingdom more into line with mainstream European thinking on equal opportunities, but to a large extent Labour was only picking what it wanted from the EU agenda. It signed up to the parental leave directive, which it claimed would encourage family-friendly and flexible working patterns by giving all employees a basic right to three months' leave following the birth or adoption of a child, and the right to time off work for urgent family reasons. It also agreed to implement Council Directive 93/104/EC on the organization of working time. This is a good example, however, of the way in which Labour's approach, when stripped of the enthusiastic rhetoric, is almost as cautious as that of their Conservative predecessors. The provisions of the directive were potentially costly, as working hours in the United Kingdom were longer than anywhere else in the EU: 10 per cent of the British labour force work a 'standard' 40-hour week, compared to 25 per cent in Germany, and 45 per cent in France and Italy (HM Treasury, 1997a, p. 22). Labour may have confirmed its intention to implement the measure, but it also stressed that 'the Directive includes a range of flexibilities, and it will be impor-tant to make sure that these are used to advantage so that arrangements are sufficiently flexible not to impose an undue burden upon industry' (HM Treasury, 1997b, §88).

A similar stance can be seen in Labour's endorsement of a minimum wage, which is relevant to equal opportunities since women are in the majority among low-paid workers and, therefore, stand to benefit most. The government announced its commitment to the introduction of a National Minimum Wage, but declared that it would only set the level according to the economic circumstances of the time and with the advice of an independent Low Pay Commission. In its own evidence to the commission, the government drew attention to the perceived costs of a minimum wage: 'the higher the level of the minimum wage, the greater the risk of an adverse effect on employment, inflation and the Public Sector Borrowing Requirement'. It emphasized the advantages of differential rates: 'we should consider having lower rates of the mini-mum wage for younger workers' (HM Treasury, 1997b, §86). Whilst abiding by its commitments, having opted-in to the Agreement on Social Policy, Labour made clear that it intended to exploit any oppor-tunities to minimize costs: the rhetoric may have changed, but the reali-ties of policy delivery are unaltered from the Conservative strategy of using soft law to minimize any increase in labour market costs.

In some areas, the equal opportunities agenda, as defined by the Equal Opportunities Commission, was more advanced, notably with regard to what could be described as reconciliation policies, although Labour have preferred to talk about measures to help families 'balance work and home' (Home Office, 1998, pp. 24–9). The Equal Opportunities Commission relaunched the 'Equality Agenda', which it had drawn up in 1991. The agenda called for a national strategy for childcare, based on a partnership between government, employers and parents, and for a family policy which would address flexible working for women and men with young children. The agenda had been virtually ignored by previous governments. The relaunched version advocated a mainstreaming approach to equal opportunities in line with the new EU agenda, implying that responsibility for equal opportunities must be held by all parts of an organization, and all policies, procedures and practices must be considered and appraised for equal opportunities implications, an approach that the New Labour government undertook to promote throughout its various departments.

Labour made great play of its decision to introduce the first ever National Childcare Strategy. Specific pledges were given to provide free education places for all four-year-olds, previously only available to those aged five and above, and additional funding was to be provided for preschool and out-of-school clubs. A new childcare tax credit was proposed, the aim being to give access to childcare for low-income working families by meeting 70 per cent of eligible childcare costs up to a maximum figure depending on the number of children (HM Treasury, 1998a, §1.30). The New Deal packages were expected to provide about 50 000 suitable people with opportunities to work in childcare. Lone parents (mothers) would be trained to help in the expansion of childcare. Lone mothers were a priority problem for Labour: over one in five of all families with children in the United Kingdom were headed by a lone parent in 1997 (one of the highest proportions in the world); only 41 per cent of lone parents in the United Kingdom were, however, in employment, compared to 82 per cent in France and 60 per cent in the United States (Department of Social Security, 1997, p. 7). Consequently, in addition to childcare employment opportunities, a national programme of help for all single parents in searching for employment and job-skill training was introduced in October 1998. Labour was careful to emphasize that: 'the government cannot deliver this strategy on our own. We need childcare providers, parents, local authorities, employers, colleges and others to work together' (Department of Education and Employment, 1998, p. 7).

Childcare may make it easier for women to take up full or part-time employment, but Labour was well aware that the British tax and benefit system could combine to make low-paid work unattractive if, as was often the case, it resulted in loss of benefit. One of the main changes proposed was a reform of the Family Credit system, introduced in 1988 as an in-work benefit for low-income families. Labour announced in its March 1998 Budget that Family Credit would be replaced from October 1999 with a new Working Family Tax Credit. Influenced by the US Earned Income Tax Credit, in operation since 1975, the Working Family Tax Credit was intended to guarantee a minimum income for families on low earnings (HM Treasury, 1998a, §1.30). Families were to be able to choose whether the mother or father received the benefit. If couples could not agree, the woman would have the final choice. The new approach was seen as an important step towards greater integration of the tax and benefit system. Almost 500 000 families were paying income tax to the Inland Revenue while receiving Family Credit as a Social Security benefit; the net effect of Working Family Tax Credit was expected to be that 97 per cent of these families would be taken out of tax (HM Treasury, 1998b, p. 4). Child Benefit was to remain as a universal benefit, although Labour clearly signalled that it intended to tax the benefit, at least among higher earners. From April 1999, the level of Child Benefit was to be increased by as much as 20 per cent for many low-earner recipients. Taken together with the new Working Family Tax Credit, Labour estimated the poorest households with children would be the main beneficiaries.

These changes were consistent with Labour's overall strategy, encapsulated in its slogan for modernizing welfare in Britain: 'work for those who can; security for those who cannot'. Labour continuously stressed that people must realize that their rights are matched by responsibilities. This theme was echoed in the 1998 White Paper on the National Health Service: whilst it is the government's responsibility to tackle the underlying causes of ill-health like unemployment, social exclusion and low educational standards, citizens must take responsibility for raising the health standards of their own families and communities. The same thinking can be seen in education. Labour's Education Minister announced the government would be 'as tough as nails' on parents who failed to take responsibility for their children, and the 1998 Crime and Disorder Bill provided for parents to be compelled to attend 'parenting' classes if their children were persistent truants or offenders.

The most comprehensive statement of intent with regard to the reconciliation of paid work with family life is to be found in the consultation document, issued in November 1998, on 'supporting families' (Home Office, 1998). In it the Home Secretary, as chair of the Ministerial Group on the Family, sets out the government's commitment to 'sensible and pragmatic measures which will strengthen the family', but is careful to note that government is not 'interfering in family life', which remains the responsibility of parents, except if intervention is necessary to protect children (Home Office, 1998, pp. 3–4). If the government was contemplating acting to help families balance work and home, it was doing so in the interests of families, business, the economy and society. A family-friendly framework of employee rights and practices was to be promoted through flexible working arrangements, but on the condition that they would not entail costs for employers. The government also confirmed its intention to implement the European directives on working time, part-time work and parental leave, and improve maternity rights. It proposed to do so by setting a baseline of rights and opportunities, relying on voluntary co-operation between employees and management. The benefits to employers were to come through direct savings on training and recruitment costs by enhancing the retention of experienced staff, reducing absenteeism and encouraging employee loyalty. Parents stood to benefit through the greater choice given to both mothers and fathers to spend more time at home. The supply of well-qualified labour was expected to increase, women would gain greater financial independence, productivity would improve, and society would benefit from greater family stability.

Over the long term, Labour, like its Conservative predecessors, has shown it is engaged in engineering a shift in responsibility from state to individual. In many important respects, it is effectively families rather than individuals that are meant to assume responsibilities for securing their own financial future, or, in the case of parents, the responsibility for raising 'good citizens', who have the skills and attitudes deemed necessary in an era of global competition for jobs. While the EU was developing recommendations aimed at helping parents to reconcile work and family life, the New Labour government in the United Kingdom was using family support measures as a means of relieving the pressure on the state and promoting family responsibility.

CULTURE CLASHES

This analysis of progress on equality and reconciliation from the 1970s to 1990s demonstrates that the impact of EU initiatives on equal opportunities in the United Kingdom has been limited, and that the objectives set by the EU, particularly on reconciliation, have not been fully met.

The problems that have arisen can be categorized in three phases: 1970–79, when they were largely due to implementation mechanisms; 1979–97, when they stemmed from a wider ideological stance inimical to social and economic intervention on the part of the state; and from 1997 on, when New Labour introduced a more receptive stance to the idea of intervention to secure equality and reconciliation, but only when it does not conflict with the 'higher order' priority of preserving a relatively low-cost labour market.

Particular ideological perspectives have clearly impacted on policy delivery, quite dramatically so during the Thatcher years, but also during the 1990s as both Conservative and Labour governments accepted the essentials of a market approach and committed themselves to preserving the United Kingdom's competitive position in a global labour market. As governments changed, so did attitudes towards reconciliation policy. For example, Labour's determination to reduce the role of the state, especially in welfare provision, with its concomitant desire to maximize employment, can be credited with promoting new opportunities for mothers to enter and remain in employment. Labour has, however, been reluctant to shoulder any further costs arising from measures for reconciling paid work with family life, either in the form of increased public spending or higher labour costs in the private sector. In such a context, the attitudes of private sector employers assume crucial importance. Where employers have decided to pursue initiatives, particularly in the realm of reconciliation of paid work and family life, governments have not resisted and, indeed, have usually offered encouragement, but not money. In areas where private sector employers have been more reluctant to introduce change, British governments of both political persuasions have been content to let them lag behind the European vision. The imperative is overwhelmingly economic; if employers perceive more flexible working patterns to be to their economic advantage, then (the Thatcher years aside) British governments will endorse their initiatives with some enthusiasm. If employers perceive reconciliation measures to be driving up non-wage labour costs, however, then they have little to fear in the way of compulsion from governments of either of Britain's major parties.

As this chapter has shown, even when the British government has not been overtly hostile to supranational guidance and leadership, significant implementation gaps have remained. Other chapters in this volume indicate that the United Kingdom has not been alone in its opposition to European rulings, or in failing to match rhetorical commitment with actual policy delivery. In relative terms, its record on implementation is good. In addition, Chapter 2 illustrates how British civil servants and politicians have actively promoted gender policies from within the European Commission and European Parliament. One factor that is, arguably, unique to the United Kingdom, and has impeded rather than facilitated the equality and reconciliation agenda, is the institutional setting of government. In comparison with other EU member states, central government in the United Kingdom is so powerful that even a combination of vocal pressure groups and codified rights has not been enough to produce significant societal change when it was not backed by central government. The apparent lack of effectiveness of gender policy can be attributed to differences in political culture: the individualization inherent in the British approach has meant that, even where opportunities for redress or advancement have been provided by EU directives, their impact in societal rather than individual terms has been limited. This is not to argue that the law has not, and cannot, play an important part in the improvement of opportunities for women. The fact that EU law appears to have had relatively little impact on national legislation since British membership may be due not simply to the inherent limitations of legal instruments, but also to the indifference of those who formulate the laws and those who interpret them.

8 Reconciliation Policies in Spain

Celia Valiente

Equal pay and equal treatment for working men and women have been on the policy agenda in Spain since the mid-1970s. Over this period, Spain has built up a strong body of equal opportunities legislation, thereby extending the rights of women as paid workers, partly as a result of Spain's entry into the European Community (EC) in 1986 (Threlfall, 1997). Relatively few measures have been introduced, however, to help parents combine employment and family life (Tobío, 1994, 1996a, 1996b). Several reasons may help to explain why reconciliation policies have not been developed further. Firstly, labour surpluses have been a permanent feature of the Spanish labour market. Therefore, from a strictly economic point of view, policies are not needed to enable women to participate in the workforce. Secondly, apart from health and education services, historically, the Spanish welfare state has developed a strong emphasis on monetary transfers rather than care services. It has been easier to expand monetary benefits, for instance for maternity, than establish childcare services. Thirdly, societal views about childrearing emphasize the value of the care provided by mothers and family members and mistrust public childcare centres for very young children. Fourthly, actors who have demanded more extensive reconciliation policies, namely the feminist movement, women's policy machineries (Stetson and Mazur, 1995), and feminists in trade unions have been too weak to influence the policy process. The first two sections of the chapter analyse the policy context and the role play by policy actors in formulating and implementing reconciliation policies. The third section examines policies designed to assist men and women in reconciling paid work and family life in Spain.

THE POLICY CONTEXT

In Spain, the main contextual factors that have impeded the progress of equality policy and, more especially, measures to help parents combine

143

paid work with family responsibilities concern the situation in the labour market, the welfare system and societal attitudes towards child-rearing. The political parties have played an important role in setting the policy agenda and in pushing forward, or hindering, the adoption of reconciliation policies.

Supply and demand for labour

In other European countries, the shortage of labour was a major reason explaining why women joined the working population, and why governments extended childcare provision and introduced other reconciliation policies. Policy, in these circumstances, has been aimed at making it easier for married women with children to become economically active, since they form the most important available reserve of labour (apart from immigrants). Between the mid-1970s and 1990s, Spain did not suffer from labour shortages. On the contrary, it recorded a large labour surplus: since 1982 the unemployment rate has not fallen below 16 per cent. This has meant that policies have not been needed to encourage female labour force participation for economic reasons, although they could be justified on grounds of gender equality or social justice.

Labour surpluses have coincided with a low participation rate for women in the labour market: 47 per cent of women were economically active in 1997, in comparison to the average of 58 per cent in the European Union (EU). The unemployment rate for Spanish women (28 per cent) was more than twice the EU average. The Spanish labour market is also characterized by a relatively high level of temporary and informal employment. In the same year, the proportion of wage-earners on temporary contracts (34 per cent) was not only by far the highest in the EU, but was double that of the second highest (17 per cent for Finland) and almost three times the EU average of 12 per cent (Eurostat, 1998a, pp. 4–5). The same firm or administrative service in the public sector often employs both permanent and temporary workers. They may even perform the same tasks, but workers with temporary contracts are characterized by a high turn-over, and the conversion rate of temporary into permanent contracts is very low: about 10–15 per cent in the early and mid-1990s (Dolado and Bentolila, 1992, p. 15).

In the mid-1980s, between 1.5 and 2.5 million people worked in the informal sector (Pérez-Díaz and Rodríguez, 1994, p. 31), although the number was probably lower in the 1990s. In the mid-1980s, roughly the same number of men and women were employed in the informal economy, whereas about 75 per cent of jobs in the formal sector were performed by men. Informal jobs are more prevalent among very young women, married women, and the least educated women (Ruesga, 1991). The existence of a large informal sector is an obstacle to the effectiveness of reconciliation policies, since work-related benefits apply only to workers who are formally covered by social insurance. The combination of a high level of fixed-term jobs and very high unemployment rates precludes the implementation of reconciliation measures. Temporary workers are less prone than permanent workers to protest against the infringements of legal provisions, especially when they know that they risk becoming unemployed (or even long-term unemployed).

The characteristics of the labour market have made it difficult both to develop and implement reconciliation measures. Generally speaking, employers are not interested in reconciliation policies that cost them money and cause them problems in work organization. Given the large labour surplus, a woman worker who has problems in combining paid work and family responsibilities is easily replaceable.

Welfare delivery

Since the social protection system in Spain is based on the provision of employment-related insurance benefits for workers and their dependants, as in many other continental welfare systems (Esping-Andersen, 1990), it does not directly cover the population excluded from the labour force. Health care and compulsory schooling are universal benefits and are provided free of charge, but most other benefits are directed towards workers. People who are unable to earn an income in the labour market due to illness, old age, invalidity or involuntary unemployment, but have previously worked and paid insurance contributions, are entitled to receive benefits. However, very few social services are provided in kind. Individuals who have caring responsibilities (usually women) for children or older relatives receive little assistance from the state to enable them to combine their professional and family responsibilities (Carrasco *et al.*, 1997; Guillén, 1997).

Social attitudes

In addition, mothers are considered as the best providers of care for very small children, which means that working mothers are not encouraged by policy measures to combine paid work and family responsibilities. It is widely assumed that care by the mother is indispensable, at least during the first few years of the child's life. Women are believed to have a natural caring instinct for their children, which men lack. Fathers or the staff in childcare centres may provide some assistance, but they are not an acceptable substitute for a mother's care. Many Spaniards firmly believe that the full-time employment of mothers endangers the upbringing of small children (Escario *et al.*, 1987, pp. 55, 84–8; Juste *et al.*, 1991, pp. 38–9).

In a survey carried out in 1990, 55 per cent of the Spanish adult population of both sexes agreed with the statement: 'a child under six is likely to suffer if her/his mother works'. When the same question was asked not just about small children, but about children of any age, there was greater acceptance of working mothers; 61 per cent of respondents agreed with the statement that 'a working mother can have as warm and secure a relationship with her children as a housewife' (Alberdi *et al.*, 1994, pp. 98–101).

The view is widely held in Spain that public childcare should not be used for very young children, and that childcare centres are one of the least desirable options for parents, particularly when children are under the age of three. Maternal care is the preferred option. When the mother does not stay at home night and day to take care of her offspring, the second preference is for an arrangement which is closest to the full-time housewife-mother, namely that children are looked after by a female relative. Grandmothers are frequently available to look after their grandchildren because most older women are full-time housewives, and young parents tend to live in the same area as their parents. Alternatively, another woman, often from a lower social class, is paid to replace the working mother in the home. This option is only available to couples in higher income groups (Escario *et al.*, 1987, pp. 89–94; Juste *et al.*, 1991, pp. 43–4).

POLITICAL PARTIES

In combination, the labour market situation for women, the lack of publicly provided services and the strong support for the male-breadwinner model imply that women in Spain can expect to receive little assistance from the state in reconciling family life with paid work outside the home. Most policy-makers obtain their positions because they are members of, or close to, political parties. In addition, parties are important vehicles for agenda building. Electoral programmes usually present a maximum in terms of the policies that a party is willing to implement once in office, but they do give an indication of the issues politicians identify as important (Cobb and Elder, 1972, p. 91). The main parties have not demonstrated a strong commitment to reconciliation policies.

The centre-right Unión de centro democrático (UCD) held government from 1977 to 1982. The party was, on the whole, not interested in reconciliation policies, as can be seen from its programmes.[1] The 1977 UCD electoral programme said nothing about reconciliation measures, as the concept was not used at the time. Nor were they mentioned in the 1979 programme, with the exception of a reference to childcare. In the section on education, free schooling was intended to cover all children aged four and five. Although this objective was not achieved during the UCD mandate, by 1979 childcare policies were being defined as measures that chiefly benefit children and not as services that help working parents to combine family responsibilities with paid work (Valiente, 1995a).

The UCD programmes did contain references to the principle of equality in employment for women and men. The 1979 programme demanded the integration of women into the army. These electoral commitments were reflected in policy-making. Governments of different ideological persuasions have been more active in dismantling discriminatory labour legislation put in place during the Franco era and in developing gender-neutral labour law than in establishing reconciliation measures.

The social democratic Partido Socialista Obrero Español (PSOE) was the main opposition party up to 1982. It held power between 1982 and 1986, and was again in opposition following its defeat in 1996. PSOE policy documents[2] contain a clear commitment to the principle of equality in employment for women and men. However, the way reconciliation policies are treated in PSOE electoral programmes and in the resolutions passed at federal congresses is more complicated. Broadly speaking, they contain a commitment to develop a comprehensive catalogue of reconciliation policies (a commitment not completely fulfilled in the 14 years the PSOE was in power).

---

1. UCD electoral programmes for general elections: 1977, 1979.
2. PSOE electoral programmes for general elections: 1977, 1979, 1982, 1986, 1989, 1993, 1996; federal congress resolutions: 1976, 1979, 1981, 1984, 1988, 1990, 1994.

Reconciliation policies were not always presented in PSOE documents as gender equality measures, but as instruments for increasing social justice. This point can be illustrated with the example of childcare. A common theme running through PSOE policy documents is the commitment to develop programmes for children under the age of six, conceptualized as educational policies. Preschool programmes are presented as an instrument to ensure greater equality between social groups. According to this view, children from underprivileged social backgrounds should be enrolled in public preschool programmes so that they acquire the educational skills necessary to be successful in elementary school, and to reduce cultural differences between children from different socio-economic backgrounds. All these ideas reflect the PSOE leaderships' opinion that the educational system should serve as an efficient mechanism to combat social inequalities.

PSOE documents also contain some references to childcare in the sections relating to gender equality, although they are less frequent than in the sections on education. The PSOE commitment to childcare as a gender equality policy is striking, if it is remembered that the PSOE has been a social-democratic party in which (as in other countries) most party members have been more concerned with class inequalities than with gender differences.

The Partido Popular (PP) came to power in 1996 and was the main opposition party between 1982 and 1996 under the names of Alianza Popular, Coalición Popular and Partido Popular. As in PSOE documents, PP electoral programmes[3] contain a clear commitment to the principle of equality of female and male workers before the law, but the party does not commit itself to developing reconciliation policies to the same extent as in PSOE programmes. The 1977 and 1979 PP programmes did not contain a section on women. Other sections set out the demand for the abolition of gender discrimination in employment. Part-time work was presented as a good solution for enabling married women to participate in the labour market at the same time as fulfilling household responsibilities. The 1982, 1993 and 1996 programmes contained a section on women, but the 1986 and 1989 programmes did not. The 1986 electoral programme (p. 10) stated that 'the PP has not considered pertinent the inclusion of a chapter on women in its electoral programme, considering that, in this way, the PP can more effectively contribute to putting women's rights and duties on a par with those of

---

3.	PP electoral programmes for general elections: 1977, 1979, 1982, 1986, 1989, 1993, 1996.

men'. The appearance and disappearance of women's issues reflect the PP's ambivalence and reluctance to make a strong commitment to gender equality. The 1993 and 1996 programmes contain references to reconciliation measures, such as flexible working hours. They present part-time work as a useful measure for women, but not for men, and affirm that women, not men, must have the freedom to choose the type of life they want to live. The implication is that women have two equally valid options: trying to combine employment and family responsibilities, and staying at home to fulfil family commitments. The PP has also proposed the extension of the preschool programmes already in place, presenting them mainly as educational programmes, and to a much lesser extent as gender equality measures, and/or family policies.

POLICY ACTORS

The unfavourable socio-economic context may go some way to explaining the limitations of reconciliation policies in post-authoritarian Spain. A less important reason is that the actors who could have campaigned for policies to support parents with young children – the feminist movement, women's policy machineries, and feminists within unions and political parties – were not strong enough to have an impact on the policy process. A further exacerbating factor was that the attitudes of these actors towards reconciliation measures were often ambivalent. Some political parties were not interested in reconciliation measures. Despite the unfavourable policy environment, others were interested in certain measures, for instance the extension of maternity leave. The same parties have often, though not always, shown only a rhetorical interest in measures such as the provision of childcare as a reconciliation policy rather than an education policy.

The feminist movement

The extension of reconciliation policies has not been the top priority of the feminist movement since the 1970s (Threlfall, 1985; Durán and Gallego, 1986; Kaplan, 1992; Escario *et al.*, 1996). Even if the contrary had been the case, it is unlikely that the movement would have obtained satisfaction in this respect. In comparison with other West European countries, the movement in Spain has been weaker, though not insignificant. It has not achieved such high visibility in the mass media;

nor has it initiated much public debate, or had as much impact on the policy process as in some other EU member states.

Feminist activists in Spain have seen the combination of paid work and family responsibilities as an important problem that many women face. Despite this awareness, since the 1970s most Spanish feminist groups have not included reconciliation policies amongst their most urgent and pressing demands, although they have given the question some attention. This is reflected not only in the rhetoric of the movement, in which the demand for reconciliation measures is often present, but also in the real battles that have been fought, where it is often absent. The question can be asked as to why the Spanish feminist movement has not mobilized around the reconciliation issue. From the 1930s until 1975, Spain was governed by a rightwing authoritarian regime that actively opposed the advancement of women's rights and status. After 1975, the feminist movement had to tackle a whole raft of issues simultaneously, including equal political rights for citizens of both sexes; equality of women and men before the law; reproductive rights; divorce law reform (passed in 1981); and the punishment of sexual violence against women. The decriminalization of the sale and promotion of contraceptives was achieved in 1978, and the decriminalization of abortion in 1985, on ethical, therapeutic and eugenic grounds. In view of the large number of areas where women's rights had to be established, it was reasonable for feminists to concentrate their efforts on certain demands and to leave others aside. Another explanation for the lack of mobilization over reconciliation policies is that the feminist movement in Spain is divided. It has two branches. One, representing the minority view, is unwilling to co-operate with formal institutions, because its members see the state as patriarchal. They are not demanding reconciliation measures from the state. The other branch, representing the majority, is willing to co-operate with formal institutions (Escario *et al.*, 1996). The demands presented in their programmes, pamphlets, and other written materials usually include reconciliation policies, but mobilization has tended to be in pursuit of other priorities.

In choosing to pay relatively little attention to the issue of reconciliation of employment and family life, feminists in Spain were rejecting a very problematic past. The official doctrine of the rightwing authoritarian regime (1936–75) defined motherhood as the main duty of women towards the state and society, and affirmed that the role of mothering was incompatible with other activities, such as paid employment (Gallego, 1983; Nash, 1991, p. 160). Many feminist groups had been formed in Spain in the late 1960s and early 1970s. Together with other (illegal) political organizations, they had opposed the authoritarian regime (Scanlon, 1990, p. 94). After almost 40 years of being confronted with the idea of mothering and caring as the most important task in women's lives, Spanish feminists were extremely reluctant to turn their attention to the issue of family responsibilities. The aims of women's liberation were to broaden the range of concerns that define women's lives, such as waged work, or control over their own bodies. They carefully avoided the question of motherhood, childcare and family responsibilities.

Women's policy machineries

Women's policy machineries have existed in Spain since the late 1970s. Nevertheless, the main bureaucracy for women at the level of the central state, the Instituto de la Mujer, was not founded until October 1983, six years after the first democratic elections were held in Spain, and one year after the PSOE first came to power. The Institute's programmatic objectives are set out in three equality plans (Valiente, 1995b; Threlfall, 1996, 1998).

Elsewhere, women's policy machineries have lobbied hard for the establishment of reconciliation policies. In Spain, the Instituto de la Mujer, like the feminist movement, has not considered the demand for reconciliation policies to be a top priority but an issue of moderate importance. In general, members of the Instituto de la Mujer and feminists have been overwhelmed by the number of demands they have felt obliged to promote. Equally, they have wanted to distance themselves from the very problematic past of the authoritarian regime. As a result, the institute has had some impact on reconciliation measures such as maternity and parental leave, but no impact whatsoever on the provision of services such as childcare (Valiente, 1995a).

Women's departments in political parties and trade unions

The PSOE commitment to gender equality was the result of the pressure exerted by socialist feminists. In 1976, a women's caucus, Mujer y Socialismo, was formed within the party. In 1981, a member of the caucus was elected to the PSOE's executive committee, and other appointments followed. In December 1984, the women's caucus was raised by the party to the status of a women's secretariat at federal executive level (Threlfall, 1985, pp. 48–9). The feminist socialists managed to introduce demands for more public childcare services (and other reconciliation programmes) in PSOE policy documents, but they were not strong enough to convince PSOE policy-makers of the need to implement reconciliation measures. Their commitment, therefore, remained at the rhetorical level. In contrast to the PSOE, neither the UCD nor the conservative PP has an organized group of rank and file and high-ranking feminist women members.

The two major Spanish trade unions, the Unión General de Trabajadores (UGT) and Comisiones Obreras (CCOO), both have departments dedicated to women's affairs. According to high-ranking feminists in the two unions, members of these departments have often publicly expressed their concerns about the obstacles that many working women face in trying to combine paid work and unpaid domestic and caring duties. They have also argued that the welfare state does not provide social services to help working women (Muriana, 1987; Vilches, 1992; Villegas, 1992).

Nevertheless, the staff of the UGT and CCOO women's departments have not successfully lobbied for the inclusion of the demand for more reconciliation measures in public policy, collective bargaining, and in the negotiation of bipartite and tripartite agreements with employers and/or the state. The reason is that the position of departments for women's affairs within the unions has always been very weak. This weakness is reflected in the small number of people they employ to deal with women's questions, and in their limited capacity to influence the discourse and practice of mainstream trade unionists. Feminist trade unionists have had to convince not only very reluctant employers and policy-makers but also the majority of male trade unionists of the need for reconciliation measures.

Most collective agreements contain no reference to the reconciliation of family life and paid work (Pérez del Río, 1997), which is hardly surprising given the collective bargaining process. When union delegates negotiate with employers, reconciliation issues are rarely mentioned. On very few occasions, normally when a feminist trade unionist participates in the negotiations, reference is made to the question. The other workers' representatives are prone to allow any demands in this area to be among the first to be abandoned, if they are to achieve gains in areas they consider to be really important, for example higher salaries, the reduction of working hours, and stability of employment.

Reconciliation measures may be the unintended by-product of bargaining between trade union representatives who are trying to obtain general improvements in working conditions, rather than devices to help parents combine their family responsibilities with paid work. This has been the case with one of the priorities of mainstream trade union representatives in collective bargaining, namely the reduction in working hours. Although shorter working hours could provide a means of combining work and caring duties, mainstream trade unionists do not conceptualize the measure as a reconciliation strategy. Rather, they see it as a means of improving working conditions and reducing the exploitation of workers. The relative indifference of trade unionists towards reconciliation issues is reflected in the absence of any reference to the question in most trade union documents.[4] The resolutions at general congresses of the UGT and CCOO since the mid-1980s rarely make reference to the question.

RECONCILIATION POLICIES

Given the socio-economic context in which policy is formulated and implemented, it is interesting to find that governments of different ideological persuasions have developed reconciliation policies. The primary concern of governments has been to dismantle discriminatory labour law inherited from the Franco era. As might be expected, the measures enacted provide modest, though not negligible, assistance to parents who are seeking to combine paid work and family responsibilities.

Social and political actors have devoted more attention to establishing the principle of equality of female and male workers before the law, which is a commitment contained in most electoral programmes of parties whatever their ideological persuasion. The main measures in equality policy have been the prohibition of sex discrimination, and the revision of discriminatory legislation. The 1978 Constitution included a blanket prohibition on gender discrimination (Article 14) in the labour market and the civil service (Article 35.1). Legislation inherited from the Franco era was revised to eliminate its discriminatory aspects, and the process had still not been completed by the late 1990s. In practice, the amendments meant that women were allowed to perform some types of work which they were prevented from doing in the past, such as night work, jobs in the police force, army or mining. In 1995, the concept of

---

4. UGT federal congress resolutions: 1986, 1990, 1994. CCOO federal congress resolutions: 1984, 1988, 1991.

wage equality was broadened to include not only the principle of equal pay for equal work but also that of equal pay for work of equal value, to bring national legislation into line with EU directives. Since 1989, women who believe that they have been discriminated against can take their case to court, and the burden of proof falls on the employer.

The principle of equality for all citizens before the law informs general legislation, although discriminatory clauses remain in collective agreements negotiated between representatives of employers and workers. Wage discrimination is one of the most common forms of gender discrimination, and applies to labour categories that include only or mainly women. Women workers tend to be paid less than men either in mixed, or male categories. Many job offers are also discriminatory, because they are directed towards only one sex, as can be seen from advertisements in newspapers (Sáez, 1994, p. 139; De la Fuente and Crespán, 1995).

The prohibition of sex discrimination before the law, the revision of discriminatory legislation and the subsequent approval of gender-neutral new legislation have been important reforms. Legislators have sent society a clear message that overt gender discrimination is no longer tolerated (at least in general legislation). Women may now use the law to fight for or defend their position in the labour market. Nevertheless, the importance of the reform should not be overstated. Equality provisions in the law are often violated. When this happens, very few women initiate legal proceedings for gender discrimination (Sáez, 1994, p. 29; De la Fuente and Crespán, 1995, p. 1). Again, high rates of unemployment and temporary employment work against the implementation of non-discriminatory labour legislation.

Although equality policy has had an impact on opportunities for women in the labour market, it has been pursued largely independently from reconciliation measures. PSOE governments (1982–96) have been more active than governments led by the UCD (1977–82) and the PP (from 1996) with regard to reconciliation measures. The PP has, for example, supported part-time work as a reconciliation strategy to a greater extent than the PSOE. The provisions made at national level are, however, minimum standards established by labour law. Collective agreements negotiated by representatives of workers and employers can offer higher standards.

Paid maternity leave and preschool services are the two main reconciliation measures available in Spain. In 1989, the PSOE government extended maternity leave by four weeks (Act 3/1989 of 3 March 1989). As a result of this and other reforms, working mothers who have previously been employed and have contributed to the social security system for at least 180 days within the five years preceding childbirth are entitled to 16 uninterrupted weeks of paid leave. The number of years contributed and the level of contributions, which is proportional to salary, are used to calculate the basis of entitlement (*base reguladora*). The right to reinstatement is guaranteed. Also, since 1989, if both parents are in paid work, the father may take up to four of the final weeks of the leave period, and in this case the mother must return to work. The number of fathers who take the last weeks of maternity leave is extremely low. The Spanish Labour Force Survey (Encuesta de Población Activa) provides data disaggregated by sex showing wage-earners who are not working during the week when the survey questionnaire is administered. In the first quarter of 1998, 96.4 per cent of wage-earners who were not working because they were on maternity leave were women (Instituto Nacional de Estadística, 1998, p. 204). Fathers in employment are entitled to two days on full pay for childbirth, or four days if they need to travel to visit their wife during confinement.

The 1986 PSOE electoral programme included a commitment to extend maternity leave, which proved difficult to implement for a variety of reasons, among them the opposition from employers, as predicted by parliamentarians in the Conservative Party. In the parliamentary debate prior to the approval of Act 3/1989, the conservative member of parliament Celia Villalobos argued against the extension of maternity leave from 14 to 16 weeks, on the grounds that employers would be less willing to recruit women, since they would be absent from work for longer periods. Employers would, she went on, see female workers as problematic to a greater extent than in the past (Comisión de Política Social, *Diario de Sesiones del Congreso de los Diputados*, 16 November 1998, p. 12806). Employers' perceptions (or misperceptions) regarding women have been identified as a major obstacle to the advancement of women in the labour market (Threlfall, 1997). The special treatment afforded to women as workers through the enactment of reconciliation measures has reinforced the misperceptions of employers by providing justification for their view that women are less 'reliable' employees.

Paid maternity leave was eventually extended only because the proposal was in line with other social measures which have been implemented, such as old age and invalidity pensions and unemployment benefits. Maternity leave with pay is, essentially, an income maintenance programme for women who are not in paid work because they have recently given birth, but who have previously worked and have contributed, together with their employers, to the financing of welfare.

The main policies for children under six (when compulsory schooling begins) are educational preschool programmes for children aged four or above. In the academic year 1995–96, 70.3 per cent of children aged five, 69.5 per cent of children aged four, and 38.3 per cent of children aged three, were in publicly provided preschool classes. By contrast, the percentage of children aged two or under cared for in public childcare facilities was very low: 0.4 per cent for those under one year old; 1.7 per cent for children aged over one; and 4.7 per cent for children aged two. Children of two or under were not provided for in private childcare centres either (calculated by the author from Instituto Nacional de Estadística, 1997, p. 157; Ministerio de Educación y Cultura, 1998, p. 155).

In practical terms, this means that, after the 16 weeks of maternity leave and before the child reaches the age of three, childcare is considered to be a private matter that parents (or mothers) have to solve by themselves. In comparison to some other countries, Spain may appear to make relatively generous provision of preschool places for four and five-year-olds (Cousins, 1994, p. 51). However, preschool programmes are, as indicated above, educational programmes with the purpose of achieving greater equality between children from different social backgrounds. They are not intended as gender equality programmes providing childcare for working parents. Since most women in Spain who are economically active work full-time, preschool arrangements cannot be used by parents as a substitute for childcare; the hours are shorter than working hours, and the day is interrupted by a break. Parents themselves see preschool services as educational programmes. Whereas many parents are prepared to leave their children aged three or over in preschool centres for educational reasons, these same parents are reluctant to leave younger children in childcare centres because they believe that maternal care is the best option for very young children.

Apart from paid maternity leave and preschool services, which are the two main reconciliation measures, other much less important reconciliation measures are available. Provision is made for up to three years of unpaid parental leave for working parents, but no leave is granted for parents to care for a sick child. The right to reinstatement is guaranteed during the first year of parental leave, and the right to return to a job in the same occupational category is guaranteed during the second and third years of leave. The period of leave is counted as time effectively worked in calculating rights accrued due to seniority. After a period of leave, however, as in other continental welfare systems, working parents receive very little help from the state to combine paid work and family responsibilities. In Spain, maternity and parental leave can, therefore, be seen as a substitute for childcare rather than as a complement to it (O'Oconnor, 1993).

As early as 1900, working women were given the right to take breaks during the working day to feed their babies. A century later, nursing breaks consist of a one-hour break, or two breaks of 30 minutes each, or a reduction of 30 minutes from the working day. These breaks are always counted as time effectively worked. Since 1989, the father may also take nursing breaks in place of the mother if both are working, but the two parents cannot both take breaks. As in the case of childbirth, workers are also entitled to two days off work on full pay (four days if travel is involved) in the event of a serious illness or death of a relative within the second degree of kinship. No provision is made for other less serious illnesses.

All these reconciliation measures are, in theory, available to all economically active parents. However, practice differs greatly from theory. Reconciliation measures are available to workers in the formal economy, but not to those who work in the informal sector. Within the formal sector, permanent workers probably benefit from reconciliation measures to a greater extent than temporary workers, who are afraid of loosing their jobs. Workers in the public sector benefit from provisions to a larger extent than workers in the private sector, because of their greater job security. Those who pay personal income tax (*Impuesto sobre la Renta de las Personas Físicas*) can benefit from tax exemptions for 15 per cent of the amount of childcare expenses for children aged under three, up to a maximum level. In the fiscal year 1994, only 110 153 tax payers benefited from this tax exemption. The average exemption over the year was about 6 per cent of the average monthly wage for employees and workers in industry and the service sector in 1994 (calculated by the author from Instituto Nacional de Estadística, 1995, p. 71; Ministerio de Economía y Hacienda, 1997, p. 117).

Part-time work has not been adopted in Spain as a widespread reconciliation strategy. It accounts for 18 per cent of employment for women, 3 per cent for men, and 8 per cent of total employment, which is about half the EU average (Eurostat, 1998a, pp. 4–9). The proportion of part-time work increased rapidly in the 1990s, as a result of reforms introducing regulations that made it more attractive to employers. PP programmes show a preference for this type of work as an instrument for reconciling paid work with family obligations, and it seems likely that this policy option will be pursued further.

DO-IT-YOURSELF SOLUTIONS

Since the mid-1970s, an extensive revision of discriminatory labour legislation has taken place in Spain. Broadly speaking, Spanish labour law has become gender neutral. In this respect, Spain is at a level comparable to that in other West European countries, and ahead of some of them. In contrast to the efforts to revise discriminatory legislation inherited from the Franco era, post-authoritarian policy-makers have paid little attention to developing policies that would help parents combine professional and family duties. As a result, parents, and especially mothers, who try, simultaneously, to carry out labour market and domestic duties receive relatively little practical support from the state after the 16 weeks of paid maternity leave, with the exception of preschool services provided for children aged four or over.

Studies of the strategies used by Spaniards to combine family and employment responsibilities show that public policy measures are only one among the many resources used by women. They rely heavily on the help provided mainly by female relatives, and much less on the assistance of male partners and domestic helpers. They are dependent on their own ability to organize strict and careful time planning and to simplify domestic duties. Reducing the standard of domestic work is another strategy available to them. They also resort to absenteeism (Tobío, 1996b). For most Spanish women, it would be impossible to combine paid and unpaid work if they had to rely solely on reconciliation measures provided by the state.

The prevailing economic and political climate has not been conducive to reconciliation policies. A serious labour surplus has characterized the labour market since 1975. Traditionally, the welfare state has limited its efforts to transfer payments rather than making provision for services in kind, though some progress has been made with preschool education. In addition, societal views about childrearing have legitimized care by mothers and undervalued public provision. The feminist movement, women's policy machineries and feminists within trade unions and political parties have adopted an ambivalent stance towards reconciliation policies and/or have been too weak to influence the policy process. Political parties have not presented themselves to public opinion as being strongly interested in reconciliation issues, although measures such as maternity and parental leave have been introduced.

In Spain, it has been difficult to create an environment conducive to combining family building with employment outside the home. Spanish fertility rates are among the lowest in the world. In some countries, the decline in fertility has been an incentive for policy-makers to introduce reconciliation measures, with pronatalist objectives, but this has not been the case in Spain, mainly due to the negative associations of policies promoting higher fertility rates with the repression of the Franco regime. The historical context has, however, provided incentives for the revision of discriminatory legislation established during the Franco years (1936–75) or earlier, as in the case of gender-neutral labour law. The low fertility rate could be seen as a consequence of the lack of effective reconciliation measures. Many women under the age of 45 are trying to combine paid work and family life. Unlike their mothers, they belong to a generation that has not left the labour market after marriage or the births of their children. Since their partners have not become more involved in domestic and caring duties, these young women are combining former roles (as mothers and wives) and new roles (as waged workers). The provision made in policy for measures to apply to both men and women has not brought about any noticeable change in the distribution of domestic tasks.

The prospects for developing more effective reconciliation policies are not encouraging. The EU is continuing to exert pressure on governments to introduce measures to help parents combine paid and unpaid work, while also pushing them to meet the criteria for Economic and Monetary Union. Even if further legislation on reconciliation measures seems unlikely, collective actors may play an important role in implementing existing labour law, and could use this as a platform for the inclusion in collective agreements of measures to enable parents to reconcile their different activities.

9 Adaptation or Diffusion of the Swedish Gender Model?

Christina Bergqvist and Ann-Cathrine Jungar

In the late 1980s, Helga Maria Hernes (1987) formulated the thesis that the Scandinavian welfare states have gone further than other welfare states in achieving equality between the sexes. Since then, Sweden has joined the European Union (EU), and questions have been raised about the extent to which EU membership may change the Swedish gender model and/or influence thinking on gender issues in other member states and at EU level. Hernes (1987, p. 135) was not claiming that equality had been fully achieved, only that the Nordic welfare states were potentially women-friendly. An important aspect of women-friendly policies is that they give women the opportunity to participate in public life and to reconcile motherhood with paid work. Compared to most EU member states, Sweden has a long history of policies encouraging women's participation in the labour market and enabling parents to combine family life and employment.

The 1970s and 1980s brought major changes in the political mobilization, participation and representation of women at all levels of politics in Sweden, with the result that only small differences remain between women and men in these areas. By 1998, women accounted for between 40 and 50 per cent of elected representatives at local, regional and central level, and made up half the members of the Swedish Social Democratic government. The high proportion of women in national political administration and decision-making bodies has also spilled over into Swedish representation in the EU. The first commissioner Sweden was entitled to nominate to the European Commission was a senior woman politician, Anita Gradin. About 40 per cent of European parliamentarians from Sweden in the late 1990s were women, and they formed the majority of the Swedish civil servants employed in EU institutions (Regeringens skrivelse, 1996/97:41, p. 72).

Membership and representation in unions and in corporatist decision-making bodies has also increased markedly (Bergqvist, 1995).

Like the other Nordic states, Sweden has a strong public sector, which funds and runs most childcare and eldercare services. Under the parental insurance scheme, either parent can take paid leave from work to look after young children. This does not mean that gender segregation has been eliminated in the labour market or in the home. In the labour market, unlike the situation in politics, men are still dominant in managerial positions. They earn more and are in the majority in higher status positions. In the home, women continue to hold the main responsibility for reproductive work. Many women, particularly those with children under the age of seven and older women, therefore, work part-time. In general, women, especially those on low incomes and lone mothers, have been affected more than men by the changes in the welfare system and financial crises (SOU, 1998:6).

Despite these shortcomings, Sweden has served as a role model together with the other Nordic states. Gender equality and women's rights have long been priority issues for Sweden in the international arena. Irrespective of the indicators used to measure gender equality in comparative studies, the Nordic countries always come first in the rank order. When Sweden and Finland joined the EU, it was anticipated that greater attention would be given to gender issues at European level and that new policies would be formulated to promote gender equality (SOU, 1993:117; Regeringens proposition, 1994/95:19, p. 217; Rees, 1998, p. 5). While other states have had to reshape their policies in response to European directives and decisions from the European Court of Justice (ECJ), in Sweden pressure was exerted to bring reconciliation onto the political agenda within the context of equal opportunities well before the topic became an issue for the EU.

Two of the basic pillars in Swedish equality policy have been public childcare and paid parental insurance. Governments support childcare and parental leave in many other countries (see Chapter 3), but Sweden is distinguished by the broad field of application and general thrust of policy and the high level of benefits provided, which are intended to make it easier for both women and men to combine parenthood and gainful employment.

In the past, studies tended to focus either on women's political participation and representation or on the design of welfare policies and their effect on gender equality. Hernes' (1987) work is an example of how women's access to, and influence on, political decision-making and the development of the welfare state can be analyzed fruitfully within the same framework. Central to Hernes' thesis is 'the way in which advanced Nordic welfare states, through their policies, have "pulled" women into the public sphere, and how women then began to "push" developments in accordance with their own interests' (Hernes, 1987, p. 9). Hernes suggests that it was welfare and labour market policy that provided the institutional framework 'pulling' women into the labour market, while also increasing women's opportunities and motivation to act as 'pushers', or political actors.

The problems involved in combining family responsibilities with gainful employment have become major issues for debate in Swedish welfare policy, due mainly to women's political participation and representation. The first part of this chapter analyses the vision of equal parenthood, which became public policy in the 1970s, and asks whether this vision is still alive and being realized. The reforms of paid parental leave and public childcare are taken as examples of policies that increase gender equality. The aim is also to focus on women as political actors and co-designers of policies. The importance of public childcare for women's participation in the labour force has long been recognized, but little has been said about the role of women in formulating policies. Rather, a tacit understanding has developed that men are the policy-makers and women the policy-takers. Studies of the role of actors rather than structures are showing that women's organizations, female actors and politicians have an interest in, and influence over, government attitudes towards reproduction (Bergqvist, 1994; Karvonen and Selle, 1995; Wängnerud, 1998).

In the second part of the chapter, Sweden is situated within the European context. Firstly, the implications of Swedish membership of the EU are examined for equal rights and opportunities. Then, the activities of the Swedish government in the EU are discussed with regard to gender policy. Two simultaneous developments are identified. On the one hand, the Swedish (and Nordic) engagement in the EU has meant that EU gender equality policy and practice have, to a certain extent, come to resemble the Nordic model. On the other, as a consequence of the existing body of legal tools available for promoting gender equality by law in the EU, Swedish legislation on equal opportunities has been levelled up. Consequently, Swedish membership has meant that the Nordic model for promoting gender equality has been diffused to the EU, whereas an adaptation has taken place at the national level with regard to judicial review of gender equality legislation.

EQUAL SHARING OF FAMILY RESPONSIBILITIES

In the Nordic states, the male breadwinner model has gradually developed into a dual-breadwinner, or individual model (Sainsbury, 1996). Birte Siim (1997, p. 140) claims that one of the most significant changes in society since the 1970s has been 'the move from a male-breadwinner to a dual-breadwinner norm, according to which the public and cultural expectation are that both women and men will be wage workers'. The fact that the dual-breadwinner family has developed more rapidly in Sweden than in most other EU member states is no accident; rather, it is the result of deliberate political decisions. Preconditions for this development were the elimination of joint taxation at the beginning of the 1970s, access to public childcare and the possibility for parents to share paid parental leave. In many cases, women in labour market organizations, women's political associations and political parties on the left were the driving force behind the changes. As the Social Democratic Party has been in power for most of the time since 1932, it has had the main responsibility for shaping the Swedish gender and welfare model.

In an article analysing the public/private dichotomy in the late 1980s, Carole Pateman (1989, p. 135) wrote that Western feminists were, for the first time, developing a theory of social practice which includes women and men equally, based on the interrelationship between individual and collective life, or personal and political life, instead of their separation and opposition. At a practical level, this means, according to Pateman (1989), that women and men must share household work and childcare. She insisted that equality within a relationship could only be understood by reference to the organization of working life and the role played by the public sector. The gender policies pursued since the 1960s in Sweden correspond to what Pateman describes as 'feminist practical politics'. When parental insurance was introduced in 1974, it was argued that its aims were to contribute to equality between men and women (Bergqvist 1994, p. 168). The proposal was based on the dual-breadwinner philosophy, whereby both parents are seen as economically independent individuals who have duties and rights in relation to children and to the labour market.

With the introduction of parental insurance, this view of gender relations was institutionalized; through government regulation, the feminist idea was legitimized. Not only mothers but also fathers could and should be responsible for the care of children. This involved a break in a long-established tradition and practice. The historian Ann-

Sofie Ohlander (1989, p. 186) saw this as an extremely important change. She argued that the conflict between reproduction and production is made visible, and is not seen solely as a problem and responsibility for women, but also as a conflict and a responsibility for men (Ohlander, 1989). The law on parental leave meant an important shift away from the idea of the male breadwinner. Although full equality in real life has still not been achieved, the reform opened up new opportunities for more equal parenthood and brought closer the possibility for men and women to combine parental responsibilities and gainful employment. As suggested by Arnlaug Leira (1993, p. 333), parental insurance is important not only because it gives parents practical support, but also 'as evidence of an interesting shift in the conceptualisation of "the worker", such that the demands of social reproduction take priority over those of production'.

The question of sharing in the private sphere is raised in a more explicit way in the case of parental leave than in that of public childcare. Childcare and leave for mothers can be seen as policies making it possible for women to combine motherhood and gainful employment without interfering in the private relationship between the sexes, or changing the role of the father. At a general level, any support for children and women would have some emancipatory effects resulting in greater autonomy, but, if the traditional distribution of work in the home remains unaffected, any changes in the public sphere become more problematic. Shared parental leave can be seen as a way of eradicating the effects that an unequal gender relationship would have for women's and men's chances of advancement at work. If fathers were to take an equal amount of paid parental leave, this could have an impact on the organization of work and the attitude towards gender in the workplace.

Public or private childcare

At the beginning of the 1960s, the party political arena in Sweden was divided between those who wanted to uphold the male breadwinner model and those who wanted public policy to support an individual model with two breadwinners in the family. In practice, the question was whether housewives should be subsidized through a care allowance to look after their own children, or whether dual-breadwinner families should be supported through extended public childcare facilities. The dividing line was also present inside the governing Social Democratic Party and their women's organization, even though the party soon moved to support public childcare.

In 1963, the Conservative (Höger) Party, later to be called the Moderate Party, stated that it was, in principle, 'unacceptable that the natural function of parenthood should be paid for by the state', and voiced its opposition to the proposal for a care allowance (Hinnfors, 1992, p. 99). By the beginning of the 1970s, the party had changed its view and was recommending the introduction of a care allowance in preference to public childcare facilities. At the same time, the Social Democratic Party decided to advocate an extension of public childcare provision. The moderates joined the Centre Party line in supporting the care allowance. The third non-socialist party in parliament, the Liberal Party, made childcare facilities a priority (Hinnfors, 1992). No clear dividing line can, therefore, be distinguished between the socialist and non-socialist blocs. Even though the non-socialist parties supported a care allowance, they did not, in principle, oppose public measures to make it easier for women to combine family responsibilities and gainful employment.

Advocates of the individual model argued that it offered all adults the possibility of supporting themselves financially, forming the basis for individual independence and freedom. They maintained that previous sex roles should be abandoned and replaced by new more equal roles: both women and men should have the same responsibility for care and the same opportunity to combine parenthood with paid work. At the ideological level, radical changes were demanded in attitudes and perceptions of the duties and tasks of each of the sexes. At the political level, radical reforms were called for to make it possible for men and women to lead their lives free from the shackles of traditional sex roles. Such a reform required a massive extension of public childcare to enable women to participate in the labour market. A report in 1969 from a Social Democratic Party/trade union working group (*Jämlikhet*), led by Alva Myrdal, strongly recommended that a 'continued extension of childcare centres on a large scale' was one of the most important reforms needed to achieve equality in the family. The same policies were advocated in the programme produced by the Social Democratic Women's Organization.

The economic activity rate of women with children below seven years of age increased from 32 per cent in 1960 to 50 per cent in 1970 and 60 per cent in 1975 (Hinnfors, 1992, p. 289). Despite the political support for day care, the real expansion of public childcare facilities did not come until the 1970s. In 1966, no childcare provision was available outside the home for 90 per cent of children under seven. In 1979, the figure was still as high as 61 per cent (Hinnfors, 1992, p. 49). Many mothers with small children had, thus, joined the labour market long before any public childcare was available.

Women participated actively in drafting policy documents and in the debates leading to decisions in parliament regarding the extension of public childcare. A number of women were members of public commissions on childcare, representing strong positive views on the need to extend childcare facilities, not only for reasons of equality but also to achieve social and pedagogical ends. At the time, women were already relatively well represented in politics compared to other non-Nordic countries. Between 1965 and 1970, some 20 per cent of the Social Democrats elected to parliament were women. The 1970 cabinet contained two women who supported equal rights and conditions for women and men: Alva Myrdal and Camilla Odhnoff, with the latter responsible for family policy. Even though the equality arguments were important for women's groups, it was the need for women's labour that dominated among male participants in the debate (Hinnfors, 1992, p. 9; Bergqvist, 1994).

In sum, a remarkable degree of consensus can be found in the political debate about the state's economic responsibility for childcare. Even if the non-socialist parties have often questioned certain aspects of childcare policy, they have not as a rule opposed increased public funding. It was not until the late 1980s that the non-socialists, and above all the moderates, began to question any further extension of public childcare (Uddhammar, 1993, pp. 250–1).

From maternity subsidy to parental insurance

With the growing interest in equal opportunities and the heightened debate over the relative merits of childcare services versus care allowances, the question arose as to who should take care of babies and young children. An increasing number of working mothers were able to have their children minded in day-care centres as a result of policies promoting dual-breadwinner families. The question then arose as to whether only mothers should be enabled to stay at home when their children were too small to go to day-care centres. In 1974, maternity insurance was replaced by parental insurance providing six months' cover for the birth of a child or adoption. In the following year, the period was extended to seven months. Parents were left to decide for themselves who should stay home and for how long, and they could share the period between them. The basic principle, which has been retained, is that parental insurance should cover loss of pay and be income related. In addition, a guaranteed basic allowance is paid to those whose health insurance benefit does not exceed the minimum, for example students and homemakers.

Parental insurance reform signalled a new approach to gender relations, expressing and institutionalizing two radically new attitudes to gender relations. First, not only mothers but also fathers should take responsibility for the care of small children. Second, the concept of the male breadwinner was to be abandoned in favour of the dual-breadwinner family.

In line with the Swedish tradition of broad-based public inquiries, involving representatives from political parties, organized interest groups, public administration and specialist advisers, the question of parental leave had been carefully prepared by the Family Policy Committee. When it reported in 1972, the committee claimed that parental insurance was likely to bring about an improvement in the sharing of work in the home and, thereby, improve opportunities for women to strengthen their position in the labour market. It recommended that fathers should be encouraged to share parental leave, but accepted that take-up was more likely to be by mothers. It did not suggest that the sharing of parental insurance benefit should be regulated (SOU, 1972:34).

The minister, Camilla Odhnoff, and all the bodies and organizations to which the report had been sent for comment supported the committee's recommendations. The proposed legislation provides a good illustration of the principles being developed: namely that equality and family policy should be based on the individual model and the idea of gender neutrality. Instead of talking about equality of opportunity, official discourse had shifted to *jämställdhet* (equality) between women and men. By widening the area of public policy and extending the reproductive sphere to comprise both women and men, it was clear that policy-makers were prepared to abandon traditional concepts of differences between the sexes.

Differentiated parental leave

When it was first introduced, parental insurance was unique and radical. In one respect, it was not consistent with the social democratic model of universalism, since it was based on the family as a group rather than on the individual. Parents were expected to bargain over how to share parental leave between them. A completely individual and gender-neutral design would have given parents an independent right to a certain number of months of paid leave, which would not be transferable to the other party. However, policy-makers seem to have been in agreement about the need to preserve parents' rights to decide for themselves how to divide parental leave. It is interesting to note that, in 1973, two women, who were Centre Party members of parliament, were the first to suggest that one parent should not be allowed to take the whole of parental leave. In their view, existing differentials in wages and career prospects would lead to the mother being the one to stay at home, which would run counter to the purpose of the reform. Instead, they proposed 12 months parental leave with neither parent being allowed to use more than eight months, with exceptions only for single parents (Motion 1973:1686, pp. 9–10).

The Family Support Committee was given the task by the Social Democratic government of responding to the problem raised by the women in the Centre Party. It was charged with evaluating the outcome of the new rules and considering whether the benefit period should be extended. At the suggestion of the Social Democratic Women's Organization, the committee was also instructed to investigate whether a longer period of paid leave could be combined with a requirement that part of the period must be used by the child's father. In its report, the commission proposed that the benefit period should be extended from seven to eight months, provided that no parent used more than seven of them (SOU, 1975:62), but the proposal before the government in early 1976 did not take account of the *pappamånad* (father's month). Many of the Social Democratic women members of parliament saw this as an act of treachery as far as gender equality was concerned and, therefore, mounted a coup in parliament.

According to the historian Gunnel Karlsson (1996), the coup served as a unique expression of a revolt by women against the party leadership. Contrary to the existing rules of the Social Democratic parliamentary group, 18 of the 36 Social Democratic women members of parliament tabled a motion in support of a 'father's month', but did so without informing the party leadership. According to Prime Minister Olof Palme, this was the first time that 'a substantial faction in the Social Democratic parliamentary group had ignored a decision by the leadership of the group' (Karlsson, 1996, p. 293). However, the Social Democrats did not have an opportunity to amend the parental insurance act before the 1976 election, after which the non-socialist parties formed the new government for the first time in 44 years. The incoming government did not make major changes to family policy. Instead, they reinforced the policy launched by the Social Democrats. Throughout the whole period of non-socialist coalition governments, up to 1982, no proposals were presented in support of a parental care allowance (Hinnfors, 1992, p. 166).

Improving childcare and equality despite economic recession

During the 1970s and 1980s, improvements were continuously made to public childcare services, and in 1985 a general reform of preschool education was carried out. The expansion of public childcare was not sufficient to meet the demand. The political objective of 1985 was to enable all parents wanting childcare to have a place for their children from the age of 18 months by 1991. After the fallow years of the 1980s, however, the 1990s became the decade of budget cuts and welfare retrenchment. All basic social insurance provisions and benefit levels were reduced, bringing the principles of gender equality under threat and losing sight of the vision of equal parenthood.

Childcare is still not universal, since it is not an equal right for all children in a particular age category. A step was taken in this direction under a new childcare law, which came into effect in January 1995. The principle of the dual-breadwinner family was not abandoned. The question of how to develop childcare and, more generally, how to choose the most appropriate welfare system for implementing it again became a controversial political issue following the resurgence of liberal market policies during the economic crisis and the ensuing spread of mass unemployment. After a period of relatively strong consensus since the 1960s, when the dual-breadwinner model began to be institutionalized, for the first time, in 1994 the non-socialist government introduced a *vårdnadsbidrag* (care allowance), which heralded a shift in the direction of the male-breadwinner model, even if the modern alternative was intended to be gender neutral.

The 1991 elections had brought a non-socialist government to power. Unlike the previous three-party coalitions of the 1970s and early 1980s, the new government included the Christian Democratic Party. The Centre Party found an ally interested in the introduction of a care allowance. The small Liberal Party continued to advocate equality and family policy in line with developments since the 1970s, in a stance similar to that of the Social Democrats. The moderates were successful in the elections, and their party leader, Carl Bildt, became Prime Minister. As a liberal rather than a conservative party, they had not adopted family policy as a central plank during the 1980s, and were prepared to make deals with both the left and the right. The new government did not display a united front, and the elections resulted in a substantial reduction in women's representation in parliament: falling from 38 to 33 per cent (Bergqvist, 1994, pp. 41–3.).

The Centre Party and Christian Democrats were able to gain support for a care allowance from the other parties represented in government. The benefit was introduced in July 1994, on the eve of new elections. The most common argument in favour of a care allowance was that it would increase the freedom of choice for parents to decide how their children should be looked after. Advocates of the allowance tried to dress up their arguments in gender-neutral language, but the underlying principle remained that the sexes occupied separate spheres. The Social Democrats and the former Communists (later referred to as the party of the Left) argued strongly against a care allowance (Regeringens proposition, 1993/94: 147, pp. 105, 108), and the Social Democrats dropped the idea when they returned to power in September the same year.

The father's month

In parallel with the care allowance discussion, another debate was raging, which was more in line with the 'vision of equality and parity'. It focused on the low take-up by fathers of parental insurance benefit. Despite extensive publicity campaigns aimed at making parental leave more attractive for men, the number of days used by fathers remained very low. In 1977, fathers were taking about 2 per cent of the total number of paid days of leave. By 1996, the figure had risen to around 12 per cent. However, the number of fathers who took part of the leave period increased from 7 per cent in 1977 to 30 per cent in 1994. By the late 1990s, 85 per cent of fathers were participating in changing nappies, dressing children, and other child-related tasks, compared to only about 1 per cent in the 1960s (SOU, 1998:6).

By the 1990s, men's rather than women's political organizations were supporting the campaign to encourage fathers to take a greater interest in the care of their children. The so-called 'fathers' group' in the government's equality unit played a critical role. It consisted of seven men, some with political affiliations, others representing areas such as the media. Their report offered a 'vision of the father as both present and available', where children should be made to realize 'that masculinity can also be warmth, care and responsibility', and 'both parents from the very beginning share responsibility and happiness'. They argued that 'a new parental role should be an asset in the labour market and should revolutionize working life', proposing a minimum of three months compulsory paternal leave (Ds, 1995:2).

The government that had introduced the care allowance also suggested compulsory sharing of paid parental leave, through the father's month. The Liberal Party leader, Bengt Westerberg (one of a growing number of well-known men who have taken paid parental leave), was the chief promoter of the policy. The proposal was enacted in January 1995, leaving parents free to decide how many days each parent takes, except for the 30 days earmarked for the individual. The benefit level was reduced from 90 to 80 per cent, apart from the father's/mother's month (Regeringens proposition, 1993/94:147, p. 4).

In sum, the picture of the women's situation at the end of the 1990s is mixed and difficult to grasp. On the one hand, access to political equality and democracy had improved: the marked disparity between women's and men's political participation and representation had disappeared, and the Swedish welfare society had enabled women to achieve a higher level of influence and autonomy. Policy objectives supporting the dual-breadwinner family had not been abandoned, despite the economic crises of the 1980s and 1990s. Attempts by some of the non-socialist parties to introduce changes in this area had not prevented strong support from developing for a publicly financed childcare system, while the debate about men as care-givers continued to be a political issue.

THE EU AND GENDER MOBILIZATION IN SWEDEN

A new momentum for gender equality developed in Sweden during the 1990s, due not only to the growing awareness of gender issues, but also as a consequence of a number of crosscutting domestic and international pressures, perceived as threats to gender equality. At the beginning of the 1990s, concern was being expressed about the impact of further European integration on the progress made by Swedish women. Surveys at the time showed that 40 per cent of female respondents believed that gender equality would suffer as a result of Swedish membership of the EU, whereas 12 per cent thought it would improve. Among male respondents, 34 per cent believed equality would decrease, and 13 per cent that it would improve if Sweden joined the EU (Oskarsson, 1996a, p. 129). Questions were also being raised about the impact that the economic crisis might have on gender equality, with some observers defending the argument that Sweden might be more vulnerable if it did not join than if it did (Jacobsson, 1994, p. 134; Regeringens proposition 1994/95:19, p. 217).

The possible repercussions of membership on Swedish gender equality have been analysed in a number of public inquiries and studies. A common conclusion was that, since member states retain responsibility for establishing how equality directives are implemented nationally, the formulation of equality policies would not be directly affected. It was assumed that the EU would contribute to greater economic growth, which would in turn guarantee the maintenance of the welfare state (SOU, 1993:117, pp. 61–3.). Other commentators feared that Sweden would have to dismantle its welfare structures if integration was pursued further (SOU, 1993:117; 'Europa', 1994). Although Sweden decided not to join Economic and Monetary Union (EMU) in the first phase, the criteria stipulated for joining were thought likely to force governments, even those who remained outside EMU, to make deep cuts in their budgets, with implications for the maintenance of the welfare state and, indirectly, for gender equality. The fear was also that, if wages were determined by external forces, national social partners would have less space for negotiation, and wage differentials between men and women might grow (Ilmakunnas and Julkunen, 1997, p. 24).

Notwithstanding these reservations, in 1991, Sweden applied for EU membership; in 1994, the accession treaty was concluded; and in 1995, Sweden became a full member state. Simultaneously, the country experienced the most severe economic crisis since the 1930s. Unemployment rose dramatically, the budget deficit increased. The value of the currency was strongly defended by the Bank of Sweden, which raised the interest rate to 500 per cent, before being forced to let the Swedish currency float in the autumn of 1992.

In 1991, with the fall in the representation of women in parliament, a number of well-known academic and intellectual women formed a group to mobilize opinion: Stödstrumporna (translated literally as 'support stockings').[1] Their primary aim was to increase the number of women in the Swedish Riksdag: they set out to mould opinion and exert pressure on the political parties by threatening to form a women's party. Their tactics were successful insofar as women's representation increased to an all-time high in the parliamentary elections held in

---

1.   The name Stödstrumporna is also associated with the first and only anarchic feminist in Swedish literature, Pippi Longstocking. This literary figure, created by Astrid Lindgren, is a strong but humane girl who mocks the establishment and chooses to live her life as she pleases.

September 1994, but without a party being formed. In the 1998 elections, women's share of the seats reached 43 per cent. The Stödstrumporna network did not formulate an opinion on the EU, as their strategy was not to take a public stand on issues over which they were themselves divided (Ulmanen, 1998, p. 24).

In the referendum on EU membership in November 1994, the 'yes' vote won with a majority of 52 per cent. Women were, however, in the majority among those opposing membership: 52 per cent voted against, compared to 40 per cent of the men (Oskarsson, 1996b, p. 211). In this respect, Sweden is no different from the other Nordic states, since women generally are more negative towards the EU project than men.[2] Their opposition helps to explain why gender equality has been a priority issue for the Swedish government in European negotiations: governments must demonstrate that the achievements for gender equality in Sweden are not being adversely affected by EU membership.

The economic crisis of the 1990s brought cuts in areas of welfare provision such as unemployment, sick leave and child benefits. However, some of these cuts have been reversed, and no strong evidence can be found to suggest that they affected women more than men, apart from women who are lone parents. Unemployment, in fact, hit men harder than women (Regeringens skrivelse, 1996/97:41, pp. 31–3.). Since a large proportion of women are employed in the public sector, their jobs, though less well paid than in the private sector, have been protected despite restructuring.

The most immediate effect of deeper integration with the EU was that Swedish law had to be amended to bring it into line with EU legislation, as was the case with the Swedish Equal Opportunities Act

---

2. In the Finnish referendum on EU membership, 54 per cent of women and 61 per cent of men voted 'yes'. In Norway, 43 per cent of women and 52 per cent of men voted in favour of EU membership. In Denmark, no gender differences emerged in the first referendum in 1972 but, in subsequent referenda on the amended EU treaties, Danish women were more negative than men (Oskarsson, 1996a, p. 111). It has been suggested that women determined the second Norwegian refusal to join the EU. Two explanations have been put forward for women's voting behaviour: feminist attitudes and their economic position and dependency as employees in the public sector. However, evidence is found that differences between men and women as regards values, religious leanings and ideological preferences determined the Norwegian outcome: women are more leftwing, traditional and periphery oriented (Jenssen and Bratterud, 1997).

(Riksdagens revisorer, 1997/98:4, pp. 67–9; Ahlbäck and Jungar, 1998). Indications can be found that EU membership has exerted pressure to tighten up existing legislation, and provided an incentive for bringing a larger number of gender discrimination cases before the Swedish Arbetsmarknadsdomstolen (Labour Court). As in other Nordic states, Sweden has created a separate agency to ensure the implementation and drafting of important legislation: Finland, Norway and Sweden all have Gender Equality Ombudsmen, whereas the Gender Equality Council performs the same function in Denmark and Iceland (Ryel, 1996, p. 357). Swedish legislation on gender equality, officially called the Act Concerning Equality between Men and Women, adopted in 1980, has been described as a relatively weak legal instrument compared to the legislation available in other democratic welfare states (Hobson, 1997, p. 203).

The Swedish equal opportunities act consists of two parts: prohibitions on discrimination, and regulations on active measures for promoting gender equality in working life. The act is weaker in the first respect than in the second (Singh, 1998, pp. 56–60, 65–6). It was replaced in 1992 and was further amended in 1994, partly as a consequence of European integration. The regulations on wage discrimination were tightened up, the meaning of the concept of equal work was made more precise, and regulations concerning indirect discrimination and sexual harassment were introduced (SOU, 1996:43; Regeringens skrivelse, 1996/97:41, 1997/98:60). In July 1998, a new commission of inquiry was set up by the government to investigate how Swedish equal opportunities law could be further amended. The explicit purpose was to harmonize Swedish legislation on equal opportunities with EU legislation and practice, as expressed in a number of decisions of the ECJ (Kommittédirektiv, 1998:60). Thus, EU membership has brought about much closer scrutiny of the scope of the Swedish act.

Apart from the early phase of politics on gender equality, legislation on equal opportunities in Sweden has generally been considered as complementary to policy-making in the economic and social fields. Legislation has been important, but insufficient, in promoting substantial gender equality (von Redlich, Interview, 19.8.98). The combination of decision-making at member state level with the legal order of the EU has intensified the debate, and resulted in a number of proposals for amending national legislation. Since the changes to the law in the 1990s, the Swedish Equal Opportunities Ombudsman, the JÄMO, has brought two cases of discrimination to the Labour Court. The JÄMO tests the scope of Swedish equal opportunities law where the legislative rules and practices at EU level prescribe different prerequisites for judicial decisions (Berg, Interview, 17.8.98).

The JÄMO won its first case on wage discrimination (Labour Court, 158/95, 20.12.95) for a woman economist employed in local government. Under the new legislation, it could be claimed that she did equal work to two male colleagues who were better paid. However, the second case brought by the JÄMO generated a debate over the match between Swedish and EU legislation (Eklund, 1996, p. 341). The court interpreted the wage difference between a female midwife and two male medical technicians as a case of wage discrimination, even though the work of a midwife requires a longer period of study, and they are paid less than medical technicians (Hobson, 1997, p. 204). The court did not rule that discrimination had occurred, as it could not be proven that the work of the midwife was of equal value to that of the medical technician.

As a consequence of these two cases and subsequent decisions by the ECJ, amendments were proposed to the Swedish act. Firstly, under Swedish law, cases of discrimination can only be brought before the court when the decision relates to employment. Hence, the scope is narrower than in existing EU legislative practice, where discrimination covers the whole process, including recruitment and promotion (Berg, Interview, 17.8.98). Secondly, when cases of discrimination are brought, Swedish law requires that an actual comparison be made between individual situations. With reference to EU directives and decisions by the ECJ, the JÄMO has suggested that the Swedish equal opportunities legislation should be modified so that a hypothetical comparison is sufficient, and an actual comparator is unnecessary to determine discrimination (Kommittédirektiv, 1998:60).[3] Thirdly, according to the JÄMO, Council Directive 97/80/EC on the burden of proof in cases of discrimination on the part of the defendant requires changes in Swedish law. In Sweden, such cases are usually resolved by arbitration. The incorporation of the directive determining that the defendant has to prove that a violation against equal treatment has not been committed means tightening up Swedish legislation.[4] Fourthly, the

---

3. The JÄMO was referring to Council Directive 76/207/EEC and Case C–177/88 E.J.P. Dekker v Stichting Vormingscentrum voor Jong Volwassenen (VJV-Centrum) Plus [1990].

4. Sweden and Finland provided a written statement in which they expressed the view that that the agreement should have made clear that the prosecutor does not need to prove that the defendant had

damages awarded in cases of discrimination have had to be amended as a consequence of EU membership. Where discrimination was alleged against several individuals, under Swedish law, damages were not previously determined individually. A number of cases before the ECJ have resulted in individuals receiving damages.[5] Fifthly, the concept of indirect discrimination has had to be more clearly defined to bring it into line with EU practice. When the proposal for an equal opportunities act was being discussed in 1991, prohibition on indirect discrimination was included, but the concept was not defined in the text of the law, and was not considered necessary by the Law Council. The legislative changes made since Sweden joined the EU suggest that its legal tradition of producing detailed preparatory texts, but short laws, is being altered, with the effect that Swedish laws will in future become more detailed (Riksdagens revisorer, 1997/98:4).

The conclusion can be drawn that the impact of EU legislation on national legal practice in Sweden has been to require adaptation and levelling up of the existing Swedish equal opportunities act. Whether this will, ultimately, result in a larger number of judicial reviews in cases of discrimination remains an open question. Such an outcome appears to run counter to the expectation that the EU would force Sweden to downgrade its gender policies and equal opportunities legislation.

EQUALITY AND SUBSIDIARITY

Sweden sees itself as a fervent ambassador for gender equality, which has advanced much further in Sweden than in most other EU member states. While admitting that a lot remains to be done, Commissioner Anita Gradin has claimed that the situation in the Commission resembled that in Sweden in the 1960s. Only her own stubbornness made the Commission set up a group on gender equality (*Svenska Dagbladet*, 11.8.98). Since joining the EU, Sweden has pushed hard to promote commitment to gender issues. The period of membership of

---

discriminatory aims to determine whether discrimination has taken place.
5. Case C–177/88 E.J.P. Dekker v Stichting Vormingscentrum voor Jong Volwassenen (VJV-Centrum) Plus [1990]; Case C–271/91 M.H. Marshall v Southampton and South West Hampshire Area Health Authority [1993], and Case C-180/95 Nils Draehmpaehl v Urania Immobilienservice OHG [1997].

Finland and Sweden has seen gender equality take a leap forward in the EU. At the Essen Summit in 1994 (European Council, 1994), although Sweden was still only an observer, its proposal that equality should, for the first time, be included in the final document issued by the summit was taken up (Ministry of Labour, 1997b). Mainstreaming, which was already one of Sweden's main goals at the United Nations World Conference on Women, in Beijing in 1995, was included in the Treaty of Amsterdam.

The newcomers brought a welcome impetus to policy-making on gender equality in the EU. Despite the pressure exerted on the EU by a large number of women's groups and by the European Parliament to make it more proactive regarding gender equality, the outcome had, hitherto, been rather modest (Hoskyns, 1996; Rees, 1998). The deadlock within the Council of Ministers came to an end with the enlargement of the EU and the entry of a number of gender equality-friendly member states. Swedish accession (and that of the other newcomers) thus fulfilled expectations, and the Swedish government considered their actions within this policy field to have been successful (Regeringens skrivelse, 1996/97:41). Most of the proposals the Swedish government made during the intergovernmental negotiations over the Treaty of Amsterdam were accepted. The Irish presidency, and in particular some of the smaller countries such as Austria and Finland, were supportive of the Swedish initiatives (EU-nämnden, 1995/96:11; CONF 3898/96, 1996; Svensson, 1999).

Since Sweden joined the EU, Swedish government representatives have visited a number of member states to explain Swedish gender equality policy. The Deputy Director of the Equality Affairs Division in the Ministry of Labour, Charlotte von Redlich (Interview, 19.8.98), who has considerable experience of political work on gender equality in the Swedish government, has pointed out that much effort went into explaining the Swedish model. She claims that, initially, it was difficult to get people to understand the difference between equality of opportunity for women and gender equality, and to rally support for gender equality with regard to the rights of men. The difference in outlook was reflected in the fact that some member states had ministers for equal opportunities for women and others for gender equality.

However, some commentators maintain that Sweden has not gone far enough, in particular those who hoped that the EU would serve as a springboard for promoting gender equality in member states where law and practice are weak. Sweden has, in the event, been reluctant to support reforms that would mean that rights are 'built in' at the EU level, rather than at national level, because it is unwilling to transfer competence to supranational institutions. In the case of gender equality, the explicit fear has been that Sweden may have to level down because of binding regulations at EU level (SOU, 1996:43, p. 87; von Redlich, Interview, 19.8.98). Sweden is seeking to avoid measures for which the consequences – social, economic and legal – are not predictable, and prefers to frame measures on gender equality in terms of programmes (EU-nämnden, 1995/96:11, 1995/96:642). For instance, a proposal was made during the 1996/97 Intergovernmental Conference to strengthen the non-discrimination article in the Treaty by giving the ECJ the right to supervise the observance of the principle (CONF 2500/96, pp. 15–16). However, Sweden was reluctant to approve the amendment, as it would have increased the competence of the ECJ. Following on from the Kalanke Case (C–450/93 Eckhard Kalanke v Freie Hansestadt Bremen [1995]), Sweden wanted to ensure that the right to use positive action, as practised for example in universities, should be included in the final document. With the support of Austria, the Swedish government succeeded in ensuring that a form of words was used which allowed for positive action, although it was not so precise as they would have wished (Ministry of Labour, 1997a).

Apart from the priority given to national interest and self-determination, rather than strengthening the legal instruments for implementing gender equality in Europe, the behaviour of the Swedish government in the EU can also be explained with reference to the Nordic model for promoting gender equality. The Swedish government does not consider formal rules concerning non-discrimination and equal opportunities as sufficient to achieve real change in gender equality. Although legislation and other measures for promoting gender equality are not mutually exclusive, a conflict arises over where the emphasis should be placed. According to Charlotte von Redlich (Interview, 19.8.98), who negotiated on behalf of the Swedish government during the Intergovernmental Conference, legislation on equal opportunities was important in the 1960s in Sweden, but a different approach is needed in the late 1990s. The EU seems to be moving in the same direction, suggesting some diffusion of Nordic instruments for promoting gender equality may be taking place at EU level; women's political representation, mainstreaming and positive action are the most obvious examples. The policies held to be most important for gender equality in Sweden could not easily be implemented across the EU. In the late 1990s, the Swedish government considered EU policy on employment and social policy to be of greatest importance in improving gender equality (Regeringskansliet, 1998). Sweden suggested that individual taxation should be used to enhance gender equality. However, since competence in the economic and social spheres lies at member state level, it is difficult to see how the main Swedish instruments for promoting gender equality in the short term can be promoted at EU level. The extent to which the Nordic model can influence policy-making in the EU depends on both the political will of individual member states and the way the EU develops in the future. Pressure is growing at EU level for more proactive social legislation, and EMU may provide a further push in the same direction, creating the conditions necessary for a social model closer to that practised in Sweden. Simultaneously, adaptation is taking place in Sweden: gender equality is being pursued through more intensified legislative activity. Swedish membership of the EU has had an effect on gender policy-making both at the national and the EU-level. In the late 1990s, adaptation and diffusion were proceeding in parallel in Sweden.

Interviews

Lise Berg, Assistant Equal Opportunities Ombudsman, 17 August 1998.
Charlotte von Redlich, Deputy Director, Equality Affairs Division, Ministry of Labour, 19 August 1998.

10 Taking Stock and Looking Ahead

Monica Threlfall

This chapter focuses on specific issues arising out of the reconciliation strategy adopted by the European Union (EU), drawing on the contributions in this volume to take stock and assess the political outlook for equality politics. The first section appraises the EU's equality work, arguing that, despite the distorting effect on women's policy of the EU's mandate, European institutions have overcome their limitations to a remarkable extent. It analyses reconciliation as a policy instrument, particularly in relation to its implications for fathers and its link to the question of citizenship and difference. The second section complements the country and policy-based models of reconciliation for women, developed in the present volume and in previous research, by proposing a set of models for reconciliation of paid work and family life within individual households for both sexes. The last section of the chapter looks beyond the EU, arguing that the next stage for action is primarily the domestic arena, and drawing attention to the notable extent to which gender policies are adopted as by-products of other goals or motivations of policy actors. In conclusion, it is suggested that the imperative of gender equality has moved beyond law-making to enter other terrains of action.

THE EU EQUALITY POLITICS PROCESS

One of the recurring themes in this book has been the way that policy on gender evolves and is transformed. The material presented shows that the process is non-linear and occurs at several levels simultaneously. While blatant pay discrimination for identical work has been almost completely eliminated, the battle for equal earnings per hour worked has continued unabated, since vertical and horizontal segregation persists, and what is labelled as women's work remains undervalued. Similarly, the goal of equal treatment continues to be elusive. Gender policies have expanded to tackle a host of different barriers to women's equal opportunities, from childcare to parental leave, harassment at work, and the reversal of the burden of proof of discrimination from employees to employers. Thus, the political dynamics of gender policy suggest development on several fronts, each policy advancing at a different pace, while remaining complementary to, though not dependent on, the others. This multispeed movement of gendered policies becomes more complex if the multinational dimension is introduced, as the case studies in this volume illustrate.

Another theme relates to the way in which some gendered policies have been prioritized because they fall more easily within the EU's remit and acquire a specific status within that institutional order by becoming either laws, which have to be implemented, or soft laws, which rely mainly on the political arena for their development, as in the case of childcare or sexual harassment at work. Other policies may not become part of the EU's political action plan at all, as happened with reproductive rights or the right to protection from domestic violence.

The process of European integration has, thereby, had a distorting effect on the agenda of the women's movement. Opinion on whether this is to be regretted or accepted depends on the feminist perspective from which the observation is made. Equal opportunities *per se* for women and men, and even less equal life chances, were not an explicit part of the original European project. Equal pay was only included in the Treaty of Rome because members states such as France were committed to the principle, having signed up to the International Labour Organization's Convention no. 100, and because it affected competition between member states through the use of cheaper female labour. The process could have stopped there, and indeed no steps to develop the equal pay rule were taken for over a decade. Even in the 1970s, as Catherine Hoskyns (1996) has shown, the measures adopted were not the result of a concerted attempt on the part of the founders of the European Economic Community (EEC) to implement the sex equality principle in the common market. Instead, Article 119 was invoked after industrial action by Belgian women and professional work by lawyers such as Eliane Vogel-Polsky. As for social policy, the integration project excluded joint decision-making on social security and welfare provision since they affected state budgets, expenditure commitments and revenue raising, seen as key areas of statehood, over which the member states wanted to remain sovereign.

It was only through the fledgling common market's concern with intracommunity competition that the EEC had an interest in working conditions and labour relations, to which the Commission was able to respond by developing the harmonization functions allowed in the Treaty of Rome. Such a context gave equality work an inescapably employment-centred focus and accounts for many of the limitations of the EU's social policies and equality agenda in its early decades (Hantrais, 1995). Arguably, it encouraged distortion insofar as the choice of policies to be pursued was virtually determined by whether they could be justified on the basis of the treaties and fitted into the specified competencies of the Commission, rather than being chosen according to an understanding of a theory of women's oppression, or a feminist strategy for liberation.

An awareness of this continuous underlying distorting effect of the institutional and legal framework is crucial for an appreciation of the development of EU equality policy. While feminist criticism of the limitations of EU action (Hoskyns, 1985; Ostner and Lewis, 1995; Elman, 1998) may be correct from a feminist perspective, in reality these limitations reflect, primarily, the parameters of allowable action at European level. Most importantly, equality policy has also been circumscribed by the unwillingness of interstate bargaining fora, such as the Council of Ministers and European Council, to allow the Commission further prerogatives in the field, as Maria Stratigaki claims in this book. Therefore, domestic feminist advocates have been forced to recognize, somewhat belatedly, that it was their own governments who were to blame for the slow pace of equality reform and the timidity of its agenda. This was greatly facilitated in the United Kingdom by the Thatcher government's reputation for, at best, indifference and, at worst, hostility to gender issues, which allowed the Commission and the EU generally to be perceived as an ally of national-level feminism.

Nevertheless, what emerges from this volume is the remarkable extent to which the EU has overcome its own limitations. Both Chapters 1 and 2 show just how far EU equality work has progressed from its initial basis. The European Parliament has played a particular role in raising issues considered beyond the pale, such as domestic violence. EU policy in the late 1990s, directed at its own institutions and at member state government action, aimed to tackle the socially constructed inequalities at work and in the home. In this sense, EU policy is no longer seeking merely to create a framework within which women can start to compete with men on an equal footing, only to find themselves losing out in the race for, say, higher pay, with the consequence that unequal outcomes are perpetuated. In addition and mainly through its support for the condition of parenthood, the EU is addressing the obstacles that women continue to face along the way.

It would be wrong to conclude that the European institutions have provided the main levers for gender policy advancement. The case studies show that, in countries such as France, Germany and Sweden, national measures addressing the issue of how women are to combine earning a living with parenthood had been adopted before they moved onto the European agenda. The adoption of directives has not required these states to develop new domestic legislation, nor to adapt to the laws' effects on the domestic actors targeted, be they women, men or employers. In this sense, some of the EU initiatives would seem to have had little novel impact. The role of the Commission as policy initiator should not, therefore, be overestimated. On the contrary, its role has been, essentially, to diffuse policy from one member state to another, using its regulatory power to act as a kind of equalizer, as illustrated by the way in which social policies have been extended to Southern member states such as Spain (Threlfall, 1997).

For these reasons, the feminist critique needs to develop a new approach. There is no longer a strong basis for criticizing the Commission, whatever its failings as a bureaucracy. Despite not having greater competencies, the Commission has used its prerogatives creatively, engaging with issues far beyond its ambit and working at the interstices between policies. The finer points of the debate may focus on how far it can take the credit and how far its action has been the result of pressures from feminists outside EU institutions. Even if a strong case can be made for the latter, it must be recognized that the Commission has often been at least as responsive as member state governments, if not more so.

While the Commission should not be used as a scapegoat for failings which may be largely domestic, it would be equally misguided for gender policy advocates to look to the Commission for leadership regarding the next steps to take. The long running struggle to implement the 1989 social action programme came to an end with the adoption of the directive on the burden of proof in December 1997. To get this far, the Commission had to resort to the new social partners procedure, because of the variety of objections raised by the Council of Ministers to its proposals. To circumvent these difficulties, the social partners became a new law-generating instance, which constitutes a particularly significant shift, since, through the social partners agreement, the Commission was able to get the very proposals adopted that had been blocked at the Council of Ministers by British conservative governments on the grounds that the impact on industry would be too costly. Ironically, the agents who were alleged to be most against the social measures – representatives of British industry – participated in negotiations through the Union of Industrial and Employers' Confederations of Europe (UNICE) and its committees, which approved the measures on parental leave and equal treatment for part-time workers. At first sight, the new social partners route, first devised by Directorate General V, under Commissioner Vasso Papandreou, appeared to have strengthened the Commission's regulatory hand. A closer look at the measures adopted also shows that the cost of getting them approved has been, arguably, a substantial weakening of their content and provisions.

The delayed final adoption of the burden of proof decision and the other main measures of the 1989 social action programme also signalled the end of a certain type of European protagonism in the equality field, deemed too dirigiste by its detractors. Though it may be argued that soft law measures and small-scale reinforcement of the existing regulatory framework can be just as useful as its expansion, the political reality is that the climate surrounding the development of EU social policy and gender policy in the late 1990s was timid and lacking in inspiration. For nearly a decade, the member states had been reluctant to give the Commission a green light to be bold once more (Venturini, 1997). British prime ministers inflicted a major blow in refusing to endorse the principles of the Community Charter of the Fundamental Social Rights of Workers and the Agreement on Social Policy. Just as the Commission was showing that it understood the feminist agenda better, it lost its ability to lead or to be bold, with the result that EU equality policies were deemed, in the late 1990s, to be at a 'critical juncture' (Mazey, 1998, p. 148).

THE POLICY INSTRUMENTS OF RECONCILIATION POLITICS

While the legal route to gender equality continued to be pursued over the years by the EC in the face of the obstacles described in the previous section, a new strategy was developed in the 1980s to further effective equality under the general goal of 'reconciling paid work and family life for both sexes'. This deceptively mild-sounding phrase expresses in a nutshell the ultimate aim of gender equality advocates. The phrase contains an egalitarian and gender-neutral formulation, as well as an emotive call to put aside conflicting aspirations and bring about a 'reconciliation', thus effectively using the language of human relationships. Feminist aspirations are articulated in a *faux-naïf* way so that men could, in theory at least, assume them as their own, and even, if they felt so inclined, adopt them simply as they stand.

The reconciliation of paid work and family responsibilities was introduced into European parlance when it appeared in the 1974 Council Resolution on a social action programme, but the formula was not widely used by the Commission until the 1980s. Prior to the appearance of 'sharing family responsibilities', a far vaguer term had been present in the demands of the women's movement for some time, without gaining agenda status. Sharing family responsibilities does not clearly imply making employment and care work compatible. Nor does it suggest that a structural incompatibility exists between paid employment and care work such as childrearing. By the 1990s, the new formulation of women's strategic goal had come fully into its own and had passed into the discourse of equality both in EU and non-specialist circles, ceasing to be merely Eurospeak.

The reconciliation of paid work and family life for women and men can be seen as far more than a mere policy instrument to further existing EU employment-centred legislation and efforts to aid labour market equality through positive actions. As a project, it merits some analysis on its own, since its formulation raises the crucial issue of care. As Tamara Hervey and Jo Shaw (1998, p. 50) put it, the work/care divide is an 'inescapable subtext or backdrop to the vexed issue of sex equality in the labour market'. Increasingly, feminists have argued that the central wellspring of inequality is no longer women's difficulties in earning their living, but mothers' difficulties in doing so, stressing the pervasive and lasting inequality produced by the inherent demands of parenthood for women.

When a woman becomes a parent, her paid working life is usually disrupted. The incompatibility is manifest mainly, but not solely, in the time constraints which, in many countries, prevent women from continuing in paid work and, thereby, entail a loss of income and economic independence. Parenthood leads to a new dependency of one parent on the other, whether it be a mutual dependency between equals who share care work and paid work, or a new dependency resulting from the more traditional recourse to one parent sharing his (possibly her) earnings via a monetary household allowance with the other parent, in exchange for which she (rarely he) runs the household and performs the childcare work.

This traditional strategy for managing earning a living and performing care work is institutionalized in the social protection system, but even terms such as 'family breadwinner' and 'providing for mother and child' cast a warm glow over a gender contract that can, less sentimentally, be viewed as a form of subcontracting of women to do the necessary care work in exchange only for maintenance. As María Angeles Durán (1994, p. 24) has aptly put it, 'unpaid work is trapped in a system of special, unwritten, inexplicit rules, poorly defined in family law, not openly agreed and frequently in contradiction with the general principles of paid work'. As a result, she argues, unpaid workers lack many of the social and political rights of other workers. Therefore, the reconciliation formulation opens up the debate on the fundamental issue of the gendering of the division of labour.

Furthermore, the formulation has its own subtext, since parenthood for men has traditionally been compatible with working life, so much so that male parents not only continued to work but, if anything, had a new incentive, and even justification, for increasing the time spent at work under the guise of being a better provider. The subtext here is that parenthood for men was 'compatible' with family life, not because they had it in their gift to stretch time and live a 36-hour day, but because their working time precluded them from having any time for care, and effectively freed them from most caring tasks. In the early 1990s, only 8.6 per cent of men in the 12 EC member states felt that having children is an obstacle to the working life of a man, compared to 55.9 per cent of women who saw it as an obstacle for their own sex (Malpas and Lambert, 1993, table 4.10). By having their family life reduced to the time span of evenings and weekends (amounting at most to about half their waking hours), male parents could negotiate which fragments of care work they would perform. The traditional compatibility of working and family life for fathers was, in this sense, a figment of time, a trick of the clock. Yet, fathers' *de facto* incompatibility between their work time and family time was to a large extent a satisfactory arrangement for them. As studies of men's leisure and time budgets show, paradoxically the male paid working week still allowed more time for leisure than the female week of unpaid caring work (for example Horrel, 1994).

This raises the problematic issue of the implications for men of reconciliation policy. It is not explicitly recognized at EU level that the reconciliation of paid work and family life is, ultimately, a proposal for men to spend less time at work and more time raising children, looking after sick relatives and performing household chores, as Maria Stratigaki concludes in Chapter 2. Neither is it an articulated demand of the men's movement, which has only demanded more access to, and time with, children for divorced fathers without custody; in other words, for fathers who, by virtue of their legal status, are performing only a fraction of their share of parenting work. For this reason, it is not surprising that some analysts view reconciliation policy as a threat. As Maria Stratigaki warns, if it is not targeted specifically at men, reconciliation ceases even to be an equality policy in the strict sense. If such policies are not targeted at fathers, they end up simply being policies to help women find easier ways of shouldering the double burden of combining employment with parenting, while allowing fathers to continue as before. The country case studies in this volume illustrate this pitfall insofar as only a minute proportion of fathers replace mothers in taking up the parental leave entitlement. Even when it is non-transferable and granted to each parent in turn, as in the case of the Swedish father's month, take-up has risen only from 7 per cent to over 30 per cent over two decades (see Chapter 9), showing that most fathers prefer not to take over the homemaker role. Where public childcare provision is generous, as also in Sweden, the introduction of a care allowance, enabling parents to stay at home with children, was perceived as a threat to the status of mothers in the labour market, and was quickly abolished by the Social Democrat Party.

Reconciliation of paid work and family life lends itself to more than one interpretation. A reading common in Commission circles, as Maria Stratigaki points out, is that reconciliation has implications for the reorganization of working time. In the 1980s, British officials were interested in the work of the Equal Opportunities Unit in the Commission because they perceived that reconciliation policies were linked with the flexibilization of the labour market, which the Conservative government of the day was promoting, and which neo-liberal economic thinking was demanding. Firms in many EU member states could, thereby, reduce the proportion of single-breadwinner jobs offering a 'family' wage, and increase their offer of part-time jobs, from which, by definition, an employee is incapable of earning enough to live on as an independent person. If the part-time worker were a parent, however, the job would allow reconciliation between paid work and family life.

Many combinations of hours and forms of work are possible, and they are, increasingly, promoted by specialist advocacy organizations, such as Parents at Work in the United Kingdom. All have extensive implications for the flexibilization of working hours and are spearheaded by parents. They include before-school/after-school hours work; term-time working; fractional appointments; short days/long days; night/day shifts; intensive/extensive weeks; annualized hours, jobsharing; and phased return from maternity leave (Daniels, 1996).

RECONCILIATION, CITIZENSHIP AND POWER

In the context of the debate about women's citizenship in the EU, reconciliation of paid work and family life is a deceptively simple formulation, since it can also be interpreted as a tactical instrument in the
grander, more stirring debate about citizenship. As demonstrated by the
chapters in this volume, until the concept of the reconciliation came to
be applied to both sexes, the norm addressed by the EU in its social
policy was that of 'man the worker' (Saraceno, 1997). Equality legislation was grounded in what feminist shorthand refers to as the 'deficit'
approach to equality (Cameron, 1992), implying that, if women found
it difficult to hold their own in the labour market and workplace, the
answer was to legislate to prevent discrimination and enable them to
make up the deficit by joining the ranks of 'man the worker'. The male
standard continued to be accepted as the universal norm. The feminist
critique of the EU clearly identified the shortcomings of the deficit
approach, arguing that the Commission's evaluation of progress in
Europe rested too heavily on a quantitative measure of women's labour
market participation, without paying due attention to issues of segregation, pay or equality outside the labour market (Duncan 1996).

     The debate about citizenship opened the door to broader considera-
tions of equity, such as whether authentic democracy is possible if
women are not included in the decision-making process on a par with
men, as demanded in the call for *démocratie paritaire*. In this context,
it can be asked whether reconciliation policy addresses the 'question of
gender-asymmetrical power relations both within the family and within
national and European decision-making bodies' (Saraceno 1997, p.
264). As shown in this volume, the goal of reconciliation in the EU
context already surpasses any merely quantitative approach to equality
in the labour market, yet still remains grounded in the issue of how
women are to earn their living. It is not, fundamentally, a debate about
public power, even though earning an independent living increases the
power of individuals. Still, reconciliation touches the realm of power
relations in the way it provides an (albeit bland) expression of what
Ruth Lister (1997, p.168) defines as the heart of social citizenship,
namely 'earning and caring'. Her full discussion of how to posit a
model of 'citizen the worker-carer' ties in with key elements of EU-
based reconciliation politics. In a European context, the citizenship
question brings us back to the point about the limitations of any EU-led
attempt to move towards a social citizenship for women. This limitation is the weak purchase which the EU has on questions of social

security. Apart from some social security effects of policies on equal treatment and the minimum subsistence guarantee, the member states are unwilling to agree measures requiring significant adjustment of welfare systems, which would arise from women's social citizenship.

Reconciliation of paid and unpaid work for both sexes also raises and confronts the notion of 'equality of difference', as expressed in Chapters 4 and 6. If reconciliation for women is achieved by paying women for what they already do, then difference is maintained. At the same time, the income gap is narrowed, particularly for mothers if their ability to earn their living is increased by measures such as paid parental leave. They become more equal but remain different. Reconciliation policy also confronts the question of equality in/of difference because, if mothers are paid for childrearing, a fusion of 'family life' and paid work is produced. If care work at home is paid, it becomes 'work' not 'family life'. The boundaries of the euphemistic meaning of family life (as not-work) implode, and the hitherto gendered meaning of family life for each sex collapses. When care work is paid, the carer's family life becomes coterminous with that of the traditional male provider. Other components of family life – affective relations, rest and leisure – can then come to the fore and alter its meaning.

The paragraph added to Article 119 (transformed into 141 by the Treaty of Amsterdam) refers to 'ensuring full equality in practice between men and women in working life', and even permits positive action. If applied to reconciliation measures, it should allow the Commission to adopt innovative action to reconcile paid work and family life, on the understanding that parenthood discriminates against women, even though reconciliation is formulated as gender-neutral. Nevertheless, analysts such as Tamara Hervey and Jo Shaw (1998) believe the Treaty of Amsterdam does not recognize structural discrimination against women achieving equality in employment, which arises out of the gendered roles regarding reproductive work. The Treaty does not incorporate a specific reference to 'care' nor to 'care-giving', which would, they argue, have 'made the gendered division of care a primary reference point for the interpretation of what "equality" means' (Hervey and Shaw, 1998, p. 60).

RECONCILIATION MODELS FOR BOTH SEXES

Chapter 3 defined six different concepts of reconciliation policy. The following models present the outcomes of such policies for parents.

They are based on the household division of labour between partners and the 'pay' versus 'time' deficit, which prevent access to paid work and family life and need to be overcome if both sexes are to earn a living and raise children. In the models, summarized in Figure 10.1, employment is taken to mean earnings from work paid for by a third (non-household) party. Care work is understood, primarily, as looking after children or other dependants, although it may include housework or homemaking. Reconciliation for women is understood as occurring partially, or fully, either when a woman with full care responsibilities is able to earn an income from care work within the household; or when a woman with care responsibilities is able to share them so as to engage in employment outside the household. Family life is used as a euphemism for care of others rather than as care for oneself or looking after the material conditions of the household. The models are based on the premise that a full-time worker does not have a full family life: male breadwinners have not reconciled paid work and care. For men family life in this context is taken to mean performing care work in the household, and reconciliation is taken to occur if, for instance, a male parent spends sufficient time to discharge half of the parenting requirements. The models (developing Threlfall, 1995) are drawn up from a user's rather than a policy-driven perspective. Nevertheless, some similarities emerge with respect to Simon Duncan's (1995, 1996) work. As hypothetical models, they are not prima facie based on any particular national experience nor, in the case of the second model, on existing legal arrangements.

Model 1: Public provision of wages for motherwork and care

Several EU member states have introduced or have contemplated introducing a mothers' wage for women who are homemakers. In 1955, France extended the single-earner allowance to self-employed workers in agriculture in the form of an allowance for mothers at home. The two allowances were, subsequently, absorbed into the *complément familial* (family supplement) in 1977. In the 1980s, the French *production domestique* debate shifted attention to the contribution made by households to the economy (see Chapter 4). In the United Kingdom, one of the oldest campaigns to make visible and to obtain recognition of the work that homemakers do is the Wages for Housework campaign, which began in 1972, at the time when a strand of feminism was demanding to participate freely in the labour market. They were making the radical claim that women should be paid out of

Figure 10.1	Models of full or partial reconciliation between paid work and family life for both sexes	
Model 1	Public provision of wages for motherwork and care 1 full-time employee + 1 income for parenting/care work	• payment from the state for parent/carer (societal responsibility for parenting and care needs of children and older people) • 'pay' reconciliation for parent/carer • no 'time' reconciliation for breadwinner
Model 2	The privately contracted homemaker-partner 1 full-time employee + 1 income for parenting, care and housework	• payment from the breadwinner-spouse • registered as work for tax and social insurance • public recognition for parenting and care • 'pay' reconciliation for parent/carer • no 'time' reconciliation for breadwinner
Model 3	The principal earner + secondary earner 1 full-time employee + 1 part-employee and part-parent/carer	• 1 'breadwinner' wage/salary • part-time wage + maintenance by spouse • 'pay' and 'time' reconciliation for part-timer • no 'time' reconciliation for breadwinner
Model 4	Two breadwinners 2 full-time employees + 2 'spare-time' parents/carers	• 2 breadwinner wages/salaries • privately funded child or elder care • 'pay' reconciliation for both • no 'time' reconciliation for either
Model 5	The double half-carer, half-provider 2 part-employees + part-carers	• 2 non-breadwinner wages/salaries • publicly funded childcare and/or • private care arrangements • 'pay' and 'time' reconciliation for both

public funds for the unpaid work they already do, rather than take on new types of labour, which would merely, it was argued, lead them to work a double day. The original proposal contains some points of relevance to the present discussion, not least because it served as a forerunner to the demand for reconciliation policy. The idea is not so radical as it might sound. Firstly, in addition to the example already mentioned of France, several EU member states have introduce a form of 'wages for motherwork' to allow lone parents not to have to seek employment and, instead, to live on benefit in recognition of their role as parents. Secondly, income tax systems which allow tax relief for dependants, such as a full-time spouse and children, and are particularly generous in France for family members, and in Germany for married couples, represent a financial compensation for single-earner households with full-time homemakers, and can be seen as an embryonic indirect wage for care work. Thirdly, married women carers of sick or disabled dependants receive, directly or indirectly, a variety of benefit payments from the public purse (Glendinning and McLaughlin, 1993; Millar and Warman, 1996).

To achieve full reconciliation of paid and unpaid work for women, the wages for housework concept would require the extension of existing forms of public support to all dependants engaged in care work, transforming their unpaid work into paid public work. Ironically, any proposal to extend to all full-time homemakers a state 'wage' is now perceived as utopian and consigns the proposer to the fringes of the radical feminist left, to such an extent that the Wages for Housework campaign no longer features the issue – nor even the question of wages for lone parents – in their publicity material. In the 1980s, it joined with the wider international campaign to get governments to take account of all forms of women's non-market work, as pioneered by Marilyn Waring (1989), as well as their forcibly submerged work in the sex trade, in all national statistics (Wages for Housework, 1995).

Model 2: The privately contracted homemaker-partner

A second way of reconciling paid work and family life on the basis of the work that women have done traditionally, the privately contracted homemaker spouse/partner model, is a variant of the first model. It also builds on the claim that women should be paid for the work they already do, rather than for measures to enable them to take on new types of (paid) work. This model, which is partly hypothetical, involves modernizing aspects of the legal framework of marriage, relating to mutual dependence and the obligation to succour, so that full-time homemakers/carers and breadwinner spouses benefit from being able to hold a contract resembling that of employee and employer. They become entitled to a regular sum of money fixed by agreement, replacing the traditional wife's housekeeping and pocket money with a professionalized homemaker's expenses and wages. The employer-spouse has to declare the employee-spouse or partner for tax purposes and contribute the social insurance due.

Although in certain ways this model represents a radical departure, some of the existing practices recognize the status of spouse as akin to that of employee, albeit only implicitly. They include dependants' tax allowances and the recognition of spouses who do work as employees of their husbands/wives in a business. Another example is the legal consideration given to caring for the home and children as a mainte-nance contribution to the household (rather than a marital duty) on an equal footing with providing maintenance in cash. This affects the calculation of assets in a marriage as, for example, in the German Equal Rights Act of 1957. A further example is the legal practice of recognizing care work as a woman's maintenance contribution to the costs of bringing up a child in calculating alimony payments after divorce (see Chapter 5). Some of these practices imply that the equivalent of a series of transfer payments has taken place from the wage-earner spouse to the homemaker-spouse, enabling the home-maker to put in the hours of care work and, *de facto*, earn a living.

Even though the feminist movement of the 1970s denounced marriage as something akin to a prison with forced labour, no out-standing movements appear to be demanding the formalization of marriage as an employment contract. Instead, younger couples are avoiding or postponing marriage, and women have resorted to earning their own money in the labour market.

Model 3: The principal earner + secondary earner

The third model could also be referred to as the 'one-and-a-half bread-winners' model, but is applicable to households where the principal earner may not have sufficient earning power to maintain the whole household without another income. Part-time employment for the principal carer becomes a mode of reconciliation, both in terms of pay and time. The form it takes varies according to the age of dependent children and degree of care needs of any other dependants, in some cases entailing the use of group, individual or family childcare. It may,

therefore, also require input from publicly financed sources. Employment for the main carer will be dependent on the flexibility of hours
and patterns of work being offered. In practice, in countries where part-
time working is widespread, as in Denmark, the Netherlands, Sweden
and the United Kingdom, governments have tended to look favourably
on the arrangement, though part-time workers may be vulnerable if the
flexibility afforded works primarily to the advantage of the employer,
despite equal treatment legislation. The main deficiency of this model
is that it does not allow time reconciliation for the principal earner,
who remains responsible for earning the bulk of the household income.

Model 4: Two breadwinners

The fourth model refers to the arrangements whereby both parents
work full-time. Because they are kept away from parenting for the
greater part of the day, extensive childcare services are needed. The
difficult question regarding this model is whether reconciliation is fully
achieved when a mother is able to stay in full-time work despite having
children, while the father also continues with full employment. Pay
reconciliation clearly occurs for both parents, but the time demands
made by children or other dependants are largely dealt with by others.
Family obligations are subcontracted out, thereby expanding the
service sector, but reinforcing job segregation in domestic services,
since the new jobs are performed essentially by women. However,
women's policy advocates in France and Spain look favourably on this
model as providing one of the more satisfactory forms of reconciliation
available, if sufficient help is given with childcare services and costs.

Whether the model can offer genuine time reconciliation for family
life is doubtful. If time reconciliation does not occur for male breadwinners, then it cannot do so for women either. Unless a case is made
for parenting to be shared more widely, the model will heighten anxie-
ties about the 'parenting deficit' (Wilkinson, 1997, p. 11). Analysis of
the role played by grandparents, as practised in Spain and advocated by
the British Labour government in the late 1990s, indicates that a
broader view of parenting can be taken, involving more than just two
birth parents, and relieving them of sole responsibility for parenting.

Model 5: The double half-carer, half-provider

The 'ideal' model of reconciled family life and paid work is one where
both parents share employment and care work, as proposed in the

Commission documents. Both engage in part-time work during a different span of hours over the day, so as to allow one parent at all times to be free to attend to the children. This model gains credits on the time dimension of reconciliation, but is far more risky on the income dimension, given the low pay of most part-time work. It also benefits those who are able to work at home. Furthermore, where households have got used to an income of more than one full-time worker, the loss in earnings is considerable (Joshi *et al.*, 1996). The development of the model depends on the spread of part-time and flexible working hours, job-sharing and other arrangements. It is premised on the willingness of fathers to reduce their hours of work and accept the consequent earnings and probable status losses. A good indicator of the model's take-up would be the number of males with dependent children working reduced hours out of choice. Here, the available data, reported in the contributions to this volume and by Jeanne Fagnani (1996, p. 136), suggest that the model is not at all widely adopted.

Issues raised by the models

New policies adopted in EU member states have skirted, permissively, around these first two models without confronting them. In some states (mainly Germany and the United Kingdom), care work and paid employment are sometimes put on a par and recognized by the state for social security entitlements. Enlightened employers may encourage female applicants to include periods out of the labour force spent on childcare as part of their career progression, during which useful experience, such as management skills, continue to be developed, rather than as a yawning gap in a person's human development. Governments may decide to make up the social security contributions lost by periods spent in childcare, so that a mother's record of labour force activity can remain unbroken despite time out. Public authorities may pay a compensatory income as a state benefit during childcare work. Nevertheless, none of these steps has yet tackled the fundamental problem head on of how to reward adequately the carers who do the socially necessary, yet unpaid, work in society.

The flaws in the 'paying women for what they already do' approach to the wider question of reconciling paid work and family life for both sexes are also evident. The approach institutionalizes the traditional division of labour between care work for women and labour market work for men, instead of beginning to erode it. Reconciliation for men does not occur in this model, particularly not in the private payment variant, as it implies full-time dedication to earning a sufficient income to pay for an employee over and above the bare family wage.

Secondly, if reconciliation occurs in a way that maintains the traditional division of labour, it will probably be at the cost of one sex moving from being non-paid to being merely low-paid. Care work and parenting subsidized from the public purse will most likely remain low paid, and so would private arrangements. They would, thus, constitute a limited advancement regarding women's autonomy.

Yet, the private solution of the contracted homemaker/partner model, as practised among middle to high-income couples, can provide a solution to the low-pay trap. It may also improve the homemaker's access to marital or household money and control over financial assets, especially after divorce. Countries where, upon divorce, non-earning wives are entitled to 50 per cent of all assets of the marriage implicitly recognize the homemaker spouse as being entitled to a form of 'back pay' for work performed. The payment has been 'saved up' by the employer-spouse who, until divorce, had only paid out the expenses (maintenance) part of the costs of having someone run the home and family, and is now faced with paying the real cost.

Models 1 and 2, nonetheless, offer an institutionalization of parenting and care work, which represents a step forward for many women who cannot find opportunities in the labour market, or who are able to earn only low wages. In these cases, the low pay of privately or publicly funded income for parenting or care, and associated entitlements, may be higher and more secure than the income from even lower paid labour market employment.

The question of 'paying fathers to do what they hardly did before' also needs to be considered. In cases where the mother earns more than the father or he opts to stay at home, the two models are again applicable. The male stay-at-home parents or carers are likely to be reluctant to fall into the traditional situation of complete dependence on a spouse/partner, in which the value of their care work is not counted at all, and would be even more likely than women are to seek to have their time out of the labour market recognized and remunerated as fully as possible.

Considering the models as a whole, it could be said that Models 3 and 4 are the most familiar because they are not only about reconciliation but also about the commonly expressed aspiration of women, whether mothers or not, to earn an income. Over 50 per cent of mothers with children between the ages of two and seven were economically active in all EU member states except Luxembourg in 1995 (Eurostat personal communication). Yet, if reconciliation is understood in its deeper sense of reconciling employment and care responsibilities, in terms of both pay and time, the deficiencies in Models 3 and 4 are more striking than at first sight, since time-for-care shortages remain for all principal earners and breadwinners, and pay shortages remain for most part-timers. While the question of 'paying women for what they actually do' in Models 1 and 2 appears at first sight more radical, it has certainly been gaining ground and has been implemented in a number of ways in different member states. Parental leave has been the most controversial, but by no means the only, element. Not surprisingly, the most equitable model, number 5, is also the least developed. Although the employment rates of mothers with young children have been growing steadily in most member states, mothers tend to work full-time not part-time: 60 per cent on average were working full-time in the 12 EC member states in the early 1990s, though much larger proportions of women were working part-time in the Netherlands and the United Kingdom. The proportion of fathers working part-time was very low everywhere: between 1 and 3 per cent (European Commission Network on Childcare and Other Measures to Reconcile Employment and Family Responsibilities, 1996, table 3). Until the nature of part-time work changes and all employed parents are able to work reduced and flexible hours at acceptable rates of pay without penalties or loss of status, the numbers of parents choosing to combine care with employment equitably is likely to remain very small.

While useful, models inevitably leave much out. In particular, it has not been possible to address issues of eldercare or the whole range of care requirements within the confines of this chapter. Attention to society's full range of care needs would result in a wider and possibly quite different range of models of reconciliation.

LOOKING BEYOND THE EU

The last section of this chapter considers the general outlook for women's policy advocates. A strong case can be made for believing that the future development of gendered policies will require domestic policy advocates to confront anew the task of persuading national policy actors to take action to keep up the momentum on equality policy. This is crucial, even if, as Kirsten Scheiwe suggests for Germany in Chapter 5, political consensus is lacking about the direction that equal opportunities should take. Highlighting the domestic arena is not to give credence to the view that EU instruments, especially those adopted under qualified majority voting, are measures brought in by the back door and less legitimate than if they had been fully debated in a national parliament. Recourse to the EU when gender policies fail to advance at national level is an advantage which may give rise to lucky breaks for policy advancement, but is likely to remain an instrument of last resort, needed in countries where women's policy advocates are weak or marginalized (Mazey, 1998, p. 148).

Elsewhere, the domestic arena offers opportunities. For instance, one of the striking elements present in the accounts in this volume is the extent to which steps taken towards reconciliation for women are often the almost unintended by-product of other policies or, at least, are primarily motivated by other goals, which may even be regarded as traditional and patriarchal. They may have various motives: promoting workplace rights in general, managing employer and human resources, reducing men's hours of work, creating jobs, strengthening families, and political bargaining.

The rights-based culture in the workplace helps to boost women's earnings via the minimum wage and in-service training. In France, policy-makers were, for example, able to accept that, for women to have equal rights at work, they had to have support for family responsibilities, such as childcare. Both in France and the United Kingdom, managers rather than unions have taken initiatives for equal opportunities by investing in human resources to improve management and maximize the use of available skills. Traditionalists in Germany and pronatalists in France, uneasy about women's employment, have agreed to support motherhood and pay for parental leave, under the guise of 'preserving women's freedom of choice', and are suspected of trying to persuade them to choose to stay home rather than return to work. In Germany, the decision to introduce the Long-Term Care Allowance was part of a 'grand coalition' between the Christian Democrat-Liberal government and the Social Democrats in the Bundestag, to avoid a Bundesrat veto because the *Länder* would have to shoulder the bulk of the costs. In Spain on the other hand, though the government led by the Partido Socialista Obrero Español (PSOE) was convinced by feminists of the need to extend the abortion law, it failed to make the necessary parliamentary bargain to get it through, showing how insufficient mere conviction can be. In Spain and France, measures to reduce working hours to 35 per week would, in practice, allow more workers to spend 'more time with the family', though governments and trade unions are not advocating the reduction primarily for this reason. Policy-makers anticipate that, when mothers become employed, they are bound to hire other women to do the care work, so that, for each better paid job taken, a second lower paid one is created. Governments therefore agree to support the process with some state aid, such as allowances for childminding and eldercare.

This is not to argue that women's policy advocates cannot take the credit for policy achievements. Both Maria Stratigaki in Chapter 2, and Christina Bergqvist and Ann-Cathrine Jungar in Chapter 9 show it is crucial for feminists to be present and influential on the political stage. It is important to realize, however, that the priorities and interests of other actors can be usefully harnessed to gender goals. This should allow gender policy advocates to operate in wider policy communities and think strategically on a grander scale. This process is likely to be reinforced as the practice of mainstreaming spreads.

The domestic arena is the key for addressing the concern of autonomous domestic policy actors and women's policy advocates that societal outcomes do not reflect the legal framework of equal opportunities and treatment, as many of the chapters in this volume have shown. Equal sharing of tasks in the home and desegregation of labour markets continue to be distant goals in France, despite the fact that the French government was one of the first to establish gender policies. The Italian law on positive action urged employers to act with the aid of voluntary measures to eliminate discrimination in the workplace, but was mostly ignored, or was used to the disadvantage of women. The chapter on the United Kingdom shows that laws can be circumvented in a number of ways, even in a civic culture that prides itself on being law-abiding. Indeed, all laws are subject to perverse interpretations (Delphy, 1996).

The problem of creating equity between the sexes remains alive much further down the policy implementation chain than the mere adoption at state level of the necessary laws. Consequently, the call must remain simply to step up law enforcement. But even the best efforts of policy enforcers may not result in equity for, as Sonia Mazey (1998, p. 148) points out, 'though gendered public policy analysis is no longer stuck in a ghetto, it is far from being routine practice among national (or European) policy-makers'. Beyond legislation, it is the stage of national policy enforcement, diffusion and embedding which is now the weak link for gendered policies. This stage is mostly beyond the reach of the EU: it does not police outcomes of its own laws. Nevertheless, its work in publicizing best practice comparative data on outcomes can be useful for 'naming and shaming', a practice that reinforces the advocates' arguments and moral standing.

In the domestic battle to embed equality and reconcile paid work and family life, two key areas for action stand out: the role of employers and that of fathers. The difficulties with employers are a recurrent theme in the national case study chapters and would seem to require fresh inputs of persuasive energy, such as the encouraging cost-benefit analysis of parental leave carried out by Demos (Wilkinson, 1997). Persuading fathers of the value of reconciliation policies comes up against the difficulty of 'selling' the prospect of spending more time with their children or caring for disabled or frail relatives. EU ministers for women and equality, meeting in May 1998, set themselves the task of 'finding out why men don't want to know' (Freely, 1998), while Adrienne Burgess and Sandy Ruxton (1997) argue they too face considerable obstacles.

As the contributions to this volume indicate, the difficulties of making policy effective on the ground are a pending challenge, fundamentally at national level. They are likely to engage women's policy advocates and activists in each country in different mixes of strategies, increasingly focused on law enforcement rather than law-making, on winning the human resources and economic case with employers, and on gaining allies among men who recognize the rewards that parenting brings. Such transformations in the gendered routine of living might be expected to lead to more positive outcomes for gender equality.

Bibliography

Afsa, C. (1996) 'L'activité féminine à l'épreuve de l'allocation parentale d'éducation', *Recherches et prévisions*, no. 46, pp. 1–8.

Ahlbäck, S. and Jungar, A-C. (1998) 'EUs återverkningar på nordisk demokrati', paper presented at De statsvetenskapliga institutionernas nätverk för Europaforskning, 25 August.

Alber, J. (1992) 'Social and economic policies for older people in Germany', Brussels: European Commission, V/5098/93-EN.

Alber, J. (1995) 'A framework for the comparative study of social services', *Journal of European Social Policy*, vol. 5 no. 2, pp. 131–49.

Alberdi, I., Flaquer, L. and Iglesias, J. (1994) *Parejas y matrimonios: actitudes, comportamientos y experiencias*, Madrid: Ministerio de Asuntos Sociales.

Altieri, G. (1994) 'L'occupazione femminile', in M. Paci (ed.), *Le dimensioni della disuguaglianza*, Bologna: Il Mulino, pp. 110–18.

Ascoli, U. (ed.) (1984) *Welfare State all'italiana*, Bari: Laterza.

Bäcker, G. (1991) 'Pflegebedürfigkeit und Pflegenotstand – Dimensionen eines sozialen und familiären Problems und Ansatzpunkte zur Absicherung des Pflegerisikos', *WSI-Mitteilungen*, vol. 44, pp. 88–103.

Bäcker, G., Bispinck, R., Hofemann, K. and Naegele, G. (1989) *Sozialpolitik und soziale Lage in der BRD*, vol. 2, *Gesundheit, Familie, Alter, Soziale Dienste*, Köln: Bund Verlag.

Bagilhole, B. (1997) *Equal Opportunities and Social Policy: issues of gender, race and disability*, London: Addison Wesley Longman.

Ballestrero, M.V. (1990) 'Esperienze giuridiche in materia di azioni positive: il diritto comunitario', *Pari e dispari*, Annuario no. 2, Milano: Angeli, pp. 9–16.

Ballestrero, M.V. (1995) 'Dopo la 125/9: valutazioni, esperienze e prospettive', in AA.VV., *Le azioni positive*, Milano: Angeli, pp. 76–93.

Beccalli, B. (1985) 'Le politiche del lavoro femminile: donne, sindacati e Stato tra il 1974 e il 1984', *Stato e mercato*, no. 15, pp. 423–60.

Beccalli, B. (1993) 'Tra parità e differenza', *Pari e dispari*, Annuario no. 4, Milano: Angeli, pp. 64–76.

Benz, A. (1995) *Verfassungspolitik im kooperativen Bundesstaat*, in K. Bentele, B. Reissert and R. Schettkat (eds), *Die Reformfähigkeit von Industriegesellschaften. Fritz W. Scharpf Festschrift zu seinem 60. Geburtstag*, Frankfurt a.M.: Campus Verlag, pp. 145–64.

Bergqvist, C. (1994) *Mäns makt och kvinnors intressen*, Stockholm: Almqvist and Wiksell.

Bergqvist, C. (1995) 'The declining corporatist state and the political gender dimension', in L. Karvonen and P. Selle (eds), *Women in Nordic Politics. Closing the gap*, Aldershot: Dartmouth, pp. 205–28.

Bieback, K. J. (1997) *Die mittelbare Diskriminierung wegen des Geschlechts. Ihre Grundlagen im Recht der EU und ihre Auswirkungen auf das Sozialrecht der Mitgliedstaaten*, Baden-Baden: Nomos.

Bonichot, J-C. (1988) 'Observation sur le jugement du 30 juin 1988', *Revue française de droit administratif*, November–December, pp. 976–85.

Bouillaguet-Bernard, P., Boisard, P. and Letablier, M-T. (1986) 'Le partage du travail: une politique asexuée?', *Nouvelles questions féministes*, no. 14/15, pp. 31–52.

Bradshaw, J., Kennedy, S., Kilkey, M., Hutton, S., Corden, A., Eardley, T., Holmes, H. and Neale, J. (1996) *Policy and the Employment of Lone Parents in 20 Countries. The EU report*, Brussels/University of York: European Commission/Social Policy Research Unit.

Braithwaite, M. and Byrne, C. (1994) *Women in Decision-making in Trade Unions. A study of the literature and a survey of the ETUC and its affiliated national confederations and European Industry Committees*, Brussels: ETUC.

Bundesministerium für Familie, Senioren, Frauen und Jugend (ed.) (1998) *Übersicht über die gesetzlichen Maßnahmen in den EU-Ländern bei der Erziehung von Kleinkindern*, Schriftenreihe Band 158, Stuttgart/Berlin/Köln: W. Kohlhammer.

Burgess, A. and Ruxton, S. (1997) *Men and their Children*, London: Institute of Public Policy Research.

Byrne, P. and Lovenduski, J. (1978) 'Sex equality and the law in Britain', *British Journal of Law and Society*, vol. 5, pp. 148–65.

Caesar-Wolf, B. and Eidmann, D. (1987) 'Equality for women in the regulation of the economic effects of divorce: legal concepts and family court proceedings in the FRG', *International Journal of Sociology of Law*, vol. 15, pp. 1–27.

Cameron, D. (1992) *Feminism and Linguistic Theory*, 2nd edn, London: Macmillan.

Caporoso, J.A. (1996) 'The European Union and forms of state: Westphalian regulatory or post-modern?', *Journal of Common Market Studies*, vol. 34 no. 1, pp. 29–52.

Carrasco, C., Alabart, A., Mayordomo, M. and Montagut, M. (1997) *Mujeres, trabajos y políticas sociales: una aproximación al caso español*, Madrid: Instituto de la Mujer.

Clasen, J. and Freeman, R. (eds) (1994) *Social Policy in Germany*, London:

Harvester and Wheatsheaf.

Cobb, R.W. and Elder, C. (1972) *Participation in American Politics: the dynamics of agenda-building*, Boston: Allyn and Bacon.

Cockburn, C. (1995) 'Strategies for gender democracy: women and the European social dialogue', *Social Europe,* Supplement, 4/95.

Colberg-Schrader, H. (1991) 'Kinderbetreuung. Ein Land, zwei Traditionen', *DJI-Bulletin,* no. 17, Munich: Deutsches Jugendinstitut.

Combette, J-M. (1976) 'Vers une nouvelle condition de la femme au travail', *Droit social,* no. 1, pp. 23–41.

Commission of the European Communities (1982) 'A new Community action programme on the promotion of equal opportunities for women', *Bulletin of the European Communities*, Supplement, 1/81.

Commission of the European Communities (1986) 'Equal opportunities for women. Medium-term Community programme', *Bulletin of the European Communities*, Supplement, 3/86.

Commission of the European Communities (1995) *European Union: Selected Instruments Taken from the Treaties*, book I vol. I, Luxembourg: Office for Official Publications of the European Communities.

CONF 2500/96 (1996) 'The European Union today and tomorrow. Adapting the European Union for the benefit of its peoples and preparing it for the future. A general outline for a draft revision of the Treaties', Conference of the Representatives of the Governments of the Member-States, Dublin II.

CONF 3898/96 (1996) 'Equality between women and men. Proposals for Treaty amendments', Conference of the Representatives of the Governments of the Member-States.

Conroy Jackson, P. (1993) 'Managing the mothers: the case of Ireland', in J. Lewis (ed.), *Women and Social Policies in Europe: work, family and the state*, Aldershot: Edward Elgar, pp. 72–91.

Cousins, C. (1994) 'A comparison of the labour market position of women in Spain and the UK with reference to the "flexible" labour debate', *Work, Employment and Society*, vol. 8 no. 1, pp. 45–67.

Cram, L. (1997) *Policy-making in the European Union: conceptual lenses and the integration process*, London/New York: Routledge.

Crawley, C. and Slowey, J. (1995) *Women and Europe, 1985–1995*, Birmingham: MEP Office.

Daniels, L. (1996) Parents at work, briefing to the Fawcett Society's Annual General Meeting.

De la Fuente, D. and Crespán, J. (1995) 'La problemática de la aplicación del principio de igualdad en el ámbito laboral', paper presented at the Jornadas sobre legislación y jurisprudencia en el marco de la igualdad de oportunidades de las mujeres, Madrid, Instituto de la Mujer, 13–15 December.

Delphy, C. (1996) 'The European Union and the future of feminism', in R.A. Elman (ed.), *Sexual Politics and the EU*, Oxford: Berghahn Books, pp. 147–58.

Del Re, A. (1993) 'Vers l'Europe: politiques sociales, femmes et État en Italie entre production et reproduction', in A. Gautier and J. Heinen (eds), *Le sexe des politiques sociales*, Paris: Côté-femmes éditions, pp. 37–57.

Department of Education and Employment (1997) *Sex Discrimination: a guide to the Sex Discrimination Act 1975*, London: Department of Education and Employment.

Department of Education and Employment (1998) *Green Paper. Meeting the Childcare Challenge*, CM3959, London: Stationery Office.

Department of Social Security (1997) 'Unemployment and access to work', *Welfare Reform Focus File*, no. 3, London: Stationery Office.

Devaud, M. and Lévy, M. (1980) 'Le travail des femmes en France: protection ou égalité?', *Revue internationale du travail,* vol. 119 no. 6, pp. 797–812.

Dolado, J.J. and Bentolila, S. (1992) 'Who are the insiders? Wage setting in Spanish manufacturing firms', *Documento de trabajo*, no. 92–29, Madrid: Banco de España.

Donaggio, F. (1994) 'La comunità europea e le discriminazioni di sesso', *Pari e dispari,* Annuario no. 4, Milano: Angeli, pp. 86–91.

Ds (1995:2) Pappagruppens slutrapport. Arbetsgruppen (S 1993:C) om papporna, barnen och arbetslivet, Stockholm: Ministry of Social Affairs.

Duncan, S. (1995) 'Theorizing European gender systems', *Journal of European Social Policy*, vol. 5 no. 4, pp. 263–84.

Duncan S. (1996) 'The diverse worlds of European patriarchy', in M.D. García-Ramon and J. Monk (eds), *Women of the European Union: the politics of work and family life*, London/New York: Routledge, pp. 74–110.

Durán, M.A. (1994) 'The international comparison of gross domestic products: a time and gender approach', paper presented at the Seminar on Time and Gender, European University Institute, Florence, 17 November.

Durán, M.A. and Gallego, M.T. (1986) 'The women's movement in Spain and the new Spanish democracy', in D. Dahlerup (ed.), *The New Women's Movement: feminism and political power in Europe and the USA*, London: Sage, pp. 200–16.

Eklund, R. (1996) 'The Swedish case – the promised land of sex equality', in T. Hervey and D. O'Keeffe (eds), *Sex Equality Law in the European Union*, Chicester: Wiley, pp. 337–56.

Elman, R.A. (1998) 'The EU and virtual equality', in P.H. Laurent and M.

Maresceau (eds), *The State of the European Union*, vol. 4, *Deepening and Widening*, Boulder/London: Lynne Riener Publishers, pp. 225–39.

Employment Department Group (1995) 'Equality pays. How equal opportunities can benefit your business. A guide for small employers', London: Department of Employment Group.

Equal Opportunities Commission (1990) 'Equal pay for men and women: strengthening the acts', Manchester: Equal Opportunities Commission.

Equal Opportunities Commission (1996) 'Facts about women and men in Great Britain', Manchester: Equal Opportunities Commission.

Escario, P., Alberdi, I. and Berlín, B. (1987) 'Actitudes de los varones ante el cambio familiar: informe de investigación', unpublished report, Madrid: Instituto de la Mujer.

Escario, P., Alberdi, I. and López-Accotto, A.I. (1996) *Lo personal es político: el movimiento feminista en la transición*, Madrid: Instituto de la Mujer.

Esping-Andersen, G. (1990) *The Three Worlds of Welfare Capitalism*, Cambridge: Polity.

EU-nämnden (1995/96:11) 'Stenografiska anteckningar vid EU-nämndens överläggningar rörande referingskonferensen 1996', EU Advisory Board at the Swedish Riksdag.

EU-nämnden (1995/96:642) 'Underlag för IGC-förhandlingar den 3–4 september', EU Advisory Board at the Swedish Riksdag.

Eurobarometer (1996) 'Public opinion in the European Community', *Eurobarometer*, no. 44.3.

'Europa' (1994) *Kvinnovetenskaplig Tidskrift*, no. 2.

European Commission (1994a) *A White paper – European social policy. A way forward for the Union*, COM(94) 333, 27 July 1994, Luxembourg: Office for Official Publications of the European Communities.

European Commission (1994b) *Growth, Competitiveness, and Employment: the challenges and ways forward into the 21st century (White Paper)*, Luxembourg: Office for Official Publications of the European Communities.

European Commission (1995) 'Equal opportunities for women and men. Follow-up to the White Paper on Growth, Competitiveness and Employment', Report to the European Commission's Employment Task Force (Directorate-General V), Brussels: European Commission, V/5538/95-EN.

European Commission (1996) 'Living and working in the information society: people first. Green Paper', COM(96) 389 final, 24 July 1996.

European Commission (1997a) *Equal Opportunities for Men and Women in the European Union: annual report 1996*, Luxembourg: Office for Official Publications of the European Communities.

European Commission (1997b) 'Partnership for a new organisation of work. Green Paper', COM(97) 128 final, 16 April 1997.

European Commission (1998a) *Equal Opportunities for Women and Men in the Europe Union: annual report 1997*, Luxembourg: Office for Official Publications of the European Communities.

European Commission (1998b) *Social Protection in Europe 1997*, Luxembourg: Office for Official Publications of the European Communities.

European Commission (1998c) *The 1998 Employment Guidelines. Council Resolution of 15 December 1997 on the 1998 employment guidelines*, Luxembourg: Office for Official Publications of the European Communities.

European Commission Network on Childcare and Other Measures to Reconcile Employment and Family Responsibilities (1994) 'Leave arrangements for workers with children: a review of leave arrangements in the Member States of the European Union and Austria, Finland, Norway and Sweden', Brussels: European Commission Directorate General V Equal Opportunities Unit, V/773/94-EN.

European Commission Network on Childcare and Other Measures to Reconcile Employment and Family Responsibilities (1996) 'A Review of Services for Young Children in the European Union, 1990–1995', Brussels: European Commission Directorate General V Equal Opportunities Unit.

European Council (1994) 'Essen European Council, Conclusions of the Presidency', *Bulletin of the European Union*, 12–1994, pp. 7–27.

European Council (1997) 'Luxembourg European Council, Conclusions of the Presidency', *Bulletin of the European Union*, 12–1997, pp. 8–20.

European Parliament (1994) 'Committee on Women's Rights. Review of the 1989–1994 Parliamentary Term', PE Doc 208.782.

European Parliament (1996) 'Report on implementation of equal opportunities for men and women in the civil service', PE Doc A4-0283/96 (rapporteur: Jessica Larive).

European Parliament (1997) 'Report on the Communication from the Commission – Incorporating equal opportunities for women and men into all Community policies and activities – "mainstreaming"', PE Doc A4-0251/97 (rapporteur: Angela Kokkola).

European Women's Lobby (1996) 'Position on the Communication from the Commission on incorporating equal opportunities for women and men into all Community policies and activities', July.

European Women's Lobby (1997) 'EWL lobbying strategies', *EWL Newsletter*, April–May, pp. 9–15.

Eurostat (1997a) *Demographic Statistics 1995*, Luxembourg: Office for Official Publications of the European Communities.

Eurostat (1997b) 'Family responsibilities – how are they shared in

European households?', *Statistics in Focus. Population and social conditions*, no. 5.

Eurostat (1997c) *Labour Force Survey 1995*, Luxembourg: Office for Official Publications of the European Communities.

Eurostat (1998a) 'Labour Force Survey. Principal results 1997', *Statistics in Focus. Population and social conditions*, no. 5.

Eurostat (1998b) *Social Protection Expenditure and Receipts 1980–1995*, Luxembourg: Office for Official Publications of the European Communities..

Fagnani, J. (1996) 'Family policies and working mothers: a comparison of France and West Germany', in M.D. García-Ramon and J. Monk (eds), *Women of the European Union: the politics of work and family life*, London/New York: Routledge, pp. 126–37.

Fagnani, J. (1998a) 'Lacunes, contradictions et incohérences des mesures de conciliation famille/travail: bref bilan critique', *Droit social*, no. 6, pp. 596–602.

Fagnani, J. (1998b) 'Recent changes in family policy in France: political trade-offs and economic constraints', in E. Drew, R. Emerek and E. Mahon (eds), *Women, Work and the Family in Europe*, London/New York: Routledge, pp. 58–65.

Finch, J. and Groves, D. (1983) *Labour and Love: women, work and caring*, London: Routledge.

Forbes, I. (1996) 'The privatisation of sex equality policy', in J. Lovenduski and P. Norris (eds), *Women in Politics*, Oxford: Oxford University Press, pp. 145–62.

Freely, M. (1998) 'Getting the boys on board', *Guardian*, 12 May, section 2, p. 4.

Gallego, M.T. (1983) *Mujer, Falange y franquismo*, Madrid: Taurus.

García-Ramon, M.D. and Monk, J. (eds) (1996) *Women of the European Union: the politics of work and daily life*, London/New York: Routledge.

Gardiner, F. (ed.) (1997) *Sex Equality Policy in Western Europe*, London/New York: Routledge.

Garhammer, M. (1997) 'Familiale und gesellschaftliche Arbeitsteilung – ein europäischer Vergleich', in Staatsinstitut für Familienforschung an der Universität Bamberg (ed.), *Zeitschrift für Familienforschung*, vol. 9 no. 1, Bamberg: Eigendruck, pp. 28–70.

Giammarinaro, M.G. (1997) 'Luoghi e sistemi istituzionali per il progresso delle donne', in Regione Autonoma Friuli-Venezia Guilia. Commissione pari opportunità (ed.), *Atti del Convegno: le politiche per le donne nelle nuove regioni italiane*, Trieste: Regione Friuli-Venezia Giulia, pp. 49–59.

Glendinning, C. and McLaughlin, E. (1993) *Paying for Care: lessons from*

Europe, Social Security Advisory Committee Research Paper 5, London: HMSO.

Götting, U. (1992) 'Die Politik der Kindererziehungszeiten. Eine Fallstudie', *ZeS-Working Paper no.* 2, Bremen: University of Bremen, Zentrum für Sozialpolitik.

Götting, U., Haug, K. and Hinrichs, K. (1994) 'The long road to Long-Term Care Insurance in Germany', *Journal of Public Policy*, vol. 14 no. 3, pp. 285–309.

Grandin, C., Maruani, M. and Meynaud, H. (1989) *L'inégalité profession-nelle dans les entreprises publiques à statut réglementaire*, Paris: doc GIP Mutations industrielles, no. 34.

Gregory, J. (1987) *Sex, Race and the Law*, London: Sage.

Gregory, J. (1989) *Trial by Ordeal: a study of people who lost equal pay and sex discrimination cases in the industrial tribunals during 1995 and 1996*, London: HMSO.

Groupe de recherche sur l'activité des femmes (1989) *Les plans d'égalité professionnelle, étude bilan, 1983–1988*, Paris: La Documentation française (Collection Droits des femmes).

Guerder, P. (1995) 'La poursuite et la répression pénales des discrimina-tions en droit du travail', *Droit social*, no. 5, pp. 447–53.

Guillén, A.M. (1997) 'Regímenes de bienestar y roles familiares: un análisis del caso español', *Papers: Revista de sociología*, no. 53, pp. 45–63.

Hantrais, L. (1995) *Social Policy in the European Union*, London: Macmillan.

Hantrais, L. and Letablier, M-T. (1996) *Families and Family Policies in Europe*, Harlow/New York: Addison Wesley Longman.

Haut conseil de la population et de la famille (1987) *Vie professionnelle et vie familiale, de nouveaux équilibres à construire*, Paris: La Documen-tation française.

Hernes, H.M. (1987) *Welfare State and Woman Power: essays in state feminism*, Oslo: Norwegian University Press.

Hervey, T. and Shaw, J. (1998) 'Women's work and care: women's dual role and double burden in EC sex equality law', *Journal of European Social Policy*, vol. 8 no. 1, pp. 43–63.

Hinnfors, J. (1992) *Familjepolitik. Samhällsförändringar och partistrate-gier 1960–1990*, Stockholm: Almqvist and Wiksell International.

HM Treasury (1997a) *UK Membership of the Single Currency: an assess-ment of the five economic tests*, October, London: Stationery Office.

HM Treasury (1997b) *United Kingdom Employment Action Plan*, October, London: Stationery Office.

HM Treasury (1998a) *Financial Statement and Budget Report*, March, London: Stationery Office.

HM Treasury (1998b) 'The Working Families Tax Credit and work incentives', *The Modernisation of Britain's Tax and Benefit System (Budget 98)*, no. 3, London: Stationery Office.

Hobson, B. (1997) 'Kön och missgynnnade. Svensk jämställdhetspolitik speglad i EG-domstolens policy', in SOU, 1997:115, *Ljusnande framtid eller ett långt farväl? Den svenska välfärdsstaten i jämförande belysning*. Rapport till Utredningen om fördelningen av ekonomisk makt och ekonomiska resurser mellan kvinnor och män, Stockholm: Ministry of Labour, pp. 174–218.

Holmes, L. (1997) *Post-Communism*, Durham: Duke University Press.

Holtmaat, R. (1992) *Met zorg een recht? Een analyse van het politiek-juridisch vertoog over bijstandsrecht*, Zwolle: Tjeenk Willink.

Home Office (1998) 'Supporting families: a consultation document', London: Home Office.

Horrell, S. (1994) 'Household time allocation and women's labour force participation', in M. Anderson, F. Bechhofer and J. Gershuny (eds), *The Social and Political Economy of the Household*, Oxford: Oxford University Press, pp. 198–224.

Hoskyns, C. (1985) 'Women's equality and the European Community', *Feminist Review*, no. 20, pp. 71–88.

Hoskyns, C. (1988) 'Give us equal pay and we'll open our own doors', in M. Buckley and M. Anderson (eds), *Women, Equality and Europe*, London: Macmillan, pp. 33–55.

Hoskyns, C. (1996) *Integrating Gender: women, law and politics in the European Union*, London/New York: Verso.

Hubert, A. (1998) *L'Europe et les femmes: identités en mouvement*, Rennes: L'Apogée.

Ilmakunnas, S. (1997) 'Public policy and childcare choice', in I. Persson and C. Jonung (ed.), *Economics of the Family and Family Policies*, London/New York: Routledge, pp. 178–93.

Ilmakunnas, S. and Julkunen, R. (1997) 'Euroopan talous – ja rahaliitto-sukupuolten tasa-arvon näkokulma', *Valtioneuvoston kanslian julkaisusarja 1997/14*, pp. 1–33.

Instituto Nacional de Estadística (1995) *Encuesta de salarios en la industria y los servicios: resultados correspondientes al cuarto trimestre y media mensual de 1994*, Madrid: Instituto Nacional de Estadística.

Instituto Nacional de Estadística (1997) *Movimiento natural de la población 1995*, tomo 1, *Resultados a nivel nacional y su distribución por provincias y capitales*, Madrid: Instituto Nacional de Estadística.

Instituto Nacional de Estadística (1998) *Encuesta de población activa: resultados detallados, primer trimestre 1998*, Madrid: Instituto Nacional de Estadística.

ISTAT (1997) *Rapporto sull'Italia*, Bologna: il Mulino.

Jacobsen, H. and Brittan, D. (1989) 'Equal opportunities in the 1990s. Elements for a draft third Community programme on equal opportunities', working paper, Brussels: Directorate General V, Equal Opportunities Unit.

Jacobsson, R. (1994) *Kvinnokraft i Europa*, Stockholm: Tidens förlag.

Jamieson, A. (1991) 'Community care for older people', in G. Room (ed.), *Towards a European Welfare State?*, Bristol: SAUS, pp. 107–26.

Jenson, J. and Sineau, M. (1995) *Mitterrand et les Françaises, un rendez-vous manqué*, Paris: Presses de la Fondation nationale des sciences politiques.

Jenson, J. and Sineau, M. (eds) (1997) *Qui doit garder le jeune enfant? Modes d'accueil et travail des mères dans l'Europe en crise*, Paris: Librairie générale de droit et de jurisprudence (Collection Droit et société).

Jenssen, A. T. and Bratterud, Å. (1997) 'Kvinnenes nei til EU', *Tidskrift for samfunnsforskning*, nr 1, http://www.sol.no/kulturkanalen/samf-for/9703/ (23.8.98).

Jobert, A. (1994) 'L'égalité professionnelle dans la négociation collective en France', *Travail et emploi*, no. 63, pp. 77–87.

Johnston, P. (1997) 'A woman's place is not in the boardroom', *Daily Telegraph*, 4.1.97.

Jones, B. (1995) 'Sintesi del documento di lavoro in prepazione del "memorandum" comunitario', *Pari e dispari*, Annuario no. 5, Milano: Angeli, pp. 45–83.

Joshi, H., Davies, H. and Land, H. (1996) *The Tale of Mrs Typical*, Occasional Paper 21, London: Family Policy Studies Centre.

Junter-Loiseau, A. (1997) *Equal opportunities and Collective Bargaining in the European Union. Selected agreements from France. Phase II*, Dublin: European Foundation for the Improvement of Living and Working Conditions, Working Paper, no. WP/97/15/EN.

Junter-Loiseau, A. and Tobler, C. (1999) 'Reconciliation of domestic and care work with paid work. Approaches in international legislation and policy instruments and in scientific discourse', in O. Hufton and Y. Kravaritou (eds), *Gender and the Use of Time*, The Hague: Kluwer, pp. 341–69.

Juste, M.G., Ramírez, A. and Barbadillo, P. (1991) *Actitudes y opiniones de los españoles ante la infancia*, Madrid: Centro de Investigaciones Sociológicas.

Kaplan, G. (1992) *Contemporary Western Feminism*, London: UCL Press/Allen & Unwin.

Karlsson, G. (1996) *Från broderskap till systerskap. Det social-demokratiska kvinnoförbundets kamp för inflytande och makt i SAP*,

Lund: Arkiv.

Karvonen, L. and Selle, P. (eds) (1995) *Women in Nordic Politics. Closing the gap*. Aldershot: Dartmouth.

Kilpatrick, C. (1997) 'Effective utilisation of equality rights: equal pay for work of equal value in France and the UK', in F. Gardiner (ed.), *Sex Equality Policy in Western Europe*, London/New York: Routledge, pp. 25–45.

Kommittédirektiv (1998:60) 'Översyn av vissa delar av jämställdhetslagen', Stockholm: Ministry of Labour.

Landenberger, M. (1990) *Wirkungen des Erziehungsurlaubs auf Arbeitsmarktchancen und soziale Sicherung von Frauen*, Munich: Special Research Unit 333, University of Munich, Publication project B 6.

Landenberger, M. (1994) 'Pflegeversicherung als Vorbote eines anderen Sozialstaates', *Zeitschrift für Sozialreform*, no. 5, pp. 314–42.

Lanquetin, M-T. (1994) 'De la discrimination indirecte entre les travailleurs masculins et féminins', in Collectif, *Le droit collectif du travail: études en hommage à Mme Sinay*, Francfort/Berlin/Berne/New York/Paris/Vienna: Peter Lang, pp. 415–24.

Lanquetin, M-T. (1995a) 'Égalité professionnelle: quelle effectivité?', *Les Cahiers du Mage*, no. 3/4, pp. 65–71.

Lanquetin, M-T. (1995b) 'La preuve de la discrimination: l'apport du droit communautaire', *Droit social*, no. 5, pp. 435–53.

Lanquetin, M-T. (1997) 'Egalité de traitement et discrimination entre les hommes et les femmes', *Action juridique*, no. 125, pp. 3–14.

Lanquetin, M-T. (1998a) 'L'égalité professionnelle: le droit à l'épreuve des faits', in M. Maruani (ed.), *Les nouvelles frontières de l'inégalité: hommes et femmes sur le marché du travail*, Paris: La Découverte (Collection Recherches), pp.115–25.

Lanquetin, M-T. (1998b) 'Discriminations à raison du sexe. Sur la Directive 97/80 du 15 décembre 1997 relative à la charge de la preuve', *Droit social*, no. 7/8, pp. 688–95.

Lanquetin, M-T. and Masse-Dessen, H. (1989) 'Les droits particuliers pour les femmes dans les conventions collectives (*CJCE* 25 oct. 1988)', *Droit social* no. 7/8, pp. 551–6.

Laufer, J. (1984) 'Égalité professionnelle, principes et pratiques', *Droit social*, no. 12, pp. 736–46.

Laufer, J. (1986) 'Égalité professionnelle: un atout négligé pour gérer les ressources humaines', *Revue française de gestion*, no. 55, pp. 41–53.

Laufer, J. (1992) *L'entreprise et l'égalité des chances: enjeux et démarches*, Paris: La Documentation française (Collection Droits des femmes).

Laufer, J. (1996) 'Les carrières féminines à EDF–GDF. Regards d'hier, regards d'aujourd'hui', in H-Y. Meynaud (ed.), *Les sciences sociales et l'entreprise, cinquante ans de recherches à EDF*, Paris: Editions La Découverte, pp. 287–300.

Laufer, J. (1998) 'Equal opportunity between men and women: the case of France', *Feminist Economics*, vol. 4 no. 1, pp. 53–69.

Lebras, H. (1992) *Marianne et les lapins: l'obsession démographique*, 2nd edn, Paris: Hachette.

Leira, A. (1992) *Welfare States and Working Mothers: the Scandinavian experience*, Cambridge: Cambridge University Press.

Leira, A. (1993) 'Mothers, markets and the state: a Scandinavian "model"?', *Journal of Social Policy*, vol. 22 no. 3, pp. 329–47.

Leonard, A.M. (1987) *Pyrrhic Victories: winning sex discrimination and equal pay cases in industrial tribunals, 1980–84*, London: HMSO.

Lepsius, R.M. (1990) 'Die Prägung der politischen Kultur der Bundesrepublik durch institutionelle Ordnungen', in R.M. Lepsius (ed.), *Interessen, Ideen und Institutionen*, Opladen: Westdeutscher Verlag, pp. 63–84.

Lewis, J. (1992) 'Gender and the development of welfare regimes', *Journal of European Social Policy*, vol. 2 no. 3, pp. 159–73.

Ligue des droits des femmes (1976) 'Quelques réflexions sur l'action du Secrétariat d'État à la Condition féminine', *Droit social*, no. 1, pp. 86–95.

Lister, R. (1997) *Citizenship: feminist perspectives*, London: Macmillan.

Lohkamp-Himmighofen, M. (1993) 'Länderbericht Deutschland', in Bundesministerium für Familie und Senioren (ed.), *Zwölf Wege der Familienpolitik in der Europäischen Gemeinschaft. Länderberichte*, Schriftenreihe Band 22.2, Stuttgart/Berlin/Köln: W. Kohlhammer, pp. 81–148.

Lustgarten, L. and Edwards, J. (1992) 'Racial inequality and the limits of law', in P. Braham, A. Rattansi and R. Skellington (eds), *Racism and Anti-racism: inequalities, opportunities and policies*, London: Sage, pp. 270–93.

Malpas, N. and Lambert, P-Y. (1993) 'Europeans and the Family', *Eurobarometer*, no. 39.0, V/72/94-EN.

Marks, G., Hooghe, L. and Blank, K. (1996) 'European integration from the 1980s: state-centric v. multi-level governance', *Journal of Common Market Studies*, vol. 34 no. 3, pp. 341–78.

Masse-Dessen, H. (1995) 'La résolution contentieuse des discriminations en droit du travail', *Droit social*, no. 5, pp. 442–6.

Mazey, S. (1998) 'The European Union and women's rights: from the Europeanization of national agendas to the nationalization of a European agenda?', *Journal of European Social Policy*, vol. 5 no. 1, pp. 131–52.

Mazur, G. A. (1995) *Gender Bias and the State. Symbolic reform at work in the Fifth Republic of France*, Pittsburgh: University of Pittsburgh Press.

Meehan, E. (1993a) *Citizenship and the European Community*, London: Sage.

Meehan, E. (1993b) 'Women's rights in the European Community', in J. Lewis (ed.), *Women and Social Policies in Europe: work, family and the state*, Aldershot: Edward Edgar, pp. 194–205.

Meehan, E. and Collins, E. (1996) 'Women, the European Union and Britain', in J. Lovenduski and P. Norris (eds), *Women in Politics*, Oxford: Oxford University Press, pp. 223–36.

Memoria (1983) *Il movimento femminista negli anni '70*, nos 19–20.

Meyer, T. (1994) 'Kinder, Kirche, Kapitalismus. Warum es im deutschen Sozialstaat einen Kindergartennotstand gibt', in K. Andruschow, R. Mersmann and A. Scheiber (eds), *Auf die Kitaplätze, fertig, los: Auswirkungen der Politik öffentlicher Kinderbetreuung*, Berlin: Orlanda Frauenverlag, pp. 11–27.

Meyer, T. (1996) 'Ausgerechnet jetzt. Über die Einführung des Rechtsanspruchs auf einen Kindergartenplatz in der Krise des Sozialstaates', *Diskurs*, no. 2, pp. 62–7.

Millar, J. and Warman, A. (1996) *Family Obligations in Europe*, London: Family Policy Studies Centre.

Ministerio de Economía y Hacienda (1997) *Memoria de la Administración Tributaria 1995*, Madrid: Ministerio de Economía y Hacienda.

Ministerio de Educación y Cultura (1998) *Estadística de la enseñanza en España 1992/1993 (resultados detallados, series e indicadores)*, Madrid: Ministerio de Educación y Cultura.

Ministry of Labour (1997a) 'Promemoria', 1997-05-13, unpublished report, Stockholm: Ministry of Labour.

Ministry of Labour (1997b) 'Proposal for amendments to the addition to article 119, 1997–05–05. Common standpoint presented at the IGC by Sweden and Austria', unpublished report, Stockholm: Ministry of Labour.

Moravcsik, A. (1993) 'Preferences and power in the European Community: a liberal intergovernmental approach', *Journal of Common Market Studies*, vol. 31 no. 4, pp. 473–524.

Morris, A.E. and Nott, S.M. (1991) *Working Women and the Law: equality and discrimination in theory and practice*, London/New York: Routledge.

Muriana, C. (1987) 'La integración de la mujer en los sindicatos: afiliación y participación', paper presented at the Seminario: mujer e igualdad de oportunidades en el trabajo, Menendez Pelayo University, Santander, 7-11 September.

Nash, M. (1991) 'Pronatalism and motherhood in Franco's Spain', in G. Bock and P. Thane (eds), *Maternity and the Rise of the European Welfare States, 1880s–1950s*, London/New York: Routledge, pp. 160–77.

O'Connor, J.S. (1993) 'Labour market participation in liberal welfare state regimes: dual breadwinning without dual breadwinner social policy frameworks', paper presented at the International Sociological Association Research Committee 19 Workshop on Comparative Research on Welfare States in Transition, University of Oxford, 9-12 September.

Ohlander, A-S. (1989) 'Det osynliga barnet? Kampen om den socialdemokratiska familjepolitiken', in K. Misgeld, K. Molin and K. Åmark (eds), *Socialdemokratins samhälle: SAP och Sverige under 100 år*, Stockholm: Tiden, pp. 170–90.

Ollerearnshaw, S. and Waldreck, R. (1995) 'Taking action to promote equality', *People Management*, no. 23, pp. 24–9.

Oskarsson, M. (1996a) 'Kvinnor, män och Europeiska unionen', in SOU, 1996:43, *Jämställdheten i EU Spelregler och verklighetsbilder*, Två expertrapporter till EU-96 kommittén, Stockholm: Ministry of Foreign Affairs, pp. 111–33.

Oskarsson, M. (1996b) 'Skeptiska kvinnor – Entusiastiska män', in M. Gilljam and S. Holmberg (eds), *Ett knappt ja till EU,* Stockholm: Norstedts Juridik, pp. 211–24.

Ostner, I. (1993) 'Slow motion: women, work and the family in Germany', in J. Lewis (ed.), *Women and Social Policies in Europe: work, family and the state*, Aldershot: Edward Elgar, pp. 92–115.

Ostner, I. and Lewis, J. (1995) 'Gender and the evolution of European social policies', in S. Leibfried and P. Pierson (eds), *European Social Policy: between fragmentation and integration*, Washington, D.C.: The Brookings Institution, pp. 159–93.

Pateman, C. (1989) *The Disorder of Women: democracy, feminism and political theory*, Cambridge: Polity Press.

Pérez del Río, T. (ed.) (1997) *La discriminación por razón de sexo en la negociación colectiva*, Madrid: Instituto de la Mujer.

Pérez-Díaz, V. and Rodríguez, J.C. (1994) 'Inertial choices: Spanish human resources policies and practices (1959–1993)', *Analistas Socio-Políticos*, Research Paper 2(b).

Pfarr, H. and Bertelsmann, K. (1989) *Diskriminierung im Erwerbsleben. Ungleichbehandlung von Frauen und Männern in der BRD*, Baden-Baden: Nomos.

Pierson, P. and Leibfried, S. (1995) 'Multitiered institutions and the making of social policy', in S. Leibfried and P. Pierson (eds), *European Social Policy: between fragmentation and integration*, Washington, D.C.: The Brookings Institution, pp. 1–40.

Prost, A. (1984) 'L'évolution de la politique familiale en France de 1938 à 1981', *Le mouvement social*, no. 129, pp. 7–28.

Putnam, R.D. (1988) 'Diplomacy and domestic politics: the logic of two-level games', *International Organization*, vol. 42, pp. 427–60.

Rapport public 1996 du Conseil d'État (1997) *Sur le principe d'égalité*, Paris: La Documentation française.

Rauhala, P. L., Andersson, M., Aydal, G., Ketola, O. and Warming Nielson, H. (1997) 'Why are social care services a gender issue?', in J. Sipilä (ed.), *Social Care Services: the key to the Scandinavian welfare model*, Aldershot: Ashgate, pp. 131–55.

Rees, T. (1998) *Mainstreaming Equality in the European Union: education, training and labour market policies*, London/New York: Routledge.

Regeringskansliet (1998) *Sverige och sysselsättningspolitiken i EU*, Stockholm: Ministry of Labour.

Regeringens proposition (1993/94:147) 'Delad makt delat ansvar' (government bill).

Regeringens proposition (1994/95:19) 'Sveriges medlemskap i Europeiska unionen' (government bill).

Regeringens skrivelse (1996/97:41) 'Jämställdhetspolitiken' (written communication from the government).

Regeringens skrivelse (1997/98:60) 'Berättelse om verksamheten i Europeiska Unionen under 1997' (written communication from the government).

Regierungsbericht (1990) *Bericht über die in den Jahren 1986 bis 1988 gemachten Erfahrungen mit dem Gesetz über die Gewährung von Erziehungsgeld und Erziehungsurlaub. Unterrichtung durch die Bundesregierung*, Bonn: Bundestagsdrucksache, 11/8517.

Reinalda, B. (1997) '*Dea ex machina* or the interplay between national and international policymaking: a critical analysis of women in the European Union', in F. Gardiner (ed.), *Sex Equality Policy in Western Europe*, London/New York: Routledge, pp. 197–215.

Rhodes, M. (1995) 'A regulatory conundrum: industrial relations and the social dimension', in S. Leibfried and P. Pierson (eds), *European Social Policy: between fragmentation and integration*, Washington, D.C.: The Brookings Institution, pp. 78–122.

Rice, R., Brown K. and Dempsey J. (1995) 'Women job quotas "unlawful"', *Financial Times*, 18.10.95, p. 1.

Riksdagens revisorer (1997/98:4) 'Sveriges införlivande av EG-rätten' (report from the parliamentary auditors).

Roelofs, E. (1995) 'The European equal oppportunities policy', in A. van Doorne-Huiskes, J. van Hoof and E. Roelofs (eds), *Women and the European Labour Markets*, London: Open University/Paul Chapman, pp. 122–42.

Ross, G. (1998) 'L'Union européenne. La performance d'un acteur sans rôle', in J. Jenson and M. Sineau (eds), *Qui doit garder le jeune enfant? Modes d'accueil et travail des mères dans l'Europe en crise*, Paris: Librairie générale de droit et de juriprudence (Collection Droit et societé), pp. 227–57.

Rubery, J. (1994) 'Wage determination and sex segregation in employment in the European Community', *Social Europe*, Supplement 4/94.

Ruesga, S.M. (1991) 'Las otras trabajadoras: un análisis de la participación femenina no registrada en la actividad económica', *Revista de economía y sociología del trabajo*, nos 13-14, pp. 114–28.

Ryel, A.L. (1996) 'The Nordic model of gender equality law', in T. Hervey and D. O'Keeffe (eds), *Sex Equality Law in the European Union*, Chichester: Wiley, pp. 357–63.

Saéz, C. (1994) *Mujeres y mercado de trabajo: las discriminaciones directas e indirectas*, Madrid: Consejo Económico y Social.

Sainsbury, D. (1996) *Gender, Equality and Welfare States*, Cambridge: Cambridge University Press.

Sainsbury, D. (ed.) (1994) *Gendering Welfare States*, London/Thousand Oaks/New Dehli: Sage.

Saraceno, C. (1997) 'Gender and Europe: national differences, resources and impediments to the construction of a common interest by European women', in J. Klausen and L.A. Tilly (eds), *European Integration in Social and Historical Perspective: 1850 to the present*, Boulder, New York/Oxford: Roman & Littlefield, pp. 249–66.

Scanlon, G. (1990) 'El movimiento feminista en España, 1900–1985: logros y dificultades', in J. Astelarra (ed.), *Participación política de las mujeres*, Madrid: Centro de Investigaciones Sociológicas and Siglo XXI, pp. 83–100.

Scheiwe, K. (1994a) 'EC law's unequal treatment of the family. The case-law of the European Court of Justice on rules prohibiting discrimination on grounds of sex and on grounds of nationality', *Social and Legal Studies*, vol. 3, pp. 243–65.

Scheiwe, K. (1994b) 'Labour market, welfare state and family institutions: the links to mothers' poverty risks. A comparison between Belgium, Germany and the United Kingdom', *Journal of European Social Policy*, vol. 3 no. 4, pp. 201–24.

Scheiwe, K. (1999) *Rechtsmodelle der Kinderversorgung und soziale Ungleichheiten zwischen Frauen und Männern in vier Ländern (Belgien, BRD, Schweden und Vereinigtes Königreich)*, Frankfurt a.M.: Vittorio Klostermann Verlag.

Schiersmann, C. (1991) 'Germany: recognizing the value of child rearing', in S. Kamerman and A. Kahn (eds), *Child Care, Parental Leave and the Under 3s: policy innovation in Europe*, Westport, Conn.: Auburn House, pp. 52–79.

Schunter-Kleemann, S. (1994) 'Sozialrechtliche Behandlung der Vereinbarkeit von Familie und Beruf auf EG-Ebene', in G. Bäcker and B. Stolz-Willig (eds), *Kind, Beruf, Soziale Sicherung, Zukunftsaufgabe des Sozialstaats*, Köln: Bund, pp. 197–235.

Scott, J.W. (1991) 'La travailleuse', in G. Duby et M. Perrot (eds), *Histoire des femmes*, Paris: Plon, vol. 4, *Le XIXè siècle*, pp. 419–44.

Siim, B. (1997) 'Dilemmas of citizenship in Denmark – lone mothers between work and care', in J. Lewis (ed.), *Lone Mothers in European Welfare Regimes*, London: Jessica Kingsley, pp. 140–70.

Silvera, R. (1996) *Le salaire des femmes, toutes choses inégales.... Les discriminations salariales en France et à l'étranger*, Paris: La Documentation française (Collection Droits des femmes).

Simitis, S. (1994) 'Familienrecht', in D. Simon (ed.), *Rechtswissenschaft in der Bonner Republik. Studien zur Wissenschaftsgeschichte der Jurisprudenz*, Frankfurt: Suhrkamp, pp. 390–448.

Singh, R. (1998) *Gender Autonomy in Western Europe: an imprecise revolution*, London: Macmillan.

Sofer, C. (1995) 'La mesure des discriminations de salaire', *Les Cahiers du Mage* no. 2/95, pp. 5–12.

Sohrab, J. A. (1996) *Sexing the Benefit: women, social security and financial independence in EC sex equality law*, Aldershot: Dartmouth.

SOU (1972:34) *Familjestöd*, Stockholm: Ministry of Social Affairs.

SOU (1975:62) *Förkortad arbetstid för föräldrar*, Stockholm: Ministry of Labour.

SOU (1993:117) *EG, kvinnorna och välfärden. Social välfärd och jämställdhet mellan kvinnor och män i ett europeiskt perspektiv*, Betänkande av EG-Konsekvensutredningarna: Social Välfärd och Jämställdhet, Stockholm: Ministry of Social Affairs.

SOU (1996:43) *Jämställdheten i EU. Spelregler och verklighetsbilder*, Två expertrapporter till EU-96 kommittén, Stockholm: Ministry of Foreign Affairs.

SOU (1998:6) *Ty makten är din ... Myten om det rationella arbetslivet och det jämställda Sverige*, Betänkande från Kvinnomaktutredningen, Stockholm: Ministry of Labour.

Statistisches Bundesamt (1995) *Im Blickpunkt: Familien heute*, Kusterdingen: Metzler.

Stetson, D.M. and Mazur, A.G. (eds) (1995) *Comparative State Feminism*, Thousand Oaks (California): Sage.

Strobel, P. (1997) 'Les mésaventures de Monsieur Gagnepain', in F. Ronsin, H. Le Bras and E. Zucker-Rouvillois (eds), *Démographie et politique*, Dijon: Éditions Universitaires de Dijon, pp. 175–84.

Sullerot, E. (1981) *Les modes de garde des jeunes enfants*, Paris: Conseil économique et social.

Svensson, A-C. (1999) *Negotiating the IGC 1996–97. The role of the presidency*, Doctoral Dissertation, Department of Government, Uppsala University.

Threlfall, M. (1985) 'The women's movement in Spain', *New Left Review*, no. 151, pp. 44–73.

Threlfall, M. (1995) 'El futuro de la igualdad en la uníon Europea: la reconciliaçon de la vida familiar y laboral para ambos sexos', Dirección Regional de la Mujer (ed.), *Mujeres al Norte*, Oviedo: Principado de asturias, pp. 117–28.

Threlfall, M. (1996) 'Feminist politics and social change in Spain', in M. Threlfall (ed.), *Mapping the Women's Movement: feminist politics and social transformation in the North*, London/New York: Verso, pp. 115–51.

Threlfall, M. (1997) 'Spain in social Europe: a laggard or compliant Member State?', *South European Society and Politics*, vol. 2 no. 2, pp. 1–33.

Threlfall, M. (1998) 'State feminism or party feminism? Feminist politics and the Spanish Institute of Women', *The European Journal of Women's Studies*, vol. 5 no. 1, pp. 69–93.

Tobío, C. (1994) 'The family-employment relationship in Spain', *Cross-National Research Papers*, vol. 4 no. 2, pp. 41–7.

Tobío, C. (1996a) 'Changing gender roles and family-employment strategies in Spain', *Cross-National Research Papers*, vol. 4 no. 4, pp. 79–85.

Tobío, C. (1996b) 'Estrategias de compatibilización familia-empleo: España, años noventa', unpublished report, Madrid: Instituto de la Mujer.

Uddhammar, E. (1993) *Partierna och den stora staten. En analys av statsteorier och svensk politik under 1900-talet*, Stockholm: City University Press.

Ulmanen, P. (1998) *(S)veket mot kvinnorna och hur högern stal feminismen*, Stockholm: Atlas.

United Nations Development Programme (1995) *Human Development Report 1995*, New York/Oxford: Oxford University Press.

Valiente, C. (1995a) 'Children first: central government child care policies in post-authoritarian Spain (1975-1994)', in J. Brannen and M. O'Brien (eds), *Childhood and Parenthood. Proceedings of the International Sociological Association Committee for Family Research Conference on Children and Families, 1994*, London: Institute of Education, pp. 249–66.

Valiente, C. (1995b) 'The power of persuasion: the Instituto de la Mujer in

Spain', in D.M. Stetson and A.G. Mazur (eds), *Comparative State Feminism*, Thousand Oaks (California): Sage, pp. 221–36.

Veil, M. (1997) 'Zwischen Wunsch und Wirklichkeit: Frauen im Sozialstaat. Ein Ländervergleich zwischen Frankreich, Schweden und Deutschland', in Bundeszentrale für politische Bildung (ed.), *Aus Politik und Zeitgeschichte*, Beilage zur Wochenzeitung *Das Parlament*, B 52/97, Bonn: Bundeszentrale für politische Bildung, pp. 29–38.

Venturini, P. (1997) 'The prospects for employment and European social policy in the context of the ICG and an integrating single market', keynote address to UACES Conference, Guildford, 6 January.

Vernaz, C. (1976) 'Le salaire maternel', *Droit social*, no. 1, pp. 74–80.

Vibe Lande, H. (1995) *Gender Equality – the Nordic Model*, Copenhagen: Nordic Council of Ministers.

Vilches, M.J. (1992) 'Un análisis crítico de la política de empleo general y de las experiencias específicas para las mujeres', in Fundación Dolores Ibárruri (ed.), *La supermujer, símbolo y simulacro: las mujeres en el mercado de trabajo*, Madrid: Fundación Dolores Ibárruri, pp. 61–6.

Villegas, L. (1992) 'La acción sindical por la igualdad de las mujeres', in Fundación Dolores Ibárruri (ed.), *La supermujer, símbolo y simulacro: las mujeres en el mercado de trabajo*, Madrid: Fundación Dolores Ibárruri, pp. 57–60.

Vogel-Polsky, E. (1997) 'Les femmes, l'égalité et le traité d'Amsterdam', *EUDIF Réseau Européen de Documentation et d'Information des Femmes*, no. 5.

Vogel-Polsky, E. and Vogel, J. (1991) *L'Europe sociale 1993: illusion, alibi ou réalité?*, Brussels: Éditions de l'Université de Bruxelles (Études européennes).

Waerness, K. (1984) 'Caring as women's work in the welfare state', in H. Holter (ed.), *Patriarchy in a Welfare Society*, Oslo: Universitetsforlaget, pp. 67–87.

Wages for Housework (1995) The International Wage for Housework Campaign, August.

Wängnerud, L. (1998) *Politikens andra sida. Om kvinnorepresentation i Sveriges riksdag*, Göteborg: Göteborg Studies in Politics, no. 53.

Waring, M. (1989) *If Women Counted: a new feminist economics*, London: Macmillan.

Wienand, M. (1996) 'Erfahrungen mit der Pflegeversicherung – Konfliktfelder und Lösungsansätze aus Sicht der Sozialhilfe', *Neue Zeitschrift für Sozialrecht*, vol. 5 no.1, pp. 1–9.

Wilkinson, H. (1997) *Time Out: the costs and benefits of paid parental leave*, London: Demos.

Willenbacher, B., Voegeli, W. and Müller-Alten, L. (1987) 'Auswirkungen des Ehegattenunterhaltsrechts in der Bundesrepublik Deutschland',

Zeitschrift für Rechtssoziologie, vol. 8 no. 1, pp. 98–113.

Wingen, M. (1995) 'Familienpolitik als Gesellschaftsform', in Bundeszentrale für politische Bildung (ed.), *Aus Politik und Zeitgeschichte*, Beilage zur Wochenzeitung *Das Parlament*, B 52-53/95, Bonn: Bundeszentrale für politische Bildung, pp. 26-39.

Index

abortion law, 91, 101, 198
Advisory Committee on Equal
    Opportunities for Women
    and Men, 32–3, 35, 44
affirmative action programmes,
    40
Afsa, Cédric, 62, 87
Agreement on Social Policy, 11,
    16, 28, 36, 42, 63, 135–7,
    184
Austria, 19, 24, 51, 55–9, 63–4,
    177–8

Belgium, 19, 30, 55–57, 59, 61–
    2, 65
biological difference, 71, 76
birthrate, *see* fertility rates
burden of proof of
    discrimination, 12–13, 75–6,
    116, 130, 154, 175, 181,
    183–4

care allowance, 104–5, 164–6,
    169–71, 187
caring, 12, 21–4, 34, 38, 47, 56,
    60–1, 64, 88, 89–107, 112–
    13, 130, 145–6, 151–3, 156–
    9, 163–7, 169–71, 185–200
    see also childcare
Catholics, 65, 100, 108, 112, 121
Centre Party
    in Sweden, 165, 168–70
centre-right (UCD)
    in Spain, 147
childcare
    childminding, 85, 87, 199

individual arrangements, 74,
    82–8, 89–103, 143–9, 151,
    156, 169–71, 181, 185, 191–
    5, 198
    policy, 16–17, 32–8, 50, 62–5,
    67, 136, 138, 147–9, 156–7
    public provision of, 9–10, 47,
    65, 81, 85, 98–102, 143, 146,
    152, 161–6, 169, 187, 191,
    194
    see also Council
    Recommendation on
    childcare
childrearing allowance, 62, 84–7
Christian Democrats
    in Germany, 97, 104
    in Italy, 108–9, 111–14
    in Sweden, 169–70, 198
church, 24, 71, 108, 111, 113–14
citizenship, 22–4, 70, 81, 180,
    188–9
civil servants, 32, 38, 57, 62,
    118, 142, 160
Cockburn, Cynthia, 36
collective agreement(s), 44, 51,
    55, 57–9, 69, 73, 76, 78, 111,
    127, 152, 154, 159
Commission of the European
    Communities, *see* European
    Commission
Communists
    in Italy, 111–14
    in Sweden, 170
Community Charter of the
    Fundamental Social Rights of
    Workers, 12, 16, 31, 135, 184

companies, 39, 44, 49, 57, 77–80, 114, 116–17, 135
compliance, 41, 79, 118, 129
Council Directives
on atypical work, 92/85/EEC, 12, 15, 51, 110, 130
on the burden of proof, 97/80/EC, 12, 175
on equal pay, 75/117/EEC, 11, 14, 125
on equal treatment, 76/207/EEC, 11, 14, 39, 72, 76, 128, 175
on equal treatment in social security, 79/7/EEC, 11, 14, 91; 86/378/EEC, 12, 14; 86/613/EEC, 12, 14
on parental leave, 96/34/EC, 12, 17, 41–4, 56–8, 63, 137
on part-time work, 97/81/EC, 12, 18, 28, 41–4, 140, 184
on working time, 93/104/EC, 12, 15
Council of Ministers, 4, 15, 28–30, 32–3, 40, 75, 119, 177, 182–3
Council Recommendations
on childcare, 92/241/EEC, 12, 16–17, 33, 38
on positive action, 84/635/EEC, 12, 29, 39, 116
Council Resolution concerning a social action programme (1974), 29, 49
see also social action programme
Crawley, Christine, 36, 44, 129–30
crèches, 98–100, 113
custody, 95–6, 186
Czech Republic, 50, 55–57, 59, 65

Defrenne v Belgian State (Case 80/70), 13, 29
Dekker v Stichting (C–177/88), 13, 175–6
demographics issues, 8, 21, 59, 61, 65, 68, 69
Denmark, 8–9, 22–4, 29, 37, 55–7, 59–61, 67, 173–4, 194
desegregation, 21, 27, 29, 43, 46, 78, 199
dignity of women and men at work, 12, 16
direct discrimination, 95–6, 126
directives, *see* Council Directives
Directorate General V (Employment and Social Affairs), 31–2, 42, 184
Directorate General X, 34
dismissal, 51, 55, 128
division of labour, 31, 41, 47, 61, 87, 92–6, 109, 132, 159, 186, 190, 195–6
divorce, 9, 89, 94–6, 107, 114, 122, 150, 193, 196
domestic labour, 86, 114
domestic production, 86, 190
domestic services, 87, 194
Draehmpaehl v Urania (C–180/95), 13, 131, 176
dual-breadwinner families, 60, 163–4, 166–7, 169, 171
Duncan, Simon, 10, 188, 190

East Germany, 8–9, 65, 67, 99
Economic and Monetary Union (EMU), 1, 5, 42, 159, 172, 179
education,
of children, 16, 90, 92–3, 138–9, 147–9, 158, 169
as a profession, 110, 118

of women, 2, 5, 37–8, 113,
126, 143
eldercare, 9, 39, 86, 90, 112,
161, 197, 199
employers
organizations, 33, 35, 42
see also UNICE
and equality issues, 47, 76, 87,
111, 116–17, 127, 129, 131–
3, 135, 154, 181, 183, 199
and labour costs 20, 22, 24, 71,
79, 112, 140–1, 152
and reconciliation, 9, 18, 44,
62–3, 136, 138, 141, 145,
152, 155, 157, 195, 200
employment guidelines, 28, 30–1
employment policies, 30, 47, 49,
81, 87
enlargement, 1, 19, 29, 45, 177
equal opportunities
analysis, 2, 4, 181, 199
at EU level, 1–2, 12, 14–18,
26, **27–48**
in France, 21, 68–9, 76–9, 81,
83
in Germany, 89–91, 93, 96–7,
99, 103–4, 107, 198
in Italy, 108, 110, 112–14, 117,
118–20, 122
in Spain, 143
in Sweden, 161–2, 166–7,
174–78
in the United Kingdom, 23,
124–34, 135–7, 140
Equal Opportunities
Commission (United
Kingdom), 32, 37, 39, 125,
128–31, 133, 135, 137
Equal Opportunities Unit
(European Commission), 3–
4, 36, 38, 42, 46–8, 72, 187
equal parenthood, 60, 162, 164,
169

equal pay
and EU legislation, 1, 2, 10,
11, 13–14, 22, 27–8, 30, 181
in France, 20, 66, 68–9, 75, 77
in Germany, 21
in Italy, 21, 108, 111–13
in Spain, 154
in the United Kingdom, 124–6,
129, 133
equal remuneration, 10, 68, 72,
111
equal sharing of parental
responsibilities, 19
equal treatment,
and EU legislation, 1, 2, 11–
15, 18, 21–2, 27–30, 32, 40–
1, 43, 46–7, 66, 180, 184,
194
in France, 69, 72, 74, 76–7, 83,
86
in Germany, 91, 96
in Italy, 109, 113
in Spain, 143
in Sweden, 175
in the United Kingdom, 127–8,
132, 14–15
equal value, 10, 68, 76, 94, 111,
114, 125–6, 129, 154, 175
equality directive(s), 14, 23, 30,
91, 96, 172
see also Council Directives
equality policy
in the EU, 2, 4, 27, 29, 32, 34–
9, 46–7, 182, 187, 197
in Italy, 109, 110–11
in Spain, 143, 148, 153–4
in Sweden, 25, 161
in the United Kingdom, 22–4,
32
Esping-Andersen, Gøsta, 10, 22,
145
Essen Summit, 5, 177
Eurobarometer, 8, 23

European Centre of Enterprises with Public Participation (CEEP), 12, 35, 42, 56
European Commission
  sources, 17–18, 22–3, 30, 40–1, 46
  as a gender policy actor, 4, 12–13, 15–18, 27, 29, 31–42, 45–8 , 72–4, 98, 110, 129, 133, 137–8, 142, 160, 176, 181–5, 187–9, 195, 197
European Commission Network on Childcare and Other Measures to Reconcile Employment and Family Responsibilities, 16, 38, 197
European Confederation of Trade Unions (ETUC), 12, 35–6, 42, 56
European Council, 4–5, 18, 28, 30, 116, 135, 177, 182
European Court of Justice (ECJ), 4–5, 11, 23, 28–31, 39–41, 68, 72–4, 91, 96, 125, 128, 131, 161, 174–5, 178
European integration, 3, 21, 24, 40, 60–1, 171, 174, 181
European Network on Women (ENOW), 34
European Parliament, 4, 27, 32–37, 39, 40, 42, 46, 142, 177, 182
European Structural Funds (ESF), 24, 37
European Women's Lobby (EWL), 30, 33, 35, 40–1, 45–6
Eurostat, 5, 8, 20, 23, 144, 157, 197

Fagnani, Jeanne, 61, 86, 195
family building, 8, 9, 22, 63–4, 69, 86, 159

family policy, 21, 42, 50, 56, 64, 66, 69, 81, 84–5, 100, 138, 166–9
father's month, 168, 170–1
fathers, 55–60, 62–5, 82, 140, 155, 163–4, 167, 170, 180, 186, 195–7, 200
feminism, 4, 14, 114–15, 182, 190
fertility rates, 9, 64–5, 69–70, 95, 159
Finland, 1, 8–9, 24, 30, 51, 55–7, 59–60, 67, 144, 161, 174–5, 177
fixed rate benefits, 58
flexibility, 18, 32, 40, 42–4, 49, 61, 109, 136–8, 140–1, 149, 187, 194–5
Fourth Action Programme on Equal Opportunities for Women and Men, 12, 17, 38–9, 43, 45
France, 8–9, 19–20, 22–3, 55–7, 59, 61–2, 65, **68–88**, 129, 137–8, 181, 183, 190, 192, 194, 198–99
full-time employment, 47, 63, 98, 146

gender discrimination, 50, 148, 153–4, 174
gender equality
  in the EU, 5, 8, 25–6, 30, 39, 43–4, 47, 49, 61, 180, 184, 200
  in France, 69, 80,
  in Germany, 90, 107,
  in Italy, 108
  in Spain, 144, 148–9, 151, 156,
  in Sweden, 25, 42, 47, 161–2, 168–9, 171–4, 176, 177–8
gender relations, 35, 91, 110–118, 163–4, 167

gender roles, 47, 49, 64, 108
German Democratic Republic (GDR), 65
Germany, 8–9, 19–21, 23, 55–9, 63, 65, 67, **89–107**, 137, 183, 192, 195, 197–8
Gradin, Anita, 45, 160, 176
grandparents, 64, 194
Greece, 5, 8–9, 23–4, 55, 57–9

health and safety at work, 14–15, 31, 51
homemakers, 8–9, 21–2, 62, 65, 81–2, 85, 108, 167, 187, 190, 192–3, 196
Hoskyns, Catherine, 2, 4, 10, 21, 24, 29–32, 41, 48, 56, 177, 181–2
households, 8, 10, 15, 17, 20, 23, 35, 61, 84, 95, 148, 163, 185–6, 190, 193, 196
housewives, 113, 146, 164
Hubert, Agnès, 30, 38, 48

indirect discrimination, 74–5, 79, 91, 96, 111, 113, 116–17, 126, 131, 174, 176
individual taxation, 60, 179
individualization of social rights, 47
informal care, 89–90, 102–6
Instituto de la Mujer, 24, 146, 151
International Labour Organization (ILO), 10, 68, 111, 181
Ireland, 8–9, 22–4, 29, 32, 55–9, 62–3, 67
Italy, 8–9, 19–21, 24, 55–7, 59, 64–5, **108–123**, 137

job creation, 18, 86
joint taxation, 93, 163

Kalanke v Freie Hansestadt Bremen (C–450/93), 13, 28–9, 39, 41, 45, 178
kindergartens, 64, 91, 99, 101

labour costs, 20, 28, 136, 141
labour law, 69, 71, 74, 80, 96, 117, 147, 153–4, 158–9
labour market
  activity, 8, 10, 14, 20, 22, 29, 60, 63–4, 70, 82, 84–6, 89, 95, 108, 113, 115, 119, 148, 158–9, 160–1, 165–6, 188, 190, 196
  equality, 18, 27, 31, 59, 87, 112, 153, 163, 185, 188, 193, 195, 201
  flexibility, 43–4, 88, 135–6, 187
  opportunities, 5, 11, 26, 38, 60, 79, 120, 141, 143–6, 154–5, 158, 162, 167, 187, 196
  policies, 112, 162
  reconciliation, 49, 59, 61, 171
  segregation, 8, 21–2, 27, 29, 43, 87, 132, 161, 188, 199
leave for family reasons, 17, 51, 74
Leibfried, Stephan, 3
Leira, Arnlaug, 90, 164
Lewis, Jane, 10, 21, 23, 62, 97, 182
Liberal Party
  in Sweden, 165, 169, 171
local government, 34, 99, 100, 105, 119, 138
lone mothers, 55, 82, 161
lone parenthood, 82, 96, 107, 138, 173, 192
Long-Term Care Insurance, 91, 102–7
Luxembourg, 8, 14, 18–19, 23, 55, 57–9, 63, 197

Maastricht Treaty, 16, 31, 41,
    135
mainstreaming, 1–2, 5, 18, 25,
    27–8, 30, 37–8, 44–7, 120,
    138, 178, 199
management, 34, 39, 42, 49, 78–
    80, 110, 117, 119–20, 135,
    140, 195, 198
    see also employers
Marschall v Land Nordrhein-
    Westfalen (C–409/95), 13, 40
Marshall v Southampton (C–
    271/91), 13, 128, 131, 176
maternity absence, 57–8
maternity leave, 13, 15, 51–7,
    63, 65, 74, 81, 112, 130, 149,
    154–6, 158, 187
Moss, Peter, 38
Myrdal, Alva, 165–6

Netherlands, 8, 19, 55–9, 63–4,
    194, 197
Network on Women in Decision-
    making, 34
New Opportunities for Women
    (NOW), 37
night work, 13, 15, 60, 71–3, 80,
    95, 153
non-compliance, 4
Non-Governmental
    Organizations (NGO), 34
Nonon, Jacqueline, 21, 72
non-transferability of leave, 41,
    56
Nordic states, 9, 22, 24–5, 59–
    61, 64, 67, 161, 163, 173–4
nursery schools, 81, 98, 113

Papandreou, Vasso, 35–6, 184
pappamånad, *see* father's month
parental insurance, 56, 59–60,
    161, 163, 166–8, 170
parental leave

national legislation, 50, 51, 57–
    60, 62–6, 85–7, 90, 97–8,
    109, 130, 136–7, 140, 151,
    156, 159, 161–4, 167–71,
    198
    see also Council Directive on
    parental leave
parity, 75–6, 109, 118–22, 170
part-time working
    and flexibility for employers,
    9, 18, 20, 49, 84, 86, 112,
    157, 187, 194
    and reconciliation, 8–9, 15, 17,
    44, 56–8, 60–4, 70, 87, 96,
    98–9, 130, 136, 138, 140,
    148–9, 154, 157, 161, 187,
    191, 193, 195, 197
    and working conditions, 26,
    41, 44, 74, 127, 133, 194–5,
    197
    see also Council Directive on
    part-time work
Pateman, Carole, 163
paternity leave, 50–1, 58–60, 65
pension(s), 13, 17, 22, 31, 41,
    94–7, 103, 105, 113, 128,
    155
Poland, 50, 55–9, 65
policy actors, 2–5, 23, 28–36,
    37, 40, 44–7, 110, 118–21,
    143, 149–53, 180, 197, 199
policy instruments, 27–8, 31, 90,
    180, 185–7
policy process, 1–2, 25, 27, 46,
    67, 110, 143, 149–50, 158
political actors, 1, 90–1, 101,
    153, 162
political parties, 23, 75, 113,
    115, 119, 122, 144, 146–9,
    151, 158, 163, 167, 172
political representation, 4, 21,
    39, 75–6, 119, 160–2, 170–2,
    178

Portugal, 8–9, 23–4, 55–9, 64
positive action
at EU level, 2, 12, 19, 27–30,
38–40, 185, 189,
at national level, 26, 39–40, 45,
47, 72, 74, 76–8, 99, 107,
109–10, 113–19, 127, 131–2,
178, 199
positive discrimination, 2, 13,
26, 127, 132
preschool provision, 101, 138,
148–9, 154, 156, 158, 169
pressure groups, 2, 4, 136, 142
prohibition on night work, *see*
night work
public administration, 110, 112,
114, 116, 119, 167
public sector, 39, 42, 51, 57, 61,
72, 79, 81, 117, 135, 144,
157, 161, 163, 173

qualified majority voting, 14,
130, 198

reconciliation of paid work and
family life,
individual, 180, 185–6, 188–97
policy, 2–3, 25–6, 27, 32, **49–
67**, 83–4, 86–8, 121–3, 134–
41, 150, 153–9, 160–1, 184–
7, 189
strategies, 57, 86, 102, 153–4,
157, 180, 185
recruitment, 72, 76–9, 113, 116,
140, 175
Rees, Teresa, 2, 161, 177
reinstatement, 10, 17, 50–1, 55,
57, 65, 112, 129, 155–6
reproductive work, 109, 116,
117–18, 122–3, 161, 189

Sainsbury, Diane, 10, 163

segregation, 62, 87, 109, 112,
117, 161, 180, 188, 194
see also labour market
segregation
service sector, 8, 29, 90, 110,
112, 157, 194
sex equality, 2, 21, 91–5, 107,
181, 185
sexual harassment, 37, 75, 174,
181
sharing of family
responsibilities, 15–17, 19,
56, 82, 116, 163–71
sharing of household tasks, 11,
17, 35, 61
Single European Act (SEA), 4,
14–15, 23, 130
Article 118a, 14
Smith and Others v Avdel
Systems Ltd (C–408/92), 13,
41
social action programme, 11, 14,
15, 19, 29, 31, 49, 183–5
Social Democrats
in Germany, 97, 104, 198
in Spain, 147–8, 151, 154–5
in Sweden, 160, 163–6, 168–
70, 187
social dialogue, 16, 36, 42
social movements, 83, 113
social partners, 18, 27–8, 33, 42–
4, 69, 79, 117, 172, 183
social security, 1, 11, 12–17, 20,
22, 24, 43, 71, 82, 89–90, 96,
100, 106–7, 111, 155, 181,
189, 195
see also welfare retrenchment
Socialist Party
in Spain, 198
Spain, 8–9, 23–4, 55–9, **143–59**,
183, 194, 198
Sullerot, Evelyne, 21, 83, 85

Sweden, 1, 8–9, 23–5, 30, 51, 55–61, 67, **160–79**, 183, 187, 194

take-up of leave, 43, 58, 60, 167, 170, 187
Third Action Programme on Equal Opportunities for Women and Men, 12, 16, 28, 36–39, 44–5, 47
trade unions, 35–6, 73, 77, 80, 111, 115, 117–18, 125, 134, 143, 151–2, 158, 199
training, 2, 5, 11, 14, 16, 37, 74, 76–80, 96, 113, 116–17, 119–20, 126–7, 131, 138, 140, 198
Treaty of Amsterdam, 2, 30, 40, 47, 177
Article 141, 11, 18, 41, 189
Treaty of Rome, 2, 28, 30, 46, 181–2
Article 119, 10–11, 14, 18, 20, 31, 47, 68, 74, 111, 181
Treaty on European Union, 11, 16, 24–5, 31, 41, 135

unemployment, 5, 8–9, 17, 26, 30, 50, 65, 80, 84, 86, 112, 139, 144–5, 154–5, 169, 173
unification of Germany, 65, 67, 98–9, 101, 107
Union of Industrial and Employers' Confederations of Europe (UNICE), 12, 35, 42, 56, 184
United Kingdom, 8–9, 11–12, 22–3, 29, 32, 37, 39, 42–3, 55–9, 62–3, 82, **124–42**, 182, 187, 190, 194–5, 197–9

universal rights, 68–9, 71, 76, 106

Vogel-Polsky, Eliane, 30, 181

wage discrimination, 74, 76, 174–5
welfare retrenchment, 1, 5, 103, 107, 169
welfare state, 10, 24, 71, 80, 99, 107, 143, 152, 158, 160–1, 172, 174
White Paper on European social policy, 17, 19
White Paper on Growth, Competitiveness and Employment, 30
women as working mothers, 9, 15, 50, 61, 69, 80–5, 110, 113, 121–2, 145–6, 154, 166
women-friendly policies, 36, 40, 59, 60, 160
women's economic activity, 5, 8–9, 20, 64–5, 70–2, 80–2, 84, 88, 90, 108, 122, 165
women's labour force participation, 61, 63, 65, 67, 144, 162
working conditions, 11, 14–15, 29, 51, 69, 77, 80, 105, 110, 113, 116, 153, 181
working hours, 15, 49, 56, 58, 60, 85, 98, 109, 137, 152–3, 156, 187, 198
working time, 12, 15, 17, 44, 47, 49, 58, 77, 80, 83–4, 137, 140, 186–7
see also Council Directives on atypical work, part-time work and working time